Stress

STRESS

The Nature and History of Engineered Grief

ROBERT KUGELMANN

PRAEGER

Westport, Connecticut
London

WITHDRAWN

Library of Congress Cataloging-in-Publication Data

Kugelmann, Robert, 1948–
  Stress : the nature and history of engineered grief / Robert
Kugelmann.
    p.   cm.
  Includes bibliographical references and index.
  ISBN 0–275–94271–6 (alk. paper)
  1. Stress (Psychology)—History. 2. Civilization, Modern—
Psychological aspects. 3. Social change—Psychological aspects.
4. Grief—Social aspects. I. Title.
BF575.S75K82   1992
155.9′042—dc20   92–8381

British Library Cataloguing in Publication Data is available.

Library of Congress Catalog Card Number: 92–8381
ISBN: 0–275–94271–6

First published in 1992

Praeger Publishers, 88 Post Road West, Westport, CT 06881
An imprint of Greenwood Publishing Group, Inc.

Printed in the United States of America

The paper used in this book complies with the
Permanent Paper Standard issued by the National
Information Standards Organization (Z39.48–1984).

10 9 8 7 6 5 4 3 2 1

I dedicate this work to three of my teachers, who directed me on the path I now follow: Rev. Bruce Ritter, O.F.M., Patrick Mullahy, and Elizabeth Nelson, R.N. I also dedicate this work to Laurie, my spouse and companion on this Way.

Contents

Preface

For my fundamental insights on the nature of stress I am indebted to the wealth of critical thought on the nature of modernity. It is hardly novel to suggest that modernity contains a revolutionary dynamic such that existing social and economic structures are constantly overthrown and replaced with new structures. Marx's imaginative depiction of it, "All that is solid melts into air" (which is also the title of Marshall Berman's brilliant study of modernity and its cities[1]), states the *conditio sine qua non* of stress.

In keeping with the historical spirit of this book, I want to name a few of my intellectual ancestors, who discovered some threads in the maze of modernity. The existential-phenomenologists, especially Maurice Merleau-Ponty and Erwin Straus, are beacons for my thinking regarding the complex of body and history and illness. First, I am indebted to them for their explication of the historical nature of human existence, including the historical being of things and matter. The changing nature of the life world, especially as formulated by J. H. van den Berg and Gaston Bachelard, directs psychological inquiry to the everyday world of praxis and its discourse as the location of souls. This insight into the nature of things makes possible an extraverted psychology that moves decisively beyond modernity's abandonment of the world and its one-sided, introverted psychology.[2] Second, the concept of the lived body, the body as one's own, as the subject—not the object—of human action, is fundamental to my critical approach to the phenomenon called "stress." One implication of considering the historicity of the lived body is that the scientific depiction of the body anatomically and physiologically is a situated truth; that is, it is a metaphor for the lived body, and not its only or even its fundamental truth.[3] This perspective on the body's description—taking description as having a metaphorical character—liberates our view of medical history. This historically informed view does not deny in the least the experiential basis of the medical description of bodily ailments; for example, of "overstrain of the heart." It lets us read the text as one which simultaneously describes the ailment and the mentality of the community describing the ailment. This approach to discourse is an attempt to practice what William Blake called "double vision." ("May God us keep,/from single vision and Newton's sleep.") It is an approach to discourse which avoids several extreme, if heuristically useful, positions that resemble double vision but fail to achieve a truly simultaneous study. I do not seek to dissolve stress or its predecessors into the discourse that speaks it, for I am convinced that the discourse says something. Nor do I seek to display a gradual unfolding of the truth about an unchanging reality, for I do not think "stress" is an eternal form, nor even a scientific concept that is being increasingly understood year by year. For I find that the experiential basis shifts as does the discourse. Both experience and discourse are mobile entities.

Although I name but one taproot in the complex net tying the present to the past, it will suffice. I want to turn my attention to my contemporaries, the community of friends that have helped my thinking and work mature by their interest, criticism, and wisdom. I am indebted to M. Jeanne Peterson, from whom I had the chance to learn a bit of the historian's craft during an NEH Summer Seminar in 1987. I am indebted also to present and former students and to friends, who have described faithfully their experiences of stress and have struggled with me to understand the structure of those experiences. Several people have carefully read the manuscript or big chunks of it and have given me helpful insights: Bill Arney, Ivan Illich, Dave Lavery, Jean Robert, Anson Rabinbach, and David Schwartz. I have followed their suggestions to the best of my ability. I thank also my sister, Eileen McCluskey, for editing the book manuscript with an eye for clarity and style—although she bears no responsibility for the deficiencies that remain.

One group of friends in particular has inspired my thinking about stress. It includes my colleague Bob Romanyshyn at the University of Dallas and a group that has met yearly in wonderful places like Claremont, "Foster Avenue" at Penn State, and the Institute for Traditional Acupuncture in Columbia, Maryland. These friends include Ivan Illich, Barbara Duden, Jean Robert, Dennis Slattery, Wolfgang Sachs, Bill Arney, and Dirk Boelticher. There are many others, and I beg them to accept my apologies for not mentioning them here. From these people I have learned much, but furthermore I have come to place my efforts in terms of a larger intellectual project which is fundamentally concerned with freeing people to *subsist* (to use the scholastic term that Illich has rehabilitated) in our day. At (more or less) yearly gatherings to discuss "the history of the human body," we have examined epoch-specific forms of experiencing the lived body. But the *raison d'être* of these examinations is ethical, even theological, and can be posed as a question: How can one live the good life in the face of our modern existence, of which stress is a part? So despite the historical, even historicist, cast to the work in this book, I am concerned with what is natural in a metaphysical sense to men and women. It is another example of the double vision to consider together the historicity and the nature of human existence. I hope that my book does justice to the importance of this project.

NOTES

1. Marshall Berman, *All That Is Solid Melts into Air: The Experience of Modernity* (New York: Simon & Schuster, 1982).

2. I am thinking here of depth psychology and its kin, the only psychology worthy of the name because it considers as real the soul of man. For references to J. H. van den Berg, see *Things* (Pittsburgh: Duquesne University Press, 1970), *The Changing Nature of Man* (New York: Norton, 1961), and *Divided Existence and Complex Society* (Pittsburgh: Duquesne University Press, 1974). For Gaston Bachelard, a good beginning is *The Poetics of Space* (Boston: Beacon Press, 1964). For this extraverted turn in psychology, see Robert Romanyshyn, "Psychological Language and the Voice of Things," *Dragonflies: Studies in Imaginal Psychology* 1, no. 2 (Spring 1979), 73–79.

3. I have already explored this notion in *The Windows of Soul* (Lewisburg, PA: Bucknell University Press, 1983).

Introduction

Whenever I would say that I was writing a book on stress, I would be greeted with one of two responses. The first response made me feel as if I were a St. Bernard carrying long-sought brandy over the Alps or a camel with sacks of water swaying through the desert to a lost, dusty, fly-covered soul. So I would say, "No, it's not that kind of book. It won't help you cope."

The second response made me feel as if I were yet another social (or worse, behavioral) scientist proposing yet another theory about stress, with appropriate tables filled with carefully validated data. "No," I would say, "it's not that kind of book either." I do not think that stress has the same kind of scientific merit as gravity or quantum mechanics. "Well, then, what sort of book is it?" was the next question. Here is my reply.

My inquiry into stress began in puzzlement. I had started my first full-time job after graduate school in 1978. I was hurrying across campus one cloudy Seattle day, ruminating about all I had to do, and realizing that if I planned my life in order to do it all, I would need to have 30 hours in a day. Then, just as the clouds parted to reveal a rainbow, the idea came to me: I am under stress. For some reason this struck me as a revelation. So like the Ancient Mariner, I began to tell certain people that I was under stress. They knew exactly what I meant, and many admitted that they too suffered under the same burdens: no time, no money, no energy—the trinity of stress. Then, like a pilgrim, I discovered that I could do something about it: cope, assert myself more, relax, take time to smell the flowers, get therapy, exercise, stop smoking. Oh, yes! I did all those things (though I am not now nor have I ever been addicted to healing techniques). By virtue of participating in all these stress-reducing activities, I had found a center in my being and a sense of community. That is what I thought—for a short while.

What I had found, I realized soon enough, was not the center of my being, but only what the ancients called "opinion": not true knowledge, but what "people say." In more contemporary terms, I had taken as revelation of truth a socially constructed artifact. Whatever "stress" is (and it is something), it has the peculiar quality of being a term that sounds vaguely scientific to most people, and one that sounds amorphously like a problem to be solved. The word *stress* gives hope—hope that something can be done. But what does the word mean?

To answer this question, I set myself a threefold task, which this book completes. First, what do people say they are suffering from when they say they are under stress? Chapter 1 addresses this question, and is the fruit of a phenomenological investigation of the experience of stress. Second, insofar as stress is experienced at all, how much is its experience due to the mass consumption of social science? Chapter 2 analyzes the rhetorical structure of the scientific and popular discourse on stress.

The path of thinking in these first two chapters leads to a conclusion: stress names, in a way distorted by all the debris of modern consciousness, a kind of grief unique to the modern period, which is a time of rapid and relentless change, whether for good or for ill. Stress names a grief perpetually unresolved, thus keeping the passion of mourning perpetually productive. The discourse on stress and the practices that enact it keep the grief unresolved. Hence, I propose that the "whatever it is" that we now call "stress" be given a newer, truer name: "engineered grief." For stress is the engineering of the grief of adapting to the changes of modernity, for good or for ill.

Third, this book answers these questions: How did it occur that *stress* came to name our experience of adapting to modern change? Is *stress* the name for an eternal verity? Chapters 3–6 explore these questions by tracing the construction of engineered grief backward in time. In Chapter 3, we find that only during World War II did stress become a topic of medical and psychological research and a named cause of disorders. The psychiatric difficulties of pilots and bomber crews brought stress into the open. These men, whose work took them away from the ground and made them totally dependent on both machinery and the social system that orchestrated their military missions, were the first to be "*men* under stress." Their stories are emblematic of ours. World War II was not simply the occasion for the emergence of stress; it configured the experience and discourse about stress along martial lines.

Chapter 4 looks back several more decades to World War I, when soldiers suffering from the traumas of trench warfare, gas, tanks, and shelling, came to occupy the psychosocial no-man's land that contains us all now. The generation of "The Waste Land" witnessed the breakdown of Victorian certainties, symbolized by the rise of psychological perspectives on life and health. The emergence of psychology and psychiatry as necessary responses to the suffering of no-man's land marks a break with old certainties in our culture. The rise of psychiatry and psychology also marks a "splitting of the flesh" on a mass level into the psychological interior (understood by the institutions of psychiatry and psychology) and the somatic exterior (grasped by the instruments of physical science).

It is not surprising that something like stress appeared in the nineteenth century, riding the rails into the new industrial cities. Chapter 5 presents life at high pressure, which produced nervous strain, neurasthenia, overstrain of the heart, and other pitfalls of an industrializing society.

This history is a grim tale, describing how we were once beings of the flesh, and how we have ceased to be so. Chapter 6 examines some changes in material, medical and social aspects of existence just before *strain* and *stress* became possible. The look backward stops circa 1750. Before then, human existence differed from ours in such a way that we detect no stress or anything like it. But the second half of the eighteenth century contains the seeds of stress, and there we can find the beginning of the change to our present condition. Matter was being tested for its strength, and new, modern materials were on the horizon. Clocks and watches were increasingly the bases for organizing work. The "medical gaze" was replacing the tact and taste of earlier medical practice. But perhaps the most important change that occurred was in the notion of luxury, which changed in the eighteenth century from a vice to be avoided to a virtue to be pursued vigorously. Stress has replaced luxury as the ill side effect of civilized life.

Finally, whither a people who labor under stress? Chapter 7 asks about the future. Having accounted for our being with others under stress (Chapters 1–2) and the historicity of stress (Chapters 3–6), we ask about our future under stress. Here I attack stress management as a monstrosity of modern social engineering that dooms us to the Sisyphean task of being forever under stress. The way out of stress is not to "manage" our stresses, but to cope no longer: The way out is to stop and grieve for our losses.

1

Hurrying to Be: The Age of Stress

Just after World War II, when "stress" began to proliferate in the professional literature surrounding health and illness, a revolution occurred in painting. Between 1946 and 1956 American painting suddenly achieved international recognition through the work of the Abstract Expressionists: Jackson Pollock, Franz Kline, Willem de Kooning, Mark Rothko, and others. Their nonrepresentational work portrayed a stress-filled world. Consider Pollock's work of this period. These are the years of his drip paintings, when he abandoned conventional techniques in favor of pouring paint onto canvases spread on the floor of his studio. The eye finds no resting place on a surface that pulls the gaze ever onward to discover yet another layer of color and line, while remaining on a plane without depth. Pollock's interpreters emphasize the energy of these paintings, visible in the tensions created and released in the interplay of line and color. Kline's black-on-white works present the world stripped of all but engineering realities; the beams and pillars are "abstract" only relative to a world that once existed, populated by humans and human things. Rothko gives to the stress-filled world its moment of peace and transcendence. As in the Rothko Chapel near the center of Houston, a stillness can occur only if the outer world is kept bricked out.

These paintings manifest a world that has come to be our home. That they did so was partially Pollock's intention. Absent or merely suggested imagery does not push into a background the play of line, color and structural relationships. The paintings, especially Pollock's, are "overall": They have no center; any space on the canvas is as noticeable as any other. Renaissance perspective abandoned, they leave the spectator free or abandoned to find a personal position with respect to them, to make sense or not as he chooses.

These paintings show the grid which interprets the world in terms of its stresses and strains. Content has vanished. Dynamism alone appears, rendering the relationship between points more important than the points themselves. Before the viewer is the world in perpetual flux, as "energy and motion made visible," to quote Pollock.[1] Among Pollock's corpus is *Portrait and a Dream* (1953). A transitional piece, it captures his move back to images, image fragments to be more precise. Human and animal forms surface and vanish as if created in momentary configurations. Bursts of joyous and angry energy explode on the left, the black side. The observer witnesses the origin and dissolution of things. On the right side, over an array of black paint is a human face which, if one scans from left to right, gradually emerges from the swirl of pure dynamism. The portrait, surfacing above the maelstrom, affirms that the human being has as its matrix and ground the bottomless and endless play that subtends it.

The huge face peering from the canvas is doubled. The left eye, the pupilless one, is simultaneously the right eye of a second, less defined face. This face looks to the left side, where living forms explode. The divided attention, the split in the portrait, the shadowy second face: This is an uneasy existence, split in two because of the groundlessness from which it rises. *Portrait and a Dream* presents the polarity of stress: a divided, dynamic, and groundless existence which surfaces and disappears into energy as stresses create and destroy it.

AN AGE OF STRESS

Ours is an age of stress. This means that the complexity and tempo of advanced industrial society have amplified difficulties in living. Stress occurs whenever one must adapt to change. But this is only half true, for stress happens only in our age. Stress is a real factor in our lives, but it is not just an objective condition. Primarily a nodal point in the grid through which we perceive and construct the world, stress is both natural and artificial. To the extent that the body responds viscerally to the corporeal discipline of a technological society, stress belongs to nature. To the extent that stress as a construct frames, interprets, guides, and organizes our bodies' reactions, stress belongs to artifice. The nature of stress lies in shared experience, hence it is a datum; its nature lies also in the discourse that forms experience, hence it is an artifact. "Stress" in its contemporary meaning first appeared only in the nineteenth century, when an engineering mentality took root. Only during the Second World War did stress come to be studied systematically, and only during the past two decades has stress colonized everyday life.

Stress is not a label for something that exists independently of its name. The discourse on stress acts as a demiurge on experience. The thesis that stress is both an experience and a discourse lies at the heart of this book's approach. Without doubt life events exist that we call stressful: To them stress discourse refers. Yet stress is also a discourse, a mutation of experience by the external power of speech, a power that can devour what it articulates. The power of the discourse partially emanates from, and in turn renews, the nondiscursive networks within which we live. This intersection of personal experience, discourse, and patterns of action constitutes the locus of stress. Central to the intention of this book is the breaking apart of this threesome in order to see beyond our current certainties.)

Stress belongs to a problem-solving discourse. Problem-solving discourses begin with problems and work toward solutions; thus there is, potentially, some answer which solves or eliminates the problem. Once a discourse takes root in our awareness of things, it is nearly impossible to experience outside the framework established by the discourse. Throughout this book, I shall strip away the layers of inscription in the flesh that constitute the construct of stress. I do this not in answer to a problem, but to reveal the suffering that is masked by stress. Only after having explored in depth the meaning and genesis of stress as experience, discourse, and praxis will we be able to speak beyond stress. Only then will we be able to wrest our suffering from the play of tensions and pressures, problems and coping. We shall speak of stress in terms of an existence that feeds on energy in order to sustain itself. And we will witness what we lose to the extent that we partake in that meal.

NO PLACE TO BE

To begin, here is a phenomenology of stress. Stress, like television, nuclear weapons, and freeways, is now a given. Whether or not people feel that they have too much of it, nearly all know what it is.[2] What is stress as an experience? What is the essence of this historical phenomenon? What are the features and contours of a stressful world? And how are individuals oriented such that stress exists for them? Who and what am "I" when "I" find myself under stress? What body does this "I" have? These questions guide a reading of typical experiences of stress. In this phenomenology, the way things show themselves is at issue. Scientific analyses of stress have privilege in this phenomenology only insofar as they influence our perception of and response to situations. For the purposes of this phenomenology, I set aside the social construction of the experience of stress, including the various ways in which scientific knowledge has sedimented into everyday life. What I will present is the form and dynamic of this already constituted world of stress.)

On the surface, the world of stress is geometric: tall office towers, freeways, cities partitioned into residential, commercial, and industrial zones. Stress belongs to the grid of Cartesian coordinates that is the locus of contemporary life. Stress belongs to traffic controlled by machines and rationalized procedures. This is home. It is, overall, rather comfortable: Cooled in summer, heated in winter, with plenty to eat and drink, with easy chairs and nice clothes. True, not all share in the pie: the poor, the beggars, the old exist at the margins of the stressful world. In general, though, this world is more affluent than not.

Everyone feels like he or she has to rush. On cold, clear winter mornings the air is brown over the city as the traffic jams and snarls. We measure distance in minutes as we commute to school, office, and factory. The crowded roads reflect the clogged arteries that we read about in the newspaper and see on television. Take a deep breath, relax. The ideal is to live in the country, even if the job is in the city. The schools are better, the air cleaner, the crime rate lower, out of the city.

A well-fed uneasiness persists. The spatio-temporal grid does not give the whole picture, insofar as actually living in the grid does not provide the order and rationality that it promises. The grid, arbitrarily deployed, produces chaos or allows anything to happen anywhere. When stress occurs, the world loses its proportions as perspective vanishes. "Nothing seems clear any longer, all is stretched out of proportion. That's it, 'things' have lost their shape and size."[3] The world has become "white noise," the "snow" that one sees on the television screen when no signal is being received. It is no coincidence that the most succinct image of the stressful world, white noise, is an image on a television screen. The television screen can present a "live" event everywhere at once. The origin of the event is no place in particular, bodies and scenes having been transformed into bits of information, electrical impulses, broadcast far and wide. White noise is the matrix for the particular scenes of this televised world.

A recurrent image is a busy street: more specifically, being a pedestrian on a freeway crowded with traffic, or being on foot in a parking lot. Both are orderly, rational spaces, yet they promote randomness and danger, and they produce the realization that no body belongs there. Crosswalks allow for bodies the way zoos allow for wild animals: allowance is made for what has no place in such a setting. The street and the parking lot provide emblems for the world under stress. Planned, serene, orderly in design, and made for our comfort; chaotic and hostile in effect. These spaces which we traverse every day make our white-noise world perceptible, insofar as they present clarity and proportion which is planned, but absent. Above all, these spaces exclude the body. One's bodily presence gives a primary orientation to the world, as basic and primitive as the articulations of left–right, front–back, up–down. But under stress things lose their shape and size because the world has no center; that is to say, because the space which sustains stress has been planned and built without regard for the body as lived. Quite literally the world is without places: there is no definite *here* from which to perceive things *there*. Under stress, "I" am lost without my life-support mechanisms, the automobile and other techniques that keep "me" speeding. "I" am lost without the grid's coordinates, since a world without place has no "image-ability," to use Kevin Lynch's term.[4]

A world under stress knows no boundaries of place, and this holds true temporally as well as spatially. Future tasks belonging to elsewhere crowd in the present. I do not dwell in the present, I do not simply leap ahead into a future. "As I stood in the doorway I tried to remember a time when my nerves weren't tense. Two meetings and a class this morning, fifteen minutes for lunch, then work until 9:00 P.M." The space of stress resembles a threshold at which one is perpetually poised. The desire and the need is to be in two places, two times, simultaneously. A threshold is a transitory place; under stress it becomes "neither here nor there" and is perpetually occupied. To stay in that position, speed is of the essence. As one task is being worked upon, the others insist on making their presence felt. The "I" in the doorway says that "the tips of my fingers are cold and numb." "I" have lost a grip on things; they dissolve because they have no place, no size, no limit. At the same time, the body becomes numb, meaning that it ceases to be felt. It is in the process of disappearing.

The body becomes numb because there is no feel to such a space and time. The body belongs to here and now, recalling a past and anticipating a future. To be a body is to be limited in time and place, not to be everywhere and nowhere at once, as we feel under stress. If the body is not yet numb, it ought to be: "to hell with my screaming baby ulcers, and my increasing gray hairs. Drink the Mylanta and full speed ahead." Anesthesia (psychic numbing) is the concomitant of dwelling neither here nor there. "After having been up all night writing a paper for a class, my boss calls to tell me I'm supposed to be at work. The basic feeling is a sort of harried numbness. There are too many things going on to comprehend priorities." The absence of proportion, the dissolution of place and time, and the numbing of the body are three constituents of a world under stress.

PRESSURE AND TENSION

There is thus a metamorphosis of physical presence, in which the body becomes a feeling of harried numbness. But this "empty and alone" condition is but half of the embodiment or, rather, the disembodiment of stress. If this anguish were all of it, no one would stand for it. But numbness only shadows the benefits of stress. "I do my best to become primitive, raw, and induce needed stress by getting angry." Stress, in other words, feels "numb and tight." "I" feel tight because stress comes as a boost; it propels, enabling existence within white noise. With the surge that stress brings, "I" can approach being in two places at once, doing two things at once. "It was as if the stress helped me and gave me more energy than I would have otherwise had." Under stress "I" am expansive, straddling the threshold, speeding down the street. "I" may be tense yet "I" am charged and in charge. "I eat stress with a spoon and demand more, more stress to feed the giant boiler in my stomach, to push me where there is only goal and conquest and devastation." Stress is a kind of substance that "I" can produce from within or ingest from without. It is not food, air, or water. When stress is incorporated, that is, when it becomes part of the "I," it becomes energy. Or to be more precise, the "I" becomes energized.[5] Then "I" am at home in the centerless world of "free ways." "My mind is going 90 MPH," states a person under stress, with a mixed feeling of terror and thrill.

The deformation of the world that corresponds to this strange embodiment has two poles: pressure and tension. These engineering terms capture something of the emptiness and absence of place. Pressure: "I find myself 'curling in' on myself, or holding things close to me and folding my arms." The burdens of duty weigh on the "I" of stress. But not only duties, for sometimes the pressure comes from unmasked hostility of something outside "my" safe haven: "I turned off all the lights in my apartment so he couldn't see my movements inside. I had never felt so caged before. . . . Finally he left, and my walls expanded as my relief grew." The constriction of being objectified, of being trapped in a box, all capture the pressure side of the deformed spatiality of stress.

The tension side is the inverse: Everything is stretched out, out of proportion, out of meaning. It is, in the extreme, senseless: "The star-filled sky stretched out from either side, split by the steel and concrete overpass. The night hours seemed immeasurably long, they stretched so far that time became meaningless and inconsequential." This kind of tension is a tension of fatigue. Rage is also a possibility: "I started beating on the walls until the sides of my hands bruised. As the rushing rage receded to the place where it came from, an unexpected reciprocation from the opposing side called up a different set of sensations. The powerful blurring rush and my two-fisted heart became that of the fluttering pace of a captive bird." This kind of stretching out is an explosion. The spatiality of stress—a no-place, a perpetual threshold, white noise—has a dynamic of either implosion (pressure) or explosion (tension). In either case, there is no present, nowhere to be, nowhere to make a connection between the past and the future, nowhere to meet others with hospitality.

THE GLORY AND TERROR OF ENERGY

Stress happens when work fills the day. In the landscape of white noise, work does not only mean time expended in exchange for money. An actual job represents "work" in an enlarged sense. "Work" now means any activity: thinking, worshiping, lovemaking, playing, etc. All are tasks, all have acceptable levels of performance, all entail energy consumption. "Sitting at Mass, I began to remember that I had not left a message for a sign to be posted. And I remembered that I have a paper due on Thursday. And I felt guilty that I hadn't spent enough time with my friends. I don't like the fact that I begin to think of visiting a friend as another thing on the list of 'things to do.'" Everything becomes a task, and the tasks crowd around, imploding space and time. Thus "I" feel consumed by what "I" must do: Every event costs something in terms of time and energy. People, occupations, activities of every kind consume what "I" am. But the fact that life becomes work provides a way to respond to the situation of stress. "I feel like the entire world is closing in on my head. My head begins to feel smaller and smaller and tighter and tighter. I force myself to accomplish something positive; the pressure subsides. The pressure does not just disappear, it is turned into positive energy. Eventually I begin to feel very content and relaxed." When "I" push myself into work, the pressure—the felt sense that boundaries of place and time do not exist—becomes energy that "I" consume in order to work. When finished with my work, "I" find myself in a free space of rest and relaxation, which comes to alternate with work. Hard work to complete tasks allows for "rest and relaxation," which in turn renews my store of energy for work.

In this world without boundaries of place and time, where proportion has been thrown to the wind, the image of the whirlwind recurs. "I" am to the extent that "I" keep spinning, stay wound up. A utilitarian principle dominates stress; "I" am to the extent that "I" can work. Stress begins when every action becomes work; to restate it from the point of view of the "I," when everything becomes a demand. In response, "I" become tight and numb: "Chest constricts—hold back your words.... Grit teeth—hold back your words." The pressing in of demands and the upsurge of energy in response sets all in motion. "There is a constant sensation of movement. Even when I am physically still my mind is whirling. Even in sleep, my dreams are like being caught up in a revolving door." A revolving door is a threshold that allows one to keep busy while going nowhere: a dynamic threshold. The "I" of stress feels at this moment helpless in the face of demands. "Too many problems, too much noise—hustle, bustle, go, go, go—nothing to hold on to. A total whirlwind of orders, requests, deadlines, and questions." But the location of the whirlwind is variable: When "I" am a whirlwind of activity "I" am delighted. The whirlwind is the world and the "I" becomes flux: without place, without body.

The whirlwind circles around power. If "I" am the whirlwind, "I" am superhuman. "I can't eat, it'll make me human, decrease the sharp eye-bulging edge I've gotten from stress and adrenaline." The "I" of this hurricane transcends all limitations, especially those of the flesh. In this modality of inhabiting a stressful situation, others are inferiors: clowns, fools, competitors, demanding menials, and needy children. At best they need my attention and care. "I was scared—not because I hadn't done this job before, but because I hadn't done it with these guys. And these guys made Cheech and Chong [two clowns perpetually stupid from drug taking] look like Crick and Watson!" Stress isolates one from others in a specific way: With its power coursing through me, "I" am superior. "I" am in charge, "I" control the course of events. In the formless world of white noise, "I" believe that "I" can fashion it however "I" wish. "I" am a whirlwind: energy made visible.

When the whirlwind surrounds rather than inhabits me, then "I" feel helpless. "I feel worthless because I don't have a plan of action." There no longer exists any interiority in such moments; "I" am at the mercy of external forces. "I" am drained of energy as the whirlwind of demands sucks me dry. "It's overwhelming, routine breaks down. Some sounds become irritating and distracting." In the anxiety and helplessness of such situations, "I" feel that "I" will unravel. In a variant of the whirlwind image, a man described himself as a golf ball, with its elastic bands wrapped tightly around the center. He felt that the outer layer was coming off and that the elastic bands would explode. Passive and explosive is the "I" in the midst of the whirlwind.

To state the energy issue simply: "I" want to be energy because either "I" want to pursue my "goal[s] and conquest[s]", or because "I" feel compelled to pursue them. I am what I do. In John Bradshaw's felicitous phrase, "I" am a human "doing."[6]

LISTS: THE ORDERING OF SCARCITY

The only so-called healthy way out of the situation is to make a decision. It need not be an existential choice; in fact, it is ordinarily more rudimentary. The basic rational choice in the stressful world is to make a list. "I feel the need to make lists," writes the woman for whom things lost their shape, "so that I can see it all more clearly." In a world of white noise, to make a list and establish priorities is the fundamental act. It orders the tasks that flood into the now. A list gives a plan of action and re-establishes control. With a list "I" can manage. Lists mediate between demands and the work "I" do to meet them. Listing tends to be the structure of consciousness under stress: "A respite. Time to catch up on the circulation figures on the computer, return phone calls, do billing 'over-dues,' balance the company checkbook, write correspondence, and go through my correspondence without too much overlap." A list orders randomness. Things themselves have no internal coherence; their seriation organizes the noise. The content of lists varies considerably, but in principle these lists, acts of creation in the stressful world, number four kinds of items: Time, energy, money, and information.

A list concerns the allotment of time. It orders and manages scarce commodities by defining the chaos of stress in terms of time, and by perceiving this time as limited and quantifiable. The only temporality of stress is that of the clock and the appointment book. The diffusion of this temporality—anonymous, empty, equalized—into all human activities is the precondition of stress: When this diffusion takes place, all events become work. "When awake, I am constantly confronted with clocks and calendars all reminding me of the deadline and how it is speeding up getting closer all the time." The clock time of the stressful world does not run at a uniform velocity: It accelerates. Moments of slack time occur, but primarily time picks up speed. Deadlines, which occur in many forms, orient this time and give it its quickening tempo. What deadlines entail are tasks to be done within a set period, tasks which cannot be completed within that limit unless one hurries. If a task can be done without accelerating, it does not have a deadline; its temporality may not even be quantified. A list of "things to do" orders work under the heading of deadlines.

Tied to time in this way is energy. With scarce time comes equally scarce energy. "So much to do! I don't have the time or energy to finish everything." Energy lies hidden within the person and can be evoked when the "I" is under pressure. Energy can be consciously summoned from within the "I," lifting it above the merely human. Yet energy can be measured and even purchased. "I need more energy," said a woman to the clerk in the natural food store. Energy is the force from the depths that suffuses the "I" of stress, keeping it in existence. Accomplishing the tasks on the list of life requires energy; and to replenish this energy, the "I" must be connected to the economic system. The energy that "I" need costs money, a third scarce commodity. The things that replenish energy cost dearly. The "lists" mentality that manages a stressful existence centers around the trinity of time, energy, and money, and typically the complaint made in regard to these things is "I don't have enough. . . ."

The scarcity of energy is the most crucial, for given enough energy, any lack of time and money can be accommodated. Only when it begins to run out is the scarcity of energy felt. "I found out how tired I truly was, gazing dumbly too often, realizing that I had deadlines, feeling disgusted at the thought of eating—being hungry, though." This declaration makes it clear that what "I" crave when exhausted is something more abstract, rarefied, mobile, and potent than food or drink. Under the regime of stress, food is merely a container of energy. The other sources of energy—drugs, exercise, fasting, meditation, massage, etc.—share the feature of being incarnations of energy. The absence of energy in my system is not hunger, nor is it fatigue. No, it is exhaustion, a word reverberating with *exhaust*, the dissipation, the entropy of our vehicles, factories, and power plants. Exhaustion has an edgy quality and because of this frazzled tone it does not resemble fatigue, which comes with the completion of nonstressful activity. Fatigue concerns effort to natural limits and brings with it a sense of completion, of satisfaction. Exhaustion brings no peace or fulfillment. Under stress, exhaustion inevitably hits the "I" who feels that if only "I" had more time or energy or ambition or drive, "I" would have done more. "When I finally return to my room, momentum has beaten exhaustion. I have been running on carry-over nervous energy for ten days, so there is no restful sleep. I fall asleep thinking of the day ahead. There is never enough time." Here, depletion meets the momentum of the whirlwind: Sleep, longed for and postponed, does not bathe the "I" in the waters of forgetfulness. There is no escape under these conditions from the incessant motion that "I" need to stay on top of things in the world of white noise. Occasionally, one finds an imaginal dialogue with an unnamed interlocutor:

"Sleep? Never! I've got to do this and this. Oh, no! I forgot the x meeting!"
"Go to sleep!"
"No. I have to finish. I can beat it."
"No, it never stops. Good night."

This scene presents the exhaustion of stress: Surrender to the passion of sleep is impossible for such a being, who of necessity must always maintain a vigil. "I still couldn't sleep even though I was exhausted. I couldn't stop living the nightmare of the assignment." Exhaustion, it should be clear, always entails this resistance to sleep and other passions of the flesh. The resistance is internal to exhaustion, because of the intimate relationship between the "I" and energy. This exhaustion is not merely depletion, it also entails "being wound up" with too much energy which cannot find release.

Intimately bound with the scarcity of time, energy, and money is the overabundance of information. Information consists of placeless bits that "I" must put together into a pattern. It often appears that time and energy are scarce because information abounds, and equally often it seems that we seek information from the electronic cornucopias because we desperately need a way to cope with the lack of time, money, and energy. Either way, information, like the number of neural connections in the brain, is virtually limitless, hence the need to make decisions in all areas of life, especially the need to make the decision to seek or listen to information. Phenomenologically, information is the primal stuff of the stressful world, since we list information. Under stress, "I" swim in a sea of information, and "I" simultaneously seek more of it and feel overwhelmed by it. The promise of information to the "I" of stress is access to power and energy and control. Information, being the one abundant commodity in the stressful world, holds out the greatest hope to the "I." Given that information can be construed into any pattern whatsoever, it is the picture or the pictures that "I" construct from the white noise that "I" live in. "I" am free to shape (to customize) any life "I" want from the information "I" receive. The world is meaningless, but there is plenty of information about it.

Listing is the general form of what "I" do under stress. It has many manifestations, including collecting, saving, organizing, shopping, hoarding. For example: "I held my lab notebook tightly to my chest and kept referring to it in order to gather my thoughts." The "I" gathers her body, her symbol of authority, and her thoughts in the face of objectifying eyes, in the face of feeling nervous and scattered. Centerless beings gather, list, sort. A far cry from "gather ye rosebuds while ye may," though the anxiety is in many respects the same.

THE "I" OF STRESS

The subjectivity that takes shape under stress: "I" am to the extent that "I" am energy. "I" am an ability to work (the scientific definition of energy transposed to the social world). Energy in this sense exists only within a stressful world. Moreover, the ego as energy is a valid proposition only within a world of white noise, a world of no proportions, of no bodies, because only a formless, protean "I" can survive in a formless space. The energy at the basis of the "I" is not libido, psychic energy, or the E of physics. Libido cannot be purchased or injected as this energy can be. Energy obviously relates to physics' E, but energy in the world of stress has a context and even methods of verification that have nothing to do with experimental science. One can say, however, that physics' E has trickled down into everyday life, becoming the energy of everyday parlance in the process. The energy that "I" need in order to be is the most tangible and rarefied of stuff. As a bodily sensation, it rises from within as "adrenaline" or anger or anxiety or fear. In addition to being so physical, it is felt to be only temporarily incarnated; it has no form of its own and exists everywhere. "I" draw it from the world as from a bank, using the tools that "I" use to sustain and define myself. Anything that moves or excites or empowers me or one of my tools is an energy source. All sustain the "I" in being. For example, "I" thrive on energizing foods such as bee pollen, or on stimulants like cocaine, or on a hectic schedule, or on the power of an automobile engine, etc. "I" draw power and identity from all "I" have. The "I" of stress is a development of what Erich Fromm called the "marketing character": "they constantly change their egos, according to the principle: 'I am as you desire me.' "[7] Under stress, "you" desire "me" to be ever ready for change and immediate action, for some use.

Because "I" am energy, "I" have a balloon-like being. "I work best under pressure." So the exhaustion which periodically looms has terror in its train. What gives exhaustion its edgy, frazzled quality, such that at times "I" desire to cease to be in order to make the whirlwind stop, concerns the nature of the "I." If "I" run out of gas, "I" cease to be. But since "I" cannot sustain myself in constant motion, "I" seek the oblivion of pleasure—some drug, even if it be only television—to silence the white noise.

We now realize what all the work that "I" do produces. It is not the various products that are at stake. Work produces the "I."

Can "I" imagine being without stress? Two places occur to the "I" of stress in response to this question: nature and churches. The natural setting may be pictured as external—the forest, the beach, the countryside, the primitive locales far from technology. "I'm going 98 MPH all the time, trying to make ends meet. If it were just me and my wife, I think we'd just live in the country in a tent. But we can't, because of the kids." Or nature may be internal, a longed-for still point in the center of the storm: "My mind focuses with frigid clarity and I realize the magic is gone. The magic of the work spell. I draw a Buddha breath. . . . I felt peace for the first time in a long, long time." Stresslessness has the character of a center, still and calm. It appears as a permanence, even partaking of eternity. To reach this place, "I" give up in a profound way will and work. The flux is left behind or transcended: "if I could return to a place of stillness, become grounded, become quiet for a while. . . . " The stressful world is the negative of this place, so it appears. Yet one can wonder about a tranquility that is marketed so fiercely by the entrepreneurs of stress.

The "I" of stress needs to assert itself as energy because the world to which it belongs is formless, fluctuating, and violent. "I begin to wonder if I've got what it takes." White noise is not simply shapeless and fluid, capable of being molded by the desires of an "I." It harbors violence of a particularly random sort. A journalist depicts urban stress in terms of traffic jams caused by police besieging bank robbers hiding in a hotel, a chemical truck overturned elsewhere, holiday shoppers pouring into shopping mall parking lots, fire trucks and an ambulance at an apartment complex.[8] "Traffic," that ceaseless flow of bodies hidden inside metal machines constantly in drive, constitutes an image of stress and its random violence. "This traffic is major stress. It makes you want to go home and beat your kids." One wrong move and "I" am dead, or someone else is. A pervasive terror surrounds the rationality of the world of stress.[9]

The terror and the violence primarily concern the "I" and its body. Stress causes illness in the common understanding, as Kristian Pollock also discovered in his anthropological study in Great Britain. Stress causes insomnia, depression, ulcers, nervousness, mononucleosis, hives, heart disease, cancer, etc. It also makes any disease worse and lowers one's resistance to disease. "The stress is building up. I'm going to break. It's getting real physical." At this point, various explanatory models, supplied by medical and psychological science, imbibed directly or through the media, come into play to account for how the breakdown will occur. To suffer stress in this way means therefore to experience one's body in terms of the modern life sciences. Moreover, stress thus experienced pushes "me" to the limit: "I have the shakes, I'm trembling. I can't take it." Enter a topic we shall explore in depth—stress management, to prevent the shakes and the breakdowns, to keep one going. Failing this, there is disease and disability. Are there other alternatives?

THE ABSENCE OF PASSION

The phenomenology indicates the nature of the world of stress. It presents the picture, and as a portrait it resembles Jackson Pollock's *Portrait and a*

Dream. What is more striking, however, is what is different from Pollock's image. Absent from the picture of white noise is the passion that Pollock's work contains and radiates. Is our phenomenology incomplete? Have we missed something essential? Or does Pollock express something that the stressful world cannot contain or fathom, because it lies beyond its horizons? I am inclined to think that the second question takes us closer to the heart of the matter, insofar as passion seems to be incompatible with stress. Passion absents itself from stress, and this is a profound mystery. Is it because the work of making an "I" in a formless world of white noise never ends, because the "I" must stay in constant motion at the threshold in order to be, and that this never-ending motion robs the "I" of all vitality?

All differentiation among passions is lost in stress. And undifferentiated emotion tends to feel like either rage or bliss. Passion in all its varieties including sleep and death as well as anger, joy, grief, fear, etc., has a transformative end, as James Hillman concludes:

Emotion is an activity not of the subject's own doing. Thus it is always a *passio*, a test, a crisis situation, when adaptation through reasoning or instinct or other partial functions no longer are enough. All such lesser means of survival have failed. Thus emotion reveals the truth about the peril of ourselves and the world.[10]

Under stress, "I" do not suffer transformation. Rather, "I" adapt by gaining control; failing that, "I" break down. The world of stress, in which "I" exist and through which "I" move with the aid of strategies directed by the discourse on stress, limits the possibility of experiencing the world as other than stressful. "I" do not escape the calculus of energy. The possibility of passion, that is, of being moved and transformed into another kind of being or another kind of experiential world, is thereby eclipsed. For passion requires place and body, neither of which are available under stress. As Bernd Jager eloquently observes:

Passion . . . announces the coming into being of a radical discontinuity within the light-dominated world of seeing, doing, and understanding. It refuses to be domesticated by the light of reason; it will not passively fit itself to the measure of tasks and the orderly arrangements of daily affairs. . . . Its order is the order of the flesh.[11]

The anguish of the "I" who under stress cannot sleep is emblematic of the hellish (in the Sartrean sense of no exit) nature of a stressful life. "I" want to be overpowered by sleep, but "I" cannot will sleep: Sleep is a power independent of the "I," as Merleau-Ponty remarked:

I lie down in bed . . . ; I close my eyes and breathe slowly, putting my plans out of mind. But the power of my will or consciousness stops there. As the faithful, in the Dionysian mysteries, invoke the god by miming scenes from his life, I call up the visitation of sleep by imitating the breathing and posture of the sleeper. . . . There is a moment when sleep "comes," settling on this imitation of itself which I have been offering to it.[12]

"I" fear being thus overpowered, since "I" am only to the extent that my will (as energy) sustains my being in the white noise of the stressful world.

Passion breaks the workaday world down, and for a differentiated life of passion, open, empty, unproductive times and places are necessary. Pollock's work, which gives form to passion, again provides a clue to what the stressful world obliterates—leisure. The precondition for the (especially artistic) expression of the passions, and even for ordinary surrender to that twilight world, as insomniacs and frustrated lovers know, leisure consists of "useless" occasions and events. Pollock's painting shows us the leisure that passion rests upon. One virtue of the drip paintings is the visibility of the act of painting that produced them. Their lack of polish does not suggest to the viewer an incompleteness, but rather the play that occasioned their production. Leisure is not rest, since the latter is a respite from work, a time for diversion, for recharging the batteries, for tuning up the mental and physical machinery. Leisure may entail intense activity, for at its core is play or celebration, the observation of rituals, gift-giving and feasting. And market relations are alien to celebration: Commodities vanish, quantified time is replaced by time as the fitting occasion, and social relations assume dramatic form insofar as all have parts to play in the observation of the celebration. Because celebration turns on the exchange of gifts, and on the acknowledgment of gifts received, it has a moment of joy, even if the celebration be funereal.

Finally, at the heart of the matter, death absents itself from the world of stress. Death haunts *Portrait and a Dream*, but the "I" of stress has no time for death. The self-creation of stress's "I" announces a flight from death. Violence and disease are everywhere in the white noise, but they appear as preventable, random occurrences that perhaps could have been avoided. The "I" has an aura of immortality, the eternity and indestructibility of energy. Hence no passion or celebration: Mardi Gras has such exuberance because Ash Wednesday follows. "I" spin in the whirlwind out of fear of death.

Not only do death, leisure, and passion not appear under stress, but the discourse on stress cannot discuss them. On the contrary, it conceals them from view. Our task is to peel away the structures of discourse and experience that form our world of stress and attempt to glimpse our world as if for the first time. What we find is an absence of death, and the celebration and passion that presence of death enables. Our further exploration of the world of stress will reveal the absence of the passion of grief, which the experience of loss, especially of death, occasions. Stress is a way of speaking of grief without speaking about it, without letting it occur. What can the relation between stress and grief be?

PRE-MODERN "STRESS" AND THE WORLD IT EVOKES

How did the stressful world come to be? The absence of death, leisure, and passion serves to launch a historical inquiry into the formation of the stressful world. To begin, we start with the observation that the word *stress* has not always had its current denotations and connotations. Stress itself has undergone historical change, and the analogies and differences between our stress and the stress of the pre-modern era are revealing. *Stress* existed as a word prior to its definition as a scientific term in the middle of the nineteenth century. Its current usage has dulled our ears to the metaphorical character of stress.

Stress was an aphetic form of *distress*, and the sense of the word arose both from that of *distress* ("straining, pressing tightly, strain, pressure") and from that of the Old French *estrece* ("narrowness, straitness, oppression"). The earliest sense of *stress* concerned "hardships, straits, adversity, affliction." In a related sense, *stress* signified oppressive power which forced someone to do something against his will. Along these lines, as a verb *stress* meant "to confine, incarcerate," in fourteenth-century usage. Sixteenth-century usage depersonalized the external force that oppressed, as in the commonplace "the stress of weather."[13] Only in its more generalized sense does pre-modern stress serve as touchstone and foil for our stresses: Engineering borrowed an appropriate word from the vernacular to describe how physical materials react to external force. Current popular usage, influenced though it be by the return of the scientific meaning of *stress* to the vernacular, continues to carry the resonance of distress and straits, despite assertions that some stress is beneficial. Fundamentally, stress named that which assails with great strength, which must be endured, and which depletes one's substance. Regarding the last aspect, the legal usage, dating from the fifteenth century, is instructive: "to take stresses" meant to seize the goods of someone because of debt, rent, etc., owed. In addition, "to call to stress" (fourteenth century) meant "to summon to undergo trial," and in this context, *stress* could mean bodily suffering or injury.

Stress named what was hard and had to be endured; what pressed in, constrained, burdened, and placed demands on whatever was subject to it. It named that which tested strength of endurance. *Stress* named a muscular and bony perception of the world, in that it was through the muscles and bones that one learned of the hardness of the world and the original meaning of straits, narrowness, pressure, constraint. Circumstances such as these reflected back one's own bulk, substantiality, and strength. But *stress* did not name or evoke mastery over the forces that muscled; it named trial, endurance, and ultimately, being overpowered by the forces that brought suffering.

Stress called forth trial, endurance, suffering, strength. A recurrent image was of a ship at sea subject to the stress of foul weather. The ship must ride out the storm. In this image lies the difference between the stress of modernity and that of earlier epochs. A sailing ship did not challenge the storm coming on the north wind, not in the sense of being independent of the wind for its own power. It remained dependent upon the wind and needed to respond to it. However much the captain fought the storm, outwitted it, outmuscled it to save his ship, he relied on the wind to see the ship through its voyage. Stress tested the ship and the captain, showing them to be—if they weathered the storm—seaworthy, capable of suffering and bearing the storm. Stress proved the strength, power, and virtue of ship and crew.

This brief meditation shows the former essence of stress, which is still found in our stress, albeit in radically different form. Stress constrained and distressed, subjected to trial, seized upon the substance, and so tested the fibers of the thing so subjected. Stress revealed how something endured.

The contrast with modernity's stress could not be greater. Stress now involves work, not endurance. Suffering stress, regarding it in terms of tests which prove one's virtue, sounds inappropriate today. Our stress is a flattened version of earlier stress, calling forth from us more work. Moreover, today stress never ceases, except in death, whereas pre-modern stress was not constant. One cannot imagine feast days or festivals per se as stressful. Only hardship called forth endurance, but today every event demands adaptation and energy. We cannot conceive of an activity that does not consume energy, although formerly such activities were a common occurrence.[14]

In the older sense of the term, *stress* named the burdens, the griefs, the trials of life. Indeed, *burden, grief,* and *trial* were synonyms for *stress*. They indicate that one can be under a weight, under oppression, without being under stress in the modern sense.

The older meaning of *stress* serves to remind us of the play of wills that the modern discourse on stress obscures. *Stress* named the oppression of being under the will of another. Is that less true today? Rushing to work to meet a deadline—that commonplace of modern stress—is submission to the will of an other, even if the "I" is driven by its own needs. But the technical connotations of the discourse on stress do not show the oppressive constraints of the other's will as the pre-modern sense of stress did. We would be different creatures today if it did. Our stress makes of the will a natural force, a given that cannot be conversed with, and which cannot (and should not) be escaped, but only a force to which we must adapt.

Only in the present does stress become something sought out. Formerly it was endured; now it is pursued. The daring of our architecture that defies gravity and soars upward; the thrill of working under pressure and living in the fast lane. These examples indicate again that we have become beings that feed upon stress. It draws forth our substance, which we call energy. As stress squeezes the flesh from our accelerating existence and turns us into sources of energy, we crave the energy that stress ultimately is. But the craving comes from desperation. We desire simply to survive, to have decent lives, and the options seem so few. We know that how we live is killing us, leading us into addictions, flaying our most important relationships by depriving them of time, yet we see no way out except to become pure energy.

CONCLUSION

What does a phenomenology of stress yield? It makes explicit lived dimensions of the world for people who daily know that they experience stress, that stress exists as one thing they reckon with and seek to modulate. In this world, time and energy and money are scarce quantities demanding allocation. The present provides hardly any dwelling place. Past and future, near and far crash into the dimensionless space of life. The stressful world has no fixed points of orientation. It is all white noise, a flood of information trivial and profound, true and false, a torrent of demands, deadlines and tasks, a revolving door of work and rest. In the wonderfully satirical novel *White Nosie*, Don DeLillo captures the chaos of this world, here in the words of the chairman of a university department devoted to the study of trivia:

"The flow is constant," Alfonse said. "Words, pictures, numbers, facts, graphics, statistics, specks, waves, particles, motes. Only a catastrophe gets our attention. We want them, we need them, we depend on them. As long as they happen somewhere else. This is where California comes in.... We can relax and enjoy these disasters because in our hearts we feel that California deserves whatever it gets. Californians invented the concept of life-style. This alone warrants their doom."[15]

In the face of this world, what do "I" do? The only *rational* act is list making. The list acknowledges that every action has the character of a demand, requiring the expenditure of energy and time. For all this, stress is not undesirable. In controlled amounts it is a good, for it means that "I" am productive, engaged, important, and useful, and not marginal, homeless, and underclass. Stress is ingested, transforming me into a primitive powerful being who overcomes mere human limitations.

NOTES

1. Jackson Pollock, quoted in B. H. Friedman, *Jackson Pollock: Energy Made Visible* (New York: McGraw-Hill, 1972), p. 178. Also: "Jackson Pollock's art is still an attempt to cope with urban life"; see Clement Greenberg, "The present prospects of American painting and sculpture," *Horizon* (October 1947), quoted in Friedman, p. 101.

2. "Provisional Data from the Health Promotion and Disease Prevention Supplement to the National Health Interview Survey: United States, Jan.–March, 1985," *Advance Data* no. 113 (Nov. 15, 1985), 4146 (8.114). As additional evidence of the public reality of stress, there is the important book from 1970, *Future Shock* by Alvin Toffler (New York: Random House, 1970), which presents in many respects a phenomenology of stress.

3. The quotations used in this section come from written descriptions and interviews that I have gathered over the past four years. For an overview of phenomenological psychological methodology, which I employed to gain insight into these data, see Rolf von Eckartsberg, *Life-World Experience: Existential-Phenomenological Research Approaches in Psychology* (Washington, DC: Center for Advanced Research in Phenomenology & University Press of America, 1986). I place the subject of stress (the "I") between quotation marks in order to indicate (1) that this subject is subject of the stressful world and not the ontological subject; (2) that as the noetic pole of experience, this subject co-constitutes the stressful world. "I" also avoids technical terms such as *ego* or *self* that have other connotations. "I" belongs to the tradition of William James in *The Principles of Psychology*, and even of Freud's *Ich*, a much more grounded term than the abstract *ego*.

4. Kevin Lynch, *The Image of the City* (Cambridge: MIT Press, 1960).

5. Martin Heidegger, writing on the essence of the modern age, states: "The revealing that rules in modern technology is a challenging...which puts to nature the unreasonable demand that it supply energy that can be extracted and stored as such." [In *The Question Concerning Technology and Other Essays*, trans. William Lovitt (New York: Harper Colophon Books, 1977), p. 14.] Stress, from this angle, is an application of the revealing that rules in modern technology in so far as it reveals human beings as a "standing reserve" of energy. "Stress" names the event of becoming so revealed.

6. John Bradshaw, *Healing the Shame That Binds You* (Deerfield, FL: Health Communications, 1988). Consider the following advice from a government publication: "The best strategy for avoiding stress is to learn how to relax. Unfortunately, many people try to relax at the same pace that they lead the rest of their lives. For a while, tune out your worries about time, productivity, and 'doing right.' You will find satisfaction in just *being*, without striving" [Louis E. Kopolow, "Plain Talk About Handling Stress" (Rockville, MD: National Institute of Mental Health, 1983)].

7. Erich Fromm, *To Have or to Be* (New York: Bantam Books, 1976), p. 133.

8. Dick Hitt, "Making the Best of Traffic Snarls on Dallas Roads," *Dallas Times-Herald*, 18 December 1988, p. B–1.

9. See Harold Searles, "Unconscious processes in relation to the environmental crisis," in *Countertransference and Related Subjects* (New York: International Universities Press, 1979), pp. 228–242.

10. James Hillman, *Emotion: A Comprehensive Phenomenology of Theories and Their Meaning for Therapy* (Evanston: Northwestern University Press, 1961), pp. 279–80.

11. Bernd Jager, "Transformation of the passions: Psychoanalytic and phenomenological perspectives," in *Existential-Phenomenological Perspectives in Psychology: Exploring the Breadth of Human Experience*, eds. Ronald S. Valle and Steen Halling (New York: Plenum, 1989), p. 223.

12. Maurice Merleau-Ponty, *Phenomenology of Perception*, trans. Colin Smith (New York: Humanities Press, 1962), pp. 163–64.

13. *Oxford English Dictionary* (Oxford: Clarendon Press, 1989). See also Lawrence Hinkle, "The Concept of 'Stress' in the Biological and Social Sciences," *International Journal of Psychiatry in Medicine* 5, no. 4 (1974), 337.

14. For a remnant of the earlier view, a view now marginal to the world of stress, see Rudolf Steiner, *The Child's Changing Consciousness and Waldorf Education* (Hudson, N.Y.: Anthroposophic Press, 1988), p. 73: "At this stage of childhood, the aim

should be to work with the one system in the human being that never tires throughout a person's whole life. The only system prone to fatigue is the metabolic and limb system. This system does tire and it passes on its tiredness to the other systems. But I ask you, is it possible for the rhythmic system to tire? No—this it must never do, for if the heart were not beating all through life without tiring, without suffering from fatigue, and if breathing were not going on all the time without becoming exhausted, we simply could not live. The rhythmic system does not tire."

15. Don DeLillo, *White Noise* (New York: Elizabeth Sifton Books/Viking, 1985), p. 66.

2

The Engineering of Grief

Stress has a structural place in consciousness, serving a key role in the understanding of self and of the ills that befall us. It guides institutional planning, as when a corporation begins a wellness program to reduce employee stress. It keeps consultants busy, researchers productive, exercise instructors jumping, and ordinary citizens experimenting with an increasingly complex array of diets, life-styles and technological stress-reducing gadgets. Stress has become a beacon in the treacherous waters of life.

But stress is not only a phenomenon that people experience. It is also an artifact of modern science and its popularization. What is absent in most of the commentary on stress is an analysis of how it forms perceptions of self, body, and world. Primarily, discussion centers on what causes stress, what stress causes, and if stress is a suitable concept in a model of disease etiology. These questions of causality cannot illumine the cultural or psychological meaning of stress as an artifact through which we perceive ourselves and the world. This chapter explores stress as an artifact and does so in two ways: (1) by analyzing what the rhetoric of stress seeks to persuade us to do and believe, and (2) by considering the truth as well as the falsity of the rhetoric, in order to grasp what is meant.

Allan Young, a sociologist, and Kristian Pollock, an anthropologist, have articulated ideological critiques of stress. Young argues that "while the facts about stress *are* scientific, they are also the products of certain historically determined factors, i.e., specific sets of social relations and theoretical knowledge which account for their ideological character." In the ideological background of stress lies the assumption of an essentially asocial atomistic individual. As a result: "By displacing the human subject from his place in society to a desocialized and amorphous environment, the discourse banishes the arena of conflicting class and group interests from the real conditions of existence."[1] Pollock agrees with Young's thesis that stress naturalizes the social world and thus supports existing social institutions, but he adds that the discourse on stress is ideologically more ambivalent than Young thinks. Pollock believes that stress

can be used selectively and in different contexts at both theoretical and popular levels to support different views about, for example, the nature of the social order, man's place in it, the nature of individual autonomy and self-reliance, the reciprocal responsibilities for health care of the individual, the health services of the state, and so on.[2]

Because the ideological context of stress is extremely flexible, Pollock believes "the term itself has become so vacuous that it represents an obstacle rather than an aid to research."[3]

I share Young and Pollock's thesis that stress as a construct peculiar to modern society has an ideological background that both reveals and conceals its own significance. But I think the vacuity of stress is positive: Since it has been bound up with systems thinking, it shares in the nature of that thinking.[4] Systems thinking accommodates all differences, offering opposition to none and making place for any ideological content. It can do so because it honors no external opposition. Thus there is no irony in viewing stress as reflecting both an ideology of the atomistic individual and an ideology of the primacy of social interdependence. If some "open subsystems" wish to maintain that they are social atoms, that is simply their way of relating to the embracing supersystems.[5]

Stress is neither a set of facts about disease causation nor a false consciousness about the nature of the individual. Rather, it is a distorted mirror reflecting life in contemporary society. In this glass, flexible enough to twist into any desired shape, sufficient reflection occurs to enable people to manage their lives. But its vacuity is such that it never moves people to recognize the inherent distortions. In uncovering the character of this mirror, the phenomenology of stress needs to be complemented by an analysis of the rhetoric of stress: a study of the recurrent images, metaphors, arguments, and themes in a wide spectrum of literature on stress—scientific and popular—in order to uncover what the literature invites us to take as self-evident. For despite the disagreements within the literature about theoretical formulations, much is common to all viewpoints. Rhetorical analysis concerns the commons of the stress field. There is enough truth in stress' metaphors to persuade us to perceive and act in "adaptive" ways, and our analysis of the rhetoric of stress must retrieve what is true in these metaphors. I believe that the discourse on stress does not simply set up a false consciousness: the aims are good but distorted by the biases of the day. The goal of this analysis then, is to unearth the distortions and salvage the nuggets of truth they contain; then we can ask about the history of stress as a construct and an experience, in order to free the imagination from its grip. The terms of the rhetoric of stress are: energy and boundaries, trauma, control, and loss.

A RHETORIC OF ENERGY AND BOUNDARIES

> "*Insulation*! That was the ticket. That was the term Rawlie Thorpe used. 'If you want to live in New York, ... you've got to insulate, insulate, insulate,' meaning insulate yourself from those people. ... If you could go breezing down the FDR Drive in a taxi, then why file into the trenches of the urban wars?"
>
> —Tom Wolfe, *Bonfire of the Vanities*[6]

Homeostasis is the dynamic process of maintaining a favorable internal milieu in the face of a changing environment. Stress challenges the internal balance and evokes the energies necessary to restore balance, to keep the organism self-regulated. From Cannon onward, stress has been seen largely in terms of the body's response to demands placed upon it.

In the scientific literature, Cannon's basic position has been affirmed. Burchfield says, "One of the most commonly accepted definitions of stress is that it is anything which causes an alteration of homeostatic processes."[7] According to Fleming, Baum, and Singer, "Integrated patterns of psychological and biological responses to situational demands characterize the stress process."[8] Monet and Lazarus say, "The arena that the stress area refers to consists of any event in which environmental demands, internal demands, or both *tax* or *exceed* the adaptive resources of an individual, social system, or tissue system."[9] Except for the technicality of the language, these various depictions of stress correspond to what one finds in popular literature. Under stress, a defined and discrete entity faces a changing environment. Cannon notes, in this vein, that cold-blooded animals have fewer demands to face because they do not maintain a constant internal temperature. In general, the greater the individuality, or differentiation of self from the world, the greater the potential for stress.

Let us provisionally define stress: Stress occurs when a situation evokes a response of energy production for the purposes of maintaining an individual's integrity. The demand and the reply occur at the boundaries of the individual. With sufficient energy, the person can secure the boundary between self and world.

The critical point is at the boundaries, for it is there that disease arises. Here is how this is presented in stress literature: (1) Disease does not result simply from the attack of an external force; host factors play a role in determining whether disease will occur. (2) Some diseases are primarily responses to noxious agents. Selye calls them "diseases of adaptation," indicating that that which protects also kills. (3) Chronic diseases are especially illuminated by the stress concept. "Diseases of civilization" result in part from long-endured, high-level stress; these diseases result primarily from wear and tear on the individual's systems. (4) "Illness or death would also be consequent to a failure to adapt," says Burchfield, stating an implication usually only implicit in the discourse on stress.[10]

The first three propositions reject unicausal theories of disease etiology ("the germ theory") in favor of multicausal theories in a systems approach and, in particular, an acknowledgment of the importance of host factors. Bringing the connection between stress and disease to bear on our definition, let us say that in the face of some demand, the individual responds by producing energy and mobilizing defensive measures in order to sustain his integrity, and that integrity as an ideal is called "health." Disease occurs when the boundaries of the systems defining the individual rigidify or dissolve, producing disharmony.

The fourth proposition would be hotly contested, but it is essential to the construct of stress. "A fundamental assumption of the stressful life event school," write Mestrovic and Glassner, "is . . . that health is natural—health being some sort of state of homeostasis—and that 'stress' leads to an abnormal state in the organism's relation to its surroundings."[11] The desire for a utopia without disease or death is an undercurrent in stress literature: everywhere disease and death are seen as failures of adaptation, as somehow unnatural. "Humans can adapt to almost any stress, given the use of appropriate coping strategies," writes a psychological researcher.[12] Consequently, illness and death occur whenever something prevents adaptation.

Adaptation resolves itself into a matter of boundary protection. A delicate balance is required, since too much defense is as pathogenic (allergies, rheumatoid arthritis) as too little (AIDS). Boundaries preserve the individual in a dynamic steady state. The force of the discourse on stress is to persuade the individual to adapt to change, given the discourse's mentality that the world is hostile and traumatizing, and its equation of health with boundary maintenance. Flexible but firm boundaries are the ideal. Avoiding disease and death become theoretical possibilities, if ways could only be found to secure the borders from the assaults of the alien world. Our borders are secured not by opposition to the world, but by adjustments of our various systems and their parts in the interest of maintaining the system itself. Since for the moment this goal is a practical impossibility, the continual monitoring (increasingly, self-monitoring) of our systems keeps us on the alert, adapting to change but never submitting to it in the archaic fashion of the suffering and the dying.

The boundaries defended so rigorously are viewed in this discourse as patterns of energy which define the nature of the individual organism or other system. As the phenomenological inquiry into the nature of stress revealed and the scientific literature affirms, an organism experiencing stress engages in the patterning (and processing) of energy. What matters most are patterns of energy—that is, information—rather than energy itself. Hinkle's critique of Selye's model is a case in point; for Hinkle, an organism's processing of environmental stimuli shapes the precise nature of the stress response, so that the stress response is not the generalized, nonspecific response that Selye assumed it to be. Again, Lazarus's model places cognitive processes at the origin of stress. These theories and their popular equivalents mirror the dominant technologies of the day, such as the computer, which does not, as did the steam engine, require enormous quantities of energy to be powerful.

The immediate and practical result of the rhetoric of energy and boundaries is to persuade us to seek information in order to maintain health, with the tacit allure of immortality if we comply with what the information vendors offer. The rhetoric of energy and boundaries entices us to accumulate power and knowledge. Then we are likely to act to maintain our health as we do when told about threatening weather—to use administrative language, when there is a "severe storm watch" or a "tornado warning"—be alert, keep tuned to the knowledge brokers, spend what we need on safety.

A RHETORIC OF TRAUMA

In the United States, the Vietnam War has come to symbolize stress in its pure form. With that war stress came to imply a trauma so intense that psychologists surrendered their once rock-solid belief in childhood experience as the primary cause of psychopathological symptoms. Soldiers who suffer from what has come to be called post-traumatic stress syndrome (PTSS) have been compared to concentration camp prisoners and accident victims. Finally, after some years of debate over the existence of a "Vietnam War syndrome," PTSS was officially recognized in 1980 with the publication of the *Diagnostic and Statistical Manual III* (DSM-III) by the American Psychiatric Association.[13] One reason for the delay in recognition was a bias in favor of etiologies emphasizing the childhood origins of psychopathology. This bias holds, according to Boulanger, "that a psychological defense system cannot have been adequate in the first place if it was so permanently disabled by a catastrophic event."[14] That bias no longer carries the weight it once did.

In the decade since PTSS became an accepted diagnosis, it has been applied to an ever-increasing population. Indeed, the 1980s have seen everyone become a victim of trauma and abuse.[15] DSM-III defines trauma in terms of events "beyond the normal range of human experience." Trauma has become so important that "the field of traumatic stress studies" is developing, according to Charles Figley.[16]

But what is a trauma? The notion is ambiguous. One understanding of trauma holds that certain events, such as death, combat, divorce—in general, any change for good or ill—are inherently traumatic. This "life events" school has been criticized for neglecting the meaning of events for the persons undergoing them and for neglecting the social and cultural contexts within which the events occur. Opponents of the life events theory hold that a trauma is a type of derangement of the symbolic context within which people make sense of life. To speak plainly, when the meaning of life is threatened or lost, then trauma occurs.[17] In a variant of this position, two researchers suggest that "contemporary American culture during the current transitional process impedes the development of a well-defined self and thus increases an individual's vulnerability to developing severe stress reactions in response to a traumatic event."[18] If trauma occurs more frequently today, it is because we suffer primarily from the loss of a cultural context in which to define ourselves and in which to comprehend suffering and pain. And it does appear to be the case that trauma occurs more often now.[19]

The primary rhetorical value of trauma has not been to reveal that life has become absurd. Rather, our understanding of trauma has persuaded us to believe that we are all victims. The popular embracing of being a victim had its beginnings, in American society, in the civil rights movement of the 1960s. As Christopher Lasch has noted, since the late 1960s, after the death of Martin Luther King, Jr., the tendency among those pressing for civil rights has been to argue that they have been victimized by the powerful.[20] Lasch argues that victims assume an unassailable moral position, insisting that victimizers redress the abuse of their power. The limitations of a victim's demand are its short-circuiting of dialogue, of appeals to common humanity, and its dwelling solely on the distribution of power. This political rhetoric has been echoed in the psychological disciplines, partly also in reaction to psychoanalytic notions such as the Oedipus complex, that saw the "victim" as desiring "abuse." Critics of psychoanalysis, such as Alice Miller, see Freud's intrapsychic etiological emphasis as a form of legitimation of existing power structures.[21] The status of victim holds, in short, the high moral ground, and the temptation is to generalize it endlessly.

The discourse on stress intertwines with that of victimization, for in both the emphasis is clearly on the traumatic nature of a situation. In both we find "a tendency to regard society rather than the individual as pathogenic and out of control."[22] One psychiatrist even suggests that the world has broken down, not the patient: "individuals who have lived in a psychotic environment and whose reality was beyond the scope of the ordinary life"[23] suffer from PTSS. Extreme conditions, lurking in the margins of everyday life and filling the columns of newspapers and the lead stories on the television news, can overwhelm anyone, not only those predisposed to breakdown by virtue of upbringing or heredity. The perpetual threat of trauma wreaks havoc on cherished ideas of individuality. Van der Kolk compares the symptoms of PTSS to those of borderline and narcissistic disorders, which have become the definitive psychopathologies of the day. All three disorders make evident a lack of psychological boundary between self and world, an inner emptiness, alternating feelings of impotence and omnipotence, and sense of self-worthlessness. As in a war against guerrillas or terrorists or ever-increasing crime, all distinctions of person and place dissolve. We are no longer surprised when the familiar is replaced by the fantastic.

What are we to make of the apparent increase in trauma? In part it is an inflated way of speaking, one that invites professional intervention into further areas of human life. Reflection along the lines of Lasch and Illich among others suggests that this is part of what is occurring.[24] Nevertheless, given a "cultural epidemiology," to use David Levin's term, which reveals the prevalence of narcissistic and other disorders of the differentiation of self and world, I am led to think that trauma has increased in part because our experience of the self and our experience of the world have changed. The symbolic universe has become deranged and we suffer from "a passion for the infinite," to use Durkheim's phrase.[25] Living under stress, we desire to become pure energy, to flee the flesh and the limitations of time and place. To the extent that we live under stress, we have become aliens on earth; that is, beings who need life-support systems in order to live here. For example, living in Dallas, I need my car, my phone, my electricity, my piped-in water, my air conditioner simply to survive. How far am I from the IV and the respirator? The difference between home and the intensive care unit (ICU) is one of degree, not of kind. That life-support systems are felt necessary means that one's very being has lost its center: One's living is not sustained from within, but essentially from without, by the products of mass production. One does not have to desire to be Robinson Crusoe in order to agree with Illich when he writes that beyond a certain degree, when humans do not make for themselves their own living, they lose the ability to subsist; i.e., to make themselves exist from themselves. We become appendages or parasites on the machines that supposedly serve us. Technology and institutions are thus counterproductive beyond a certain point, and our felt vulnerability to trauma indicates the extent to which we have lost an ability to subsist.[26] Thus, the rhetoric of trauma in the discourse on stress provides a distorted mirror for our situation, insofar as it points to our felt vulnerability, to the hostility of the world with its juxtaposed comforts and accidents, and to our tendency to define every aspect of life as a problem needing professional intervention.

A RHETORIC OF CONTROL

The rhetorical texture of the discourse on stress conveys attitudes about the self and the world. Thus far we have seen that if we imagine ourselves as under stress, we are enticed to perceive ourselves as victims of a traumatizing world and to accumulate power (energy, boundaries) in order to deal with it.

Now we turn to the solution to stress: taking control of one's life.[27] Three kinds of metaphors that pervade stress literature entice us to take control. Like all metaphors, they establish a common bond between different kinds of things. These metaphors link stress with three interlocking domains: engineering, administration, and the military. Their role in the discourse on stress is to instill attitudes of instrumental reason, namely a means–ends analysis or a problem-solving approach to life's difficulties. If these metaphors were intentionally presented as such, we would be amazed at their audacity; instead, we absorb them without the faintest tremor. The metaphors seem perfectly natural, given that our knowledge about stress comes largely from the academic science industry and the applied fields of health care distribution and business management. All three industries are temples of instrumental thinking.

The notion of system binds the metaphors together. The three form a whole that epitomizes the contemporary organization of living. Under the sway of a pliable notion of systems, these metaphors specify how systems should be managed. A system is a complex whole, in which the relationships between parts is of greater significance in defining the whole than the parts themselves, which are replaceable. A system may be closed, meaning that it does not exchange energy or information with anything outside of the system, or it may be open, meaning it does exchange energy and information. The universe is apparently a closed system, while organisms are open systems, in constant interaction with their environment. Systems are understood to be arranged hierarchically: one system, say an organism, is a subsystem of larger systems, such as society and the natural environment. In turn, the organism is a supersystem embracing physiological and psychological subsystems.

Because of the nature of our world, with its relatively abstract and decentralized communications, transportation, and energy systems, *system* conveys a reality to us. A system is basically a kind of object, governed by a network of energy and information exchanges. Systems theory gained such prominence in the biological sciences because it promises a way to speak about teleology or goal-directedness, which is evident in the behavior of living things, without abandoning a materialist metaphysics, which rejects teleological principles. The construct of stress fits well into systems thinking since stress names relations of force between elements in a system. And the systems framework for speaking of stresses enables an easy slide from problems of the organism to those of the environment and the social order. For the content of words like *system* and *stress* is ambiguous: They can name any kind of relationship, from those between subatomic particles to those between the superpowers.[28] Hence the binding power systems thinking has regarding the metaphors in the discourse on stress.[29] The metaphors are normative as well as descriptive: As nurses "learn a variety of relaxation, imagery, and breathing techniques ... they begin to share and feel the true experience of 'being an open system.' "[30] These relaxed open systems mediate the "high tech" ICU with "high touch" human contact and so accommodate the larger systems that encompass them.

An engineering mentality has been present since the nineteenth century, when something like stress began to appear. Questions such as "How much can one take?" and "How can we strengthen the organism or make it more flexible?" pervade our perceptions of the stressful and emanate from engineering concerns. Let me give one example of an engineering metaphor, but add that such a literal reading of the metaphor is not universally shared. Hans Eysenck, a prominent researcher, explicitly equates personality traits, such as introversion and extraversion, with the modulus of elasticity, k, in Hooke's Law (stress = $k \times$ strain), the basic formula in the scientific study of stress on material. In physics, Eysenck writes, k "depends upon the nature of the material and the type of stress used to produce the strain" and is a measure of elasticity.[31] While other theorists do not apply Hooke's Law so directly to psychological variables, they do share the value given to the implied virtue named by k: flexibility. Like strength, resilience, and hardiness, flexibility names a good toward which we ought to strive, a good influenced by the engineering mentality and the metaphors that express it.

Closely allied to engineering are military and administrative metaphors. While it is useful to distinguish the three, both engineering and the military have administrative organizations. By administration I mean technologically and bureaucratically organized activity. Administered groups emphasize procedures, roles, means–end analysis, and impartiality.[32]

Administrative metaphors proliferate in scientific literature. They convey the spirit of instrumental reason, efficiency, and cost–benefit analysis as central values. In the discourse on stress these values are enshrined and unquestioned.[33] A few examples will suffice. One set of psychological researchers describes stress in terms of "appraisal of events" and of a "response . . . mediated by a costs–rewards analysis."[34] Again: "the selection of responses is facilitated by evaluation of probable outcomes, available options, and so on."[35] "Appraisals," "costs–rewards analysis," and "evaluation of probable outcomes" suggest systematic rational analysis, connoting the managerial processes that supposedly reign in the boardroom, and which aim at efficiency and productivity. While *cope* tends to generate military considerations, it carries administrative ones as well: "Coping has been defined as the process of managing external or internal demands that are perceived as taxing or exceeding a person's resources."[36] The management of scarce resources plays a role basic to the appraisal of potentially stressful situations: "If one has a limited amount of attention or effort to invest, decisions must be made about which situations are important enough to warrant investment of time and energy."[37] A major review of the effects of stress on performance concluded that "many of the proposed explanations for stressor after-effects are" forms of the "adaptive-cost hypothesis."[38] This hypothesis states that "increased adaptive effort would deplete one's available psychic energies and would thus result in deficits in subsequent demanding tasks."[39]

There is even a recent theory of stress framed explicitly in administrative terms. Hobfalls defines psychological stress as "a reaction to the environment in which there is (a) the threat of a net loss of resources, (b) the net loss of resources, or (c) a lack of resource gain following the investment of re-sources."[40] These metaphors carry expectations which focus on "rational, efficient, and successful decisions about how to cope." For example, certain classes of people are found to engage in counterproductive measures: battered women and "black women in a traditional Black community" are cited as inadequate copers.[41]

Military metaphors are equally ubiquitous in the literature. Selye's depic-tion of the General Adaptation Syndrome (GAS) is in terms of attack, defense, coexistence, resistance, exhaustion, defeat. The GAS, with its stages of alarm, resistance, and exhaustion, is a clear description of a state of siege. Selye's model has been called a "pathogen model" described in military terms: for example, "combat threats posed by invading pathogens."[42] Throughout stress discourse, there is the omnipresent sense that stress happens in the context of threat, danger, and harm; that stress evokes defenses; and that stress takes place at the boundary of self and non-self, a boundary maintained by mech-anisms of vigilance and combat. Most important, "coping," a concept central to the construct, has its roots in warfare. The earliest usage of *cope* meant "to strike, to come to blows, encounter, join battle, . . . meet in the shock of battle or tournament."[43] In a prominent theory of psychological stress, Richard Lazarus states that stress cannot even exist unless danger or threat is appraised, appraisal being the keystone of the coping process. Once coping gets intro-duced into the discourse, it brings with it offensive as well as defensive strategies and tactics: "When we speak of *coping*, then, we are referring to that aspect of the stress process that includes individuals' attempts to resist and overcome stressors."[44] From this perspective, the potential hostility of the world is ever-present. Anything can cause the stress reaction if it is so appraised (Lazarus), or if it demands change (the life events school of Holmes and Rahe), or if it taxes resources (Hobfalls).

Military metaphors allow for considerable self-aggrandizement. In an ex-treme example, a middle-class American compared her midlife crisis to a Cambodian child's survival of Pol Pot's reign of terror. Such hyperbole comes easily when we envision life as stressful, when we are steeped in the attitudes, the mentality of stress. Our perception of our vulnerability to trauma is pronounced. Questions arise (like those Walker Percy asks in *Lost in the Cosmos: The Last Self-Help Book*[45]): (1) Are modern selves so vulnerable, or is the world so hostile, as to invite such extreme comparisons? (2) Could it be that the construct of stress disables modern selves, leading them to ex-perience themselves as helpless?

The three kinds of metaphors—administrative, military, and engineering—reflect the relationships of power that spark the concern for stress in the contemporary world. A frank appraisal of the meaning of stress occurs in the following:

We are in the middle of a national epidemic of stress disease, as clearly shown by death and health breakdown statistics. Stress directly and indirectly adds to the cost of doing business, and it detracts from the total quality of life for a very large number of American workers. . . . It is the self-interest of corporate management to understand and deal with stress. Good health is good business.[46]

Helping workers and managers deal more effectively with stress has become a necessity in the modern business world. Since "human resources constitute the most expensive form of capital for an organization,"[47] health is too valuable a commodity to be left solely to individual initiative. The metaphors, implicitly equating corporate goals and personal health, can persuade us to manage our own stresses in the service of overall productivity and efficiency. The discourse also encourages social planning and regulation in the name of an unquestionable good, namely health. If efficiency, productivity, and health form a trinity of public goods, what force can resist actions done for the good of all in their names? Through the discourse on stress we are moved to identify as our own the attitudes and values that reign in corporate and public administrative life. In this move we do not see ourselves as subordinated to externally imposed goals; on the contrary, when we act in ways that promote efficiency/health, we are seen, and see ourselves, as having "taken control of our lives."

The notion of control binds together the engineering, administrative, and military metaphors in the discourse. In an illuminating passage, George Mandler writes:

Mastery refers to the perception that the events in our personal world may be brought under our control. This sense of mastery may be important not so much because it has direct effect on our actions but because a sense of control, or mastery, colors the cognitive interpretation of our world. It is generally seen as good to be in control of our world, and as the world is appraised as good the emotional tone will be positive. . . . The objective absence of control is not necessarily seen as negative. . . . It is rather the subjective sense of control that is important rather than the objective control of the environment.[48]

This prime example of doublethink is instructive. The outer world may well be beyond the control of the individual will, or of individual wills, but no matter. So long as one has the feeling of being in control—to will in Stoic fashion that will happen anyway—stress is reduced. Herbert Lefcourt argues that "while freedom and control are both illusions, . . . illusions do have consequences."[49] He cites as example what amounts to an Aesop's fable for the Age of Stress:

With shock as the aversive stimulus, Staub, Tursky, and Schwartz (1971) found that subjects who were allowed to administer shock to themselves and to select the level of intensity of that shock reported less discomfort at higher levels of shock and endured stronger shock than did paired subjects to whom shock was administered passively.[50]

Thus do survivors and victims cope and stay on top of things. The rallying cry of "take control of your life," sanguine enough in the face of a massive sense of helplessness that underlies the modern self, is in fact largely the nurturing of an illusion. Problem-solving and the strengthening of boundaries are lubricants in the gears of modern corporate and social life, a life in which the individual needs to remain ever an open system.

While the emphasis on the perception of control opens the door to so-phisticated forms of manipulation, such as when nursing home patients are invited to feel that they control their health care by being informed of plans and by being provided information regarding procedures,[51] there is another aspect of the subjective feeling of control. Suzanne Kobasa's explanation of the importance of an internal locus of control captures the spirit:

Control allows persons to perceive many stressful life events as predictable conse-quences of their own activity and, thereby, as subject to their direction and manip-ulation. . . . But even those events that a person is not likely to have caused (e.g., death of a parent) are also best confronted in a spirit of control. . . . Persons in control should benefit from both autonomy and intention. They feel capable of acting effectively on their own. Further, they can interpret and incorporate various sorts of events into an ongoing life plan and transform these events into something consistent and not so jarring to the organism.[52]

This description partially portrays the stress-resistant or "hardy" personality who accepts the world as a network of events with definite causes and effects, and who can intervene in the process. The hardy personality is the existential hero filtered through the construct of stress. He renounces all illusions, save the one that he is in charge; and he perceives himself as being in charge, even of death.

Lefcourt summarizes the research on the locus of control issue:

Whether in response to cardiac difficulties, commuting, business disruptions, or the stressful training in medical school or Marine Corps recruitment camps, internals seem better equipped to survive their ordeals. They do not succumb as readily to dysphoric feelings and cease in their efforts to succeed at their various tasks as do those who hold external control expectancies.[53]

Primarily through mastery and a sense of control does one survive ordeals, showing clearly how stress frames the world. It reveals an absurd world in which meaning is made, not found, and in which the will of the individual is simultaneously glorified and treated as illusory. A great unresolved ambivalence shines through this notion of control. To face ordeals with equanimity, to cope without undue anguish, anxiety, or despair is the advantage of having an internal locus of control. But the underlying thrust of the rhetoric is that the sky is empty. As Aaron Antonovsky states: "Only when there is no deity, no writ, but only meaningless chaos does one's only hope lie in an internal locus of control."[54] An inner but illusory locus of control seems all that is left of the Faustian bargain in a time of systems under stress.

As a final example of the kind of perception of self and world that is currently accepted unquestioningly, I refer to Spiro's interpretation of the type of man who becomes a Buddhist monk in Burma: "Buddhist monasticism . . . is a highly efficient means for coping with the psychological problems of many Burmese men."[55] The author emphasizes that the monks are not psychotic, merely that they have found a culturally approved means for dealing with intrapsychic conflicts. The underlying message is that the monks flee a world that they cannot handle—the retreat behind the walls being a salutary coping response. The stress perspective, indifferent to the claims of Buddhism, sees only a problem of the efficient deployment of manpower. His article is the conceptual equivalent of an army converting a monastery into a command post. The commander, like Sartre's Orestes in *The Flies*, looks at the statue of the Buddha, serene in enlightenment, and sees only potential protection from the stimuli that the enemy—the outer world—hurls.

A RHETORIC OF LOSS

> In our "civilized" society the symbolic meanings of countless social interactions are continuously arousing us to fight, defend, or flight. It seems plausible that, since we rarely allow this arousal to be transformed into physical action, our voluntary and autonomic nervous systems are continuously overloaded. Beyond a certain point, this overloading leads to a stress reaction.
>
> —Aaron Beck[56]

One of the icons of the stress field is the Social Readjustment Rating Scale, developed by Holmes and Rahe back in the 1950s. While theoretically there is debate over the value of the scale, it has come to symbolize the existence of stress. Reproduced in countless textbooks in psychology and making appearances in the magazines that airlines provide free of charge, the scale contains a list of life stresses, in descending order of seriousness, to enable the reader to review life for its stresses and their relative seriousness. The list is fairly comprehensive. It begins with death of spouse (100 points) and moves through a typical set of real-life scenarios, including job loss, job promotion, vacations, Christmas, etc. All events that require change, not only "bad" events, cause stress. If after adding up your score, the number is 300 or greater, you stand an increased chance of getting sick from the stresses of your life. In a way analogous to medieval manuals for examining one's conscience, the scale invites the reader to consider the extent to which he copes with change and the risks to health that he now faces. The great majority of the items involve loss of one kind or another. The message in the accompanying text informs the reader that things can be done to cope with stress: "Take charge of your life!" which is the modern equivalent of "Repent!"

The felt need to take control stems from occupying a position of vulnerability and trauma. In the literature on stress, we find stories of the origin of stress. They all depict a fundamental and unresolved loss. In a way that mirrors and partially accounts for the contemporary absorption with the psychology of the infant—particularly with what Melanie Klein calls the depressive position[57]—stress articulates a mood of abandonment, of vanished herds, of nostalgia. At odd moments in the talk around stress this depressed mood surfaces with poignancy, especially in daily life and occasionally in the scientific literature, although there it appears as either fact or as debunked misperception. But the position of loss grounds the entire construct of stress. The basic plot of these stories says that modernity is more stressful than previous times. This commonplace (in the rhetorical sense of an argument that has become a standard) of the discourse has two variants. First, modernity is stressful because cultural and technological development have outpaced biological evolution; our instinctual responses to complex situations are still those of the jungle, and are thus inappropriate and harmful. Second, modernity is stressful because it has lost its myths and traditions, rendering life meaningless. Exploration of these accounts draws us near to the heart of stress.

The Archaic Body

Modernity is stressful because it conflicts with our archaic body. Stress evokes primitive reflex and homeostatic mechanisms which were appropriate for natural conditions and for animals who have no choice but to react physically when threatened. Unfortunately, autonomic activity increases even when fight or flight no longer makes sense. Cultural progress, having outpaced biological evolution, invalidates some of the wisdom of the body. The problem is that we cannot discharge the aroused energy (felt as stress) directly, for we live in an environment where only applying problem-solving rationality produces beneficial results.

The muscle tension, the surge of epinephrine and other hormones, and the further consequences of physiological arousal, become sustained at a level that is too high for continued health. Because stress is chronic, our bodies face the threat of breakdown from constant wear and tear. Hence the emergence of "diseases of civilization," which were virtually unknown in primitive times. These disorders, such as heart disease and some kinds of cancer, are diseases of the individual; they are not communal diseases as were the epidemics of the past. Because we live under chronic levels of unrelieved stress, we need to relax, exercise, use certain drugs, and generally manage the stress of civilized life. Let us call this commonplace argument the topic of the archaic body, in that the plot states that we suffer stress because our bodies are not designed for technologically sophisticated societies.[58]

A variant of this commonplace states that stressful situations cause psychological regression to the archaic psyche of childhood. Aaron Beck presents one version: "stressors lead to a disruption of the normal activity of the cognitive organization. In addition to erosion of the ability to concentrate, recall, and reason, and to control impulses, there is an increase in primitive (primary process) content."[59] Stress threatens "vital interests," evokes primitive egocentric cognitive schemes, and depletes "the resources for energizing secondary-process schemes."[60] Beck explicitly states that the constraints of modern society inhibit direct action that would discharge excess energy and combat stress. However, the primitive impulses are not always constrained, erupting in violence when externalized or "acted out"; in illness, depression, and suicide when internalized.

Common to these different versions of the commonplace of the archaic body is a certain passivity of the individual in the face of distinctively modern situations. Contemporary social and technological changes are viewed as unchangeable as any natural thing, such as climate (perhaps more so, given current fears for the ecology). What takes a beating in this passivity is the embodied self, viewed as a primitive in the face of modern things. Correlative to the appearance of the body as archaic is the appearance of modernized social structures as a second nature. We face them as primitives presumably faced the natural world prior to the technological domination of nature. Thomas Luckmann, writing of the irrationality of modern society, and "a certain helplessness of the individual—vis-a-vis nature and the social order," concludes:

In modern society we are faced with a curious reversal. Nature appears to be manageable rather than fateful, the social structure seems to have become unmanageable—a second nature. It can be seen today that we shall be obliged to revise the modern view of nature. But shall we be able to revise not only our *view* of society as second nature but also change what may have become a hard *fact*: that the modern social system has indeed become second nature.[61]

Along the same lines, Arnold Gehlen observed that given the complexity of the social order and the resulting lack of immediate connection between actions and their consequences, we have become psychologically like primitives in an important way:

the industrial culture shares with the magic-ritualistic cultures of primitive peoples the property of severing man from everyday existence. Between early primitivism, which spins its resilient net of fantastic accounts and rituals over the world of experience, and the later primitivism, engendered by the unbearable pressure of monotony of a narrow sector of experience, there is not much difference from the standpoint of world estrangement.[62]

While the assessments by Luckmann and Gehlen of modern helplessness concur with the topic of the archaic body, they differ in one important way. Luckmann and Gehlen compare modern with archaic helplessness, whereas the topic of the archaic body imagines that the primitive was capable of real action. The commonplace thus obscures the passivity of the individual and the helplessness at the heart of the evocation of the archaic body by encouraging a fantasy that, underneath it all, we are cavemen, that the primal beast screams for release.

Examined more closely, the image of the archaic body presents anxiety over the possibility of action in the world. The primitive in the commonplace does not turn to ritual, magic, or collective action, he confronts the terror directly and alone, and then either fights or flees. This picture of man in nature, of the noble savage, makes for comforting fantasies and random explosions of rage and violence, but it does not move us to reckon with our social order as a human creation and hence to re-imagine our social order in the service of making dwelling possible. The commonplace indulges wishful thinking but little more.

The historical roots of this wishful thinking lie in the Enlightenment of the eighteenth century, specifically in Rousseau's noble savage and the correlative view that the city and society in general are artificial in the negative sense. Also having an Enlightenment source is the desire for power through knowledge and through an inner locus of control. The discourse on stress is in large measure warmed-over Enlightenment thought, seasoned with twentieth century facts about arousal and physiological changes in extreme situations.

The topic of the archaic body does contain, however, an implicit critique of modernity, specifically of its unnaturalness. Simpler societies did not face the flood of changes that we do. Then, the pace of life was slower and real communities existed. But the critique cuts both ways. It invites a revolt of the body against the mechanization of life, especially in response to the diseases of civilization. "Over the first three-quarters of this century," writes Albrecht, "Americans have enjoyed a dramatic increase in health and a dramatic decline in wellness."[63] The needs of the archaic body have become a potent political and social rallying cry, with both public and private sectors making efforts to accommodate it among the machinery. Nevertheless, the force of the critique has not been demodernization, a path usually seen as nostalgic at best. Rather, the critique calls for an increased disciplining of the body. Albrecht, for example, recommends a "wellness triad" of relaxation, exercise, and diet, which are standard items in any stress management program. The point of these activities is to improve well-being, true, but the ultimate effect is accommodation to modern conditions. The regimen has the effect of silencing the archaic body by whipping it into shape. In Illich's terms, wellness programs belong to "shadow work," which he defines as unpaid labor necessary to keep the machinery of production and consumption going. The regimen thus moves in the direction of making the body epiphenomenal in the modern world.[64]

The theme of the archaic body flows downstream as it were to considerations such as those of wellness. The archaic body is, then, but one half of the commonplace about the origin of stress, the other half being the engineering of the archaic body through the regimen of diet, exercise, and relaxation. It is worth noting that *Men Under Stress*, the first book to deal with stress, began by invoking Daedalus and Icarus. The fliers of World War II, who were the first to experience stress, were in command of one of modernity's potent symbols:

This supertoy, this powerful, snorting, impatient but submissive machine, enables the man to escape the usual limitations of time and space. Truly godlike, the flier soars above the earth and the little men confined to its surface. He feels his mastery of space and time by means of the intense speed of modern aircraft and their ability to maneuver without obstacle into any desired position.[65]

Here we have the archaic body as Icarus: young, capable of flight beyond his wildest dreams, only to come crashing down when he went beyond the limits of the human in an act of hubris. We take visceral pleasure in the intensification of bodily power that machines give us. Nevertheless, for the most part we enact Daedalus, the personification of instrumental reason, the one who always designs a technical solution to a human problem. In fact, the topic of the archaic body belongs to the perspective of Daedalus, insofar as the archaic body is a problem for which solutions must be found.

This need to find solutions for our archaic body's plight arises from loss: loss of an ability to act, of nature as the primal setting of human action, of the body as the ground of existence. These losses find expression in the narrative about the archaic nature of the flesh. Substitutes for bodily power, such as machines or disciplinary techniques, which promise to amplify our native powers, render us more helpless and passive than we were prior to their invention. By virtue of their power to amplify physical ability, these gifts of Daedalus reveal how defective, how archaic the body is. The gifts of Daedalus, the eternal engineer, abstract us increasingly from all that can be called the familiar. The topic of the archaic body reaches this conclusion by assuming that the body is indeed archaic in its response to danger. The conclusion is that intelligence resides elsewhere than in the flesh.

The Exile

But what if the stress response were not the atavistic appearance of the caveman or the pre-Oedipal infant? What if it were not the response of "nature" at all?[66]

The second commonplace which accounts for the stress of modern life centers around meaning and order. Modernity is stressful because society has lost its myths and traditions; as a result, moderns are alienated, anomic, hypervigilant, and morbidly self-conscious. Antonovsky links stress to an experienced lack of coherence in the world. According to Antonovsky, a sense of coherence

is a global orientation that expresses the extent to which one has a pervasive, enduring though dynamic feeling of confidence that one's internal and external environments are predictable and that there is a high probability that things will work out as well as can reasonably be expected.[67]

Stress is not the occurrence of hardships per se; hardships become stressful only when they lack meaningful context. Antonovsky does not find a pervasive absence of a sense of coherence in the modern world: only the extremes of totalitarian regimes or societies of "normless libertarianism" would lack it entirely. It is not, however, a great extension of his concept to say that modernity progressively diminishes the sense of coherence, and that is precisely what this commonplace asserts. Robert Woolfolk and Paul Lehrer make the extension explicit by noting the alienation rampant in modern society, an alienation consequent on loss of values, replacement of science for religion as the ultimate authority, etc. They quote Camus's insight that modern men are disillusioned, exiles without hope for return home, as that home is now forever destroyed.[68]

We can call this version of the origin of stress the topic of the exile. "Exile" as a name for the human condition has deep roots, having Platonic, Judeo-Christian, and Gnostic variants. In the discourse on stress, this topic has a particularly modern slant, that is, a lament over alienation from community, myth, and tradition. As the topic of the archaic body has Enlightenment roots, the exile's heritage is Romantic and Victorian, when the flight of the gods, of God himself, His religion and temporal powers, were discerned with mixed delight and horror. In the discourse on stress, the theme is muted. Generally it appears in the recognition that frames of reference and community support serve as buffers, and that religious practices and beliefs play favorable roles in the coping process. Look beneath that surface, and see that stress is the suffering of the threats and burdens of life without the support of social and cosmic order; that stress is the experience of adversity and pain without an ultimate ground.

A typical presentation of the exile occurs in Friedman and Rosenman's

Type A Behavior and Your Heart. Among the causes of Type A behavior, they write, is our tendency to treat people as numbers:

A society would have little luck in trying to reduce humans to numerals or statistics if it were not for a companion tendency of the people themselves to forget their individual identity and the emotional linkages that draw them together. In times past, belief in the protective presence of a powerful God (or group of gods) allowed man to feel that he was being singled out and protected as a unique personage. Trust and pride in his particular group of fellow men, living and dead, gave him a feeling of emotional unity with them. These forces of religion and . . . patriotism, supported by myth and ritual, have been waning relentlessly even as the forces making for automaton-man have been waxing.[69]

The waning of these forces has implications for our health. The type A behavior pattern, with its habits of treating people as objects and trying to make time more productive, has been implicated in the development of some heart diseases. Friedman and Rosenman suggest that the destructive aspects of type A might be tempered by strong bonds of social feeling and public orthodoxy.[70]

The perception of the individual as an exile in a heartless technological society occurs not only in the discussion of type A behavior, but also in the discussion of other uniquely modern conditions in which stress plays an etiological role: burnout, neurosis, narcissistic personality disorders, and diseases of civilization.[71] The topic of the exile shapes self-perception among those suffering stress. Getting out of the rat race, leaving the city, communing with nature, returning to traditional values, and remaking a sense of community are common fantasies when under stress. Another typical appearance of the topic of the exile is the formation of informal support groups in a search for community and ritual.

From the perspective of the exile, modernity is stressful because it strips us of all the things that once gave meaning to life. We have lost ritual, myth, kin, and friendship; we have become the naked apes well satirized in Walker Percy's *The Thanatos Syndrome.*[72] To be more precise, this topic of the exile states that we suffer stress because we are being stripped of myth and community. The intense nostalgia that this commonplace evokes, a yearning even for the life-styles of two or three decades ago, is its feeling tone.

It is not simply the loss of tradition and community that produces stress; it is their replacement with relationships without known or even knowable norms and rules. As Gendlin astutely observes, even the "traditional emotions" are no longer evoked because the situations that would evoke them do not occur.[73] The relations between man and woman, parent and child, individual and community no longer have taken-for-granted structures that once facilitated unself-conscious social intercourse. All that was familiar has been lost, exposed as fraud, withered away, or become irrelevant. Hence we feel ourselves exiled, rudderless.

Just as the first commonplace contained a polarity between the archaic body and the engineer, so here an opposition appears: Stress arises in the modern world because we must make choices, whereas in previous ages major decisions were made for people. We have reached a critical stage of evolution, so runs one variant of the topic, entering a new age of personal growth and awareness. All personal acts will be works of creativity as each of us forges individualized myths, traditions, and families. Ties of the flesh, of the familiar, of the traditional will be discarded as worn-out garments. In explaining the stresses unique to contemporary society, Woolfolk and Lehrer write: "The removal of many of the economic and social barriers to individual growth and self-expression presents the modern individual with a dazzling array of choices, as well as an awesome set of responsibilities."[74] The exile is, to borrow Sartre's phrase, condemned to be free. Stress originates in the ambivalence between the isolation and loneliness of the loss of tradition and the heady liberation that views myth as a set of barriers to be replaced by a "dazzling array of choices."

The Familiar

But what if the basic assumption of the topic of the exile were wrong? What if our exile did not stem from renunciation, willing or otherwise, of the cultural past? What if the nature of the loss of the familiar were otherwise than that it has fled us?

Both of the preceding versions of the source of modernity's stresses reckon with loss and the constancy of change. In each case, the familiar has been lost in the ceaseless flux: indwelling the body, nature, custom, tradition, myth, community. Having abandoned or been forced to abandon what is close, we engineer solutions in the context of vast freedom of choice of paths into the future. Stress on this account names a mood concerning progress. The mood is decisively ambivalent. On the one hand is intense suffering of loss, such that bodily orientation and the forms of intimate personal relationships are confused beyond recognition; such that, as we saw in the phenomenology of stress, there is no place or time for body or for dwelling. On the other hand, the engineering of new solutions to modernity's "problems" and freedom from the shackles of past traditions and rules together intoxicate and render imaginable new and even fantastic ways of being. These new ways of being promise, in the extreme, release from the injustices, inequities, and conflicts of the past. Stress names, *nota bene*, ambivalence, since the solutions generate further problems and conflicts, as the narratives themselves recount. Stress names a type of experience in which the familiar becomes progressively uninhabitable and replaced by freely chosen, rationally considered prostheses and life-support systems. Finally, as we have seen, loss of the familiar, because it exposes us to life without meaning, renders us vulnerable to trauma. The circle closes when, victimized by trauma, we feel our individuality under attack, so we seek control, thus stripping ourselves further of the flesh.

But the "familiar" as the lost ground comes freighted with meanings in these narratives of origin. The familiar is either the primitive body untouched by culture or mind, the Noble Savage within, or the past which through myth and tradition provided a sense of coherence to life. After looking again at stress, seeing through its enmeshing rhetoric, we will ask if it is likely that the body surpassed is the archaic body and if the past surpassed is that of myth and tradition.

STRESS VERSUS GRIEF

If stress is a mood of ambivalence about loss of the familiar, then stress is akin to grief. A number of studies of the social effects of pronounced stress illustrate that people grieve when they are under stress. In a major review of the after-effects of stress, Sheldon Cohen summarizes thusly: "Overall, it appears that exposure to unpredictable and uncontrollable stress is followed by a decreased sensitivity to others. This includes a decrease in helping, a decrease in the recognition of individual differences, and an increase in aggression," as well as an increase in helplessness.[75] These are signs of bereavement, although Cohen does not call them such. Other researchers have noticed, however, that in response to traumatic stressors, such as combat and fire, and also in response to burnout following prolonged stress, people grieve. PTSS, noted one observer, "bears the hallmarks of grieving."[76] The distinctive symptom of PTSS—the re-experiencing of the trauma—refers to a past that refuses to be dead and buried, that haunts the present, so that the mourner cannot get on with living, even twenty or thirty years later. It has been widely noted that the response to stressors can at least sometimes be called grief.

Like stress, grief has been the topic of intense research in recent years, generating a minor industry of grief counseling and management. But whereas death which occasions grief is by some considered a kind of stressor, the tables have not been turned to reveal stress as a kind of grief. But that is precisely how it appears. Stress is grief in which losses are not mourned but adapted to. Moreover, in the ambivalence of the mood of stress, the implicit dictate to take control, to adapt to the new and to shed the familiar, short-circuits the work of grief. With Peter Marris, I mean grief "to refer to the psychological process of adjustment to loss.... Grieving reactions are evoked when adaptive abilities are threatened."[77] Grief is a "work" as Freud observed, of accepting the reality of lost love. Love, or "involvement," to use Marris's specific word for the precondition of grief, dies hard, especially when there are mixed feelings toward the lost object. In the course of the grief work, the bereaved undergoes a transformation. The self which loved the lost love must itself die in order to live again. "Man is but a network of relationships, and these alone matter to him," Saint-Exupery wrote;[78] when one of these relationships ends, man changes.

Marris sees in grief two opposing impulses which account for the necessity of a moratorium, a period of stilled time, to heal the wounds of loss:

Grief. . . is the expression of a profound conflict between contradictory impulses—to consolidate all that is still valuable and important in the past, and preserve it from loss; and at the same time, to re-establish a meaningful pattern of relationships, in which the loss is accepted. Each impulse checks the other, reasserting itself by painful stabs of actuality or remorse, and recalling the bereaved to face the conflict itself. Grieving is therefore a process which must work itself out, as the sufferer swings between these claims, testing what comfort they might bring, and continually being tugged back to the task of reconciling them.[79]

The resolution, Marris continues, rests upon "a sense of continuity . . . re-stored by detaching the familiar meanings of life from the relationships in which they were embodied, and re-establishing them independently of it."[80] This gradual reformulation of the self and its commitments is fraught with danger. Reconciliation is not guaranteed—the grief may never end, becoming "chronic."

Marris's lucid analysis of grief makes it possible to understand the nature of stress. Grief is the genus; stress, the species. Stress, like grief, entails loss: loss fundamentally of the familiar. Stress expresses an ambivalence, a particular case of the conflict that Marris describes for all grief. Grief is an existential condition in which one's becoming has been placed in question by loss. When someone close to me dies, I desire to hold on to the previous relationship, since it defines in part my very self. Yet death has gripped what I love, and I must let go in order to live. But I face nothing when I let go. Like Orpheus I cannot help but look back; like him I leave the realm of the dead for the sunlight. Grief is a passion in which the conflict between holding on and letting go finds expression and resolution. In the type of grieving called stress, this existential momentum which sweeps me up in passion is channeled into what feels like tension, pressure, and energy by demands that leave no place or time to let go and reconcile death with a viable future. Instead, I divert the passion of grief into productive work and consumption. These activities seem to fill my need and satiate the desire that springs from loss. The assumption that technologically driven change is natural and good, in the context of insufficient time and the absence of place in which to mourn, makes the diversion appear inevitable.

Harnessing the passion of grief indicates in part that the end of grief is endlessly deferred. While grief in one sense does not end, the passion of grieving can subside, as the mourner accepts the paradox that the death of love does not mean that love dies, but rather that it is transformed. One's particular love becomes a mirror for universal love, as described by C. S.

Lewis in his personal memoir, *A Grief Observed*. When his wife, who died of cancer, became for him a mirror reflecting the divine light, such as Beatrice was for Dante, Lewis was able to accept her absence and sense her presence. The egotism of his love was burnt out or excised through a tempering, enabling him to move "from the garden to the Gardener, from the sword to the Smith."[81] Death for him occurred within a sense of coherence, enabling the turmoil of grief to find resolution.

Thus grief, like Eros (since grief is the end of eros), is a means to insight into the whole, by stripping life, at least temporarily, of its meaning. It has, if you will, a philosophical moment. This aspect of grief may be what lies behind the observation from the Aristotlean tradition that philosophers are melancholic. Precisely that route is blocked to the extent that stress is lived as stress. The passion remains, for there is no way to resolve it; there are only means to exhaust it temporarily.

The extension of grief to non-death situations is hardly novel. For Marris, for example, grief occurs whenever meaning is lost. His book *Loss and Change* masterfully articulates how a variety of people mourn the loss of the familiar: young widows in London; Nigerians affected by a slum clearance project in Lagos; advocates of tribalism in Nigeria; entrepreneurs in Kenya; minority students at Berkely. In all settings

a conflict arises between the yearning to return to the reassuring predictability of the past, and a contradictory impulse to become the creature of circumstance, abandoning the past as if it belonged to another, now repudiated, being. Both impulses are self-destructive in themselves, but their interplay generates the process of reformulation by which the thread of continuity is retrieved. This reformulation of the essential meaning of one's experience of life is a unique reassertion of identity, which takes time to work out. In this it resembles grief: for though the circumstances are not tragic, and the gains may outweigh the losses, the threat of disintegration is similar.[82]

Not all change evokes grief, Marris writes, only that which entails the loss of meaningful attachments, yet all change (as the more inclusive category) does involve stress. He writes that since meaning is both universal (expressed in linguistic, religious, or philosophical terms) and particular (since meaning means involvement with singular persons, places, things), "whenever we cannot create or sustain this meaning...we undergo stress." Stress happens whenever we lose "confidence in our ability to handle our circumstances,"[83] because our structure of meaning is no longer reliable. Marris, then, brings stress and grief together as types of suffering, with grief being a kind of stress.

Two other approaches to stress link it with grief, but not to the extent that I am developing here. As noted earlier, Antonovsky connects stress with a loss of a sense of coherence, in that with such a sense, one's health is protected against the vicissitudes of life. A "sense of coherence" strongly

resembles Marris's conception of "structures of meaning" which make suffering bearable. For Antonovsky, change is pathogenic when undergone
without a sense of coherence, or to put it in other terms, stress happens when
we suffer loss in the decay of a coherent framework. Thus stress can be said
to exist when the cosmos loses its recognizable face.

Hobfalls's resource theory also places loss at the core of stress: "the evidence
suggests that stress is likely to ensue only when loss is evidenced: Change,
transition, and challenge are not of themselves stressful."[84] However, for
Hobfalls loss has an accounting meaning and can be offset arithmetically by
gains.

The three formulations converge with the phenomenology of stress and
the analysis of the rhetoric of the discourse on stress. Stress entails loss in
a specific sense: change in the context of white noise, i.e., in the context
of the loss of the familiar. I propose, therefore that stress be understood
as grief. In this light, the meaning of *stress* borrowed from engineering is
a misleading metaphor for a peculiarly modern form of grief. Through
this metaphor we are drawn to perceive our living and especially our suffering through the narrow lens of instrumental rationality and the con-
stricted value of efficiency. Moreover, we are invited to adapt an attitude
of the alien toward our world, to accept our alien status as normal and
good. My proposal calls for a new metaphor. What we have called *stress*
now let us call *engineered grief*, since stress is the engineering of our grief,
the managing of the uniquely modern predicament of facing continual
loss of the familiar. Grief is engineered to the extent that we are expected
to accommodate all the changes that a modern industrial and information
society makes possible by remaking ourselves and our habits. Renaming
stress *engineered grief* at least has the merit of acknowledging the ambivalence and conflict that such change evokes.

Grief, although intensely personal, is fairly predictable in its course, and
resembles a disease or a wound. Cultures ordinarily provide rituals of
mourning to give place for the conflict of grief to work itself out. In the
West, mourning has been progressively lost as a public custom. We do
not know how to deal with loss in time-honored ways through moratoria
and social rituals of mourning. Stress reflects and compounds the dilemma. Grief requires time, and a specific temporality at that. Where time
is money, grief cannot occur. Under stress, time as qualitative, as *kairos*, as
suitable for an activity, does not exist. One constantly adapts to loss and
awaits the next blow, leaving one perpetually poised on the threshold of
change, being neither here nor there. Losses accumulate, the grief work
never done. This stifled passion of our grief has been renamed *energy*,
upon which we feed. Stress, then, is a kind of grief in which the wounds
of loss are kept bleeding in order to keep the mourner energized for work
and consumption.

CONCLUDING THOUGHTS ON THE ARCHAIC BODY AND THE EXILE

The reframing of stress that we initiate here calls us back to the questions raised earlier about the nature of the archaic body and the pastness of the past. While a fuller consideration must attend the historical analysis of the construct of stress, a preliminary statement is in order.

What if stress were not the awakening of atavistic responses to danger? The body appears archaic under the reign of stress because stress invites us to see two images of the body: as a system of mechanisms and as a field of energy. When we attend to bodily mechanisms, the complex cybernetic mechanisms of bodily systems, we envision a body whose programming is set by evolution. Hence the stress reaction appears as a problem of corporeal hardware, as a throwback to primal nature. Then, the body needs modification through technological intervention, or at least it needs continual monitoring because of its inherent limitations. If we envision bodily energetics, then we regard it as a flux with unlimited potential for reprogramming, in a New Age fantasy of transcending disease and mortality through enlightenment and diet, for example. The energetic body has nothing to do with nature; it is a pure product of history and society. But the body is never simply "nature" even as it is never simply "culture."[85] If the response to white noise is grief, then it does great harm to that phenomenon to reduce the felt bodily presence to a reaction adopted from the science of the strength of materials. Grief is not a "reaction" to loss as a reflex is a reaction to a stimulus. Grief expresses or displays the meaning of loss. The yearning and the emptiness of grief make it clear that the expression concerns not simply the present moment but also the past and the future. Rather than calling this upwelling of passion *archaic*, we do the phenomenon more justice by calling it *primordial*. This passion is how human beings display the rupture in time when the present does not contain threads connecting the past to the future. It is primordial in the sense that grief asserts what is necessary for a human life, for dwelling as men and women. Thus, as primordial it is far from primitive and not in need of fixing. It demands our attention.

What if our exile did not stem from renunciation of the cultural past? What if the nature of the loss of the familiar were otherwise than that the familiar has fled us? If grief asserts the necessity for the persistence of the past in the present, then we will also have to reconsider the topic of the exile, which claims that we are uprooted from the past. Only when grief is resolved can the past be let go. Unresolved grief surrounds us with ghosts and phantoms who have not been lain to rest. The difficulty may not be that we have lost traditions, but that we have not let them go through the work of grief. Perhaps to deal with our historical consciousness and the disruptions of traditions and myths, we have, paradoxically, to bury rather than flee them into the neon lights or defensively claim their continuity. We need to bury the dead in order that we can, with their help, find continuity with them.

To these topics we shall return. But first it is necessary to inquire into the origin and development of the construct of stress in order to better grasp its historical essence.

NOTES

1. Allan Young, "The discourse on stress and the reproduction of conventional knowledge," *Social Science and Medicine* 14B (1980), 133.

2. Kristian Pollock, "On the nature of social stress: Production of a modern mythology," *Social Science and Medicine* 26, no. 3 (1988), 387.

3. Ibid., p. 390.

4. For systems thinking, see William Arney, *Experts in the Age of the System* (Albuquerque: University of New Mexico Press, 1991).

5. For systems thinking as promoting a tyranny of harmony, see William Arney and Bernard Bergen, *Medicine and the Management of Living: Taming the Last Great Beast* (Chicago: University of Chicago Press, 1984).

6. Tom Wolfe, *Bonfire of the Vanities* (New York: Farrar, Strauss & Giroux, 1987), p. 55.

7. Susan Burchfield, "The stress response: A new perspective," *Psychosomatic Medicine* 41, no. 8 (December 1979), 661.

8. Raymond Fleming, Andrew Baum, and Jerome E. Singer, "Toward an integrative approach to the study of stress," *Journal of Personality and Social Psychology* 46, no. 4 (1984), 941.

9. Alan Monat and Richard S. Lazarus, "Stress and coping—Some current issues and controversies," in A. Monat and R. S. Lazarus, eds., *Stress and Coping: An Anthology*, (New York: Columbia University Press, 1977), p. 3.

10. Burchfield, "The stress response," p. 668. See also N.J.C. Andreason, R. Noyes, and C. E. Hartford, "Factors influencing adjustments of burn patients during hospitalization," in Monat and Lazarus, eds., *Stress and Coping*, p. 227: "Strictly speaking, of course, death cannot be considered a failure to adjust, but all the patients who died had already demonstrated an adaptive failure."

11. Stjepan Mestrovic and Barry Glassner, "A Durkheimian hypothesis on stress," *Social Science and Medicine* 17, no. 18 (1983), 1322.

12. Burchfield, "The stress response," p. 668.

13. *Diagnostic and Statistical Manual of Mental Disorders: DSM–III* (Washington, DC: American Psychiatric Association, 1987). For a brief history of the battle over recognition of PTSS, see the reference in the following note.

14. Ghislaine Boulanger, "Post-traumatic stress syndrome: An old problem with a new name," in *The Trauma of War: Stress and Recovery in Viet Nam Veterans* (Washington, DC: American Psychiatric Press, 1985), 17. Further: Opposition to recognition came from the entrenched position that "the etiology of pathology lies not in adult but in childhood traumas. To argue that trauma in adult life can have profound and long-lasting psychological consequences even among individuals who were previously normal is to contradict this developmental theory" (p. 17).

15. With the etiological scales tipped again in favor of real events, victims of abuse of all kinds and children of parents who were addicted to virtually anything, to cite two leading examples, are now likely to be seen as suffering with PTSS. This model permeates the mental health and counseling domains and appears everywhere in self-help books. See, for example, John Bradshaw, *Healing the Pain That Binds You* (Deerfield, FL: Health Communications, 1988).

16. Charles Figley, "Toward a field of traumatic stress," *Journal of Traumatic Stress 1*, no. 1 (January 1988), 3–16.

17. Stjepan Mestrovic, "A sociological conceptualization of trauma," *Social Science and Medicine 21*, no. 8 (1985), 835–48.

18. Mitchell B. Young and Cassandra A. Erickson, "Cultural impediments to recovery: PTSD in contemporary America," *Journal of Traumatic Stress 1*, no. 4 (1988), 441.

19. Ibid., pp. 431–43.

20. Christopher Lasch, "Fraternalist manifesto," *Harper's Monthly 274*, no. 1643 (April 1987), 17–20.

21. Alice Miller, *The Drama of the Gifted Child* (New York: Basic Books, 1990).

22. Pollock, "On the nature," p. 388.

23. Henry Kystal, "Psychoanalytic views on human emotional damage," in *Post-Traumatic Stress Disorders: Psychological and Biological Sequelae*, ed. Bessel A. van der Kolk (Washington, DC: American Psychiatric Association, 1984), p. 22.

24. Christopher Lasch, *A Culture of Narcissism: American Life in an Age of Diminishing Expectations* (New York: Norton, 1979); Ivan Illich, "The disabling professions," in *The Disabling Professions* (Boston: Marion Boyars, 1978), pp. 11–40.

25. Durkheim, cited in Mestrovic, "A sociological conceptualization," p. 842.

26. Ivan Illich on subsistence: see *Gender* (New York: Pantheon, 1982), and "Subsistence," in *The Virtues That Make Us Human: The Foundations of Medical Ethics* (Urbana & Chicago: University of Illinois Press, 1985), 45–53.

27. The centrality of control is made clear in a recent review of health psychology: "More recent and sophisticated work has enabled researchers to identify the dimensions of events that are most likely to produce stress. Events appraised as negative, uncontrollable, unpredictable, or ambiguous are typically experienced as more stressful than those not so appraised. Research identifying the significance of these dimensions has come both from well-controlled laboratory studies . . . and from opportunistic studies of people undergoing major stressful events such as unemployment . . . or crises such as the Three Mile Island catastrophe. . . . Of the factors implicated in stress, controllability may be especially important. In studies involving stressful events, when those events were under the control of the organisms studied, those organisms showed physiological profiles similar to those of organisms undergoing no stress at all, whereas organisms experiencing the event without the experience of control showed physiological reactions indicative of anxiety and arousal." Shelley E. Taylor, "Health psychology: The science and the field," *American Psychologist 45*, no. 1 (January 1990), 43.

28. Such words are called "amoeba words" by Ivan Illich and Barry Sandlers, *ABC: The Alphabetization of the Popular Mind* (Berkeley: North Point Press, 1988).

29. See Robert Kugelmann, "The stress on 'stress' in psychology and medicine," *New Ideas in Psychology 7*, no. 1 (1989), 99–108.

30. Cornelia Kenner, Cathie E. Guzzetta, and Barbara M. Dossey, *Critical Care Nursing: Body-Mind-Spirit*, 2nd ed. (Boston: Little, Brown, 1985), p. 17.

31. Hans Eysenck, "Stress, personality, and smoking behavior," in C. D. Spielberger, I. G. Sarason, and P. B. Defares, eds., *Stress and Anxiety*, vol. 9 (Washington, DC: Hemisphere Publishing, 1985), 1985), p. 37.

32. Peter Berger, Manfried Kellner, and Brigit Berger, *The Homeless Mind: Modernization and Consciousness* (New York: Vintage Books, 1983).

33. The pioneering work of Lazarus and his colleagues has elaborated this administrative metaphor, as Taylor's summary indicates: "For example, as conceptualized by Lazarus and his associates, coping is initiated by an appraisal process secondary to the assessment of circumstances as harmful, threatening, or challenging. In this view, a person judges his or her resources, such as time or money, assesses his or her coping skills and abilities, and then determines whether or not they will be sufficient to overcome the threat or challenge posed by a stressful event" ("Health Psychology," p. 44).

34. Andrew Baum, Jerome Singer, and Carlene Baum, "Stress and the environment," *Journal of Social Issues* 37, no. 1 (1981), 7.

35. Fleming, et al., "Toward an integrative approach," p. 941.

36. Taylor, "Health psychology," p. 44. Moreover, Taylor writes: "Coping researchers are also investigating some of the costs of coping, such as the energy expenditure and physiologic arousal that may be required when people must be vigilant in response to threatening events" (pp. 44–45).

37. Fleming et al., "Toward an integrative approach," p. 943.

38. S. Cohen, "Aftereffects of stress on human performance and social behavior: A review of research and theory," *Psychological Bulletin* 88 (1980), 105.

39. Ibid., p. 97.

40. Stevan E. Hobfalls, "Conservation of resources: A new attempt at conceptualizing stress," *American Psychologist* 44, no. 3 (March 1989), 516.

41. Ibid., p. 519.

42. Baum et al., "Stress and the environment," p. 6.

43. *Oxford English Dictionary* (Oxford: Clarendon Press, 1989).

44. Fleming et al., "Toward an integrative approach," 942.

45. Walker Percy, *Lost in the Cosmos: The Last Self-Help Book* (New York: Farrar, Straus & Giroux, 1983).

46. E. M. Gherman, *Stress and the Bottom Line: A Guide to Personal Well-Being and Corporate Health* (New York: Amacom, 1981).

47. Ibid., p. 18.

48. George Mandler, "Stress and thought processes," in Leo Goldberger and Shlomo Broznitz, eds., *Handbook of Stress: Theoretical and Clinical Aspects* (New York: Free Press, 1982), pp. 97–98.

49. Herbert M. Lefcourt, "The function of the illusions of control and freedom," *American Psychologist* 28 (1973), 417.

50. Ibid., p. 419.

51. See David Reid, "Participatory control and the chronic-illness adjustment process," in *Research with the Locus of Control Construct*, vol. 3, ed. H. M. Lefcourt (New York: Academic Press, 1984), pp. 361–91.

52. Suzanne C. Kobasa, "The hardy personality: Toward a social psychology of

stress and health," in *Social Psychology of Health and Illness*, eds., G. S. Sanders and J. Sols (Hillsdale, NJ: Lawrence Erlbaum, 1982), p. 7.

53. Herbert M. Lefcourt, "The locus of control as a moderator variable: Stress," in *Research with the Locus of Control Construct*, vol. 2: *Developments and Social Problems*, ed. H. M. Lefcourt (New York: Academic Press, 1983), p. 258.

54. Aaron Antonovsky, *Health, Stress and Coping* (San Francisco: Jossey-Bass, 1979), p. 15.

55. Melford Spiro, "Religious systems as culturally constituted defense mechanisms," in *Stress and Coping: An Anthology*, p. 178.

56. Aaron Beck, "Cognitive approaches to stress," in *Principles and Practices of Stress Management*, eds., Robert Woolfolk and Paul Lehrer (New York: Guilford Press, 1984), p. 285.

57. For an overview of Melanie Klein's understanding of the depressive position and its importance in development, see Hanna Segal, *Introduction to the Work of Melanie Klein*, 2nd ed. (New York: Basic Books, 1974), pp. 67–81. Also see Donald W. Winnicott, "The depressive position in normal emotional development," in *Collected Papers: Through Paediatrics to Psycho-Analysis* (London: Tavistock, 1958), pp. 262–277.

58. For statements of this topic see for example Karl Albrecht, *Stress and the Manager* (Englewood Cliffs, NJ: Prentice-Hall, 1979), pp. 56–57; Errol Korn and Karen Johnson, *Visualization: The Uses of Imagery in the Health Professions* (Homewood, IL: Dow Jones-Irwin, 1983), p. 28; Jeanne Achterberg and G. Frank Lawlis, *Bridges of the Bodymind: Behavioral Approaches to Health Care* (Champaign, IL: Institute for Personality and Ability Testing, 1980), p. 4; Susan Burchfield, "Stress: An integrative framework," in S. Burchfield, *Stress: Psychological and Physiological Interactions* (Washington, DC: Hemisphere Publishing, 1985), p. 387; Kenneth Pelletier, *Mind as Healer, Mind as Slayer* (New York: Dell, 1977), p. 344.

59. Beck, "Cognitive approaches," p. 267.

60. Ibid., p. 266.

61. Thomas Luckmann, "On the rationality of institutions in modern life," in *Life-World and Social Realities* (London: Heinemann Educational Books, 1983), pp. 185–86.

62. Arnold Gehlen, *Man in the Age of Technology* (New York: Columbia University Press, 1980), p. 55.

63. Albrecht, *Stress and the Manager*, p. 27. He defines health negatively as the absence of symptoms and wellness as "a high level of total human functioning" (p. 30).

64. For shadow work, see Illich, *Gender*, pp 45–60.

65. Roy R. Grinker and John Spiegel, *Men Under Stress* (Philadelphia: Blakiston, 1945), p. 5.

66. See Eugene Gendlin, "A philosophical critique of narcissism: The significance of the awareness movement," in D. M. Levin, ed., *Pathologies of the Modern Self* (New York: New York University Press, 1987), pp. 251–304 for a cogent critique of the notion that the body is merely raw material for social programming, and for the possibility of attunement to the body as the ground of social critique.

67. Antonovsky, *Health, Stress and Coping*, p. 125.

68. Robert Woolfolk and Paul Lehrer, "Clinical applications," in *Principles and Practices of Stress Management* (New York: Guilford, 1984), p. 353.

69. Meyer Friedman and Ray H. Rosenman, *Type A Behavior and Your Heart* (Greenwich, CT: Fawcett Crest, 1974), p. 196.

70. For this term, see Frederick Wilhelmsen and Willmoore Kendall, "Cicero and the Politics of Public Orthodoxy," *The Intercollegiate Review* 5, no. 2 (Winter 1968–69), 84–100.

71. For the topic of the exile in (1) burnout: Francis Ianni and Elizabeth Reuss-Ianni, " 'Take this job and shove it!' A comparison of organizational stress and burnout among teachers and police," in Barry Farber, ed., *Stress and Burnout in the Human Service Professions* (New York: Pergamon Press, 1983), p. 92; and (2) neurosis: Jacques Ellul, *The Technological Society*, trans. J. Wilkinson (New York: Vintage Books, 1964), p. 331; David Levin, in *Pathologies of the Modern Self* (New York: New York University Press, 1987); Christopher Lasch, *The Minimal Self* (New York: W. W. Norton, 1984).

72. Walker Percy, *The Thanatos Syndrome* (New York: Farrar, Straus & Giroux, 1987).

73. Gendlin, pp. 251–304.

74. Woolfolk and Lehrer, "Clinical applications," p. 351.

75. Cohen, "After effects of stress," p. 95.

76. C. F. Shatan, "The grief of soldiers—Viet Nam combat veterans' self help movement," *American Journal of Orthopsychiatry* 43 (1973), 640–53.

77. Peter Marris, *Loss and Change* (London: Routledge & Kegan Paul, 1974), p. 4.

78. Antoine de Saint-Exupery, quoted in Maurice Merleau-Ponty, *Phenomenology of Perception*, trans. C. Smith (New York: Humanities Press, 1962), p. 456.

79. Marris, *Loss and Change*, pp. 31–32.

80. Ibid., p. 34.

81. C. S. Lewis, *A Grief Observed* (New York: Seabury Press, 1961), p. 50.

82. Marris, *Loss and Change*, p. 34.

83. Peter Marris, "The social impact of stress," in Louis A. Ferman and Jeanne P. Gordus, eds., *Mental Health and the Economy*, (Kalamazoo, MI: W. E. Upjohn Institute for Employment Research, 1979), p. 307.

84. Hobfalls, "Conservation of resources," p. 518.

85. Merleau-Ponty, *Phenomenology of Perception*, p. 189: "The use a man is to make of his body is transcendent in relation to that body as a mere biological entity. It is no more natural, and no less conventional, to shout in anger or to kiss in love than to call a table a 'table.' Feelings and passional conduct are invented like words.... It is impossible to superimpose on man a lower layer of behavior which one chooses to call 'natural,' followed by a manufactured cultural or spiritual world. Everything is both manufactured and natural in man."

3

The Martial Beginnings of Stress

Though stress is a construct, today it has the force of nature. It seems hardly imaginable that it has not always existed, if not in fact then at least in name. But a historical exegesis of the development of the construct shows that not only has the construct or anything like it not always existed, but that the conditions for its existence did not exist before the nineteenth century. Stress resembles in this way other products of the last two centuries—television, automobiles, air pollution, nuclear weapons. Stress did not exist either as a set of facts about human suffering or as a way of construing the suffering of loss. Much as Foucault has argued that life and sexuality are modern artifacts, products of the modern epistemological field and modern social practices,[1] so do I argue with stress, a point that may seem likely given the relationships between the three artifacts. The same mentality and practices that produced the first two gave rise to the last.

Working from the present, with a clear idea of stress, we can engage the past in dialogue in order to see if our present-day assumptions about the naturalness of stress concur with what comes from the past to meet us. We will step backward into the past in four moves and four chapters, each time going further back. I do this to witness the successive confrontation of our assumptions with progressively foreign modes of thought and action, which were in their time taken for granted. Instead of seeing a triumphant march of progress and science as knowledge replaced ignorance, we watch our own reality become more and more strange as we encounter the foreign assumptions that our forebears held. I intend to take their assumptions and practices as reasonable responses to their life experience (with all the ambiguity that

that entails, given my critical attitude toward stress) as our assumptions and practices are to us.

Now to the steps: (1) Stress comes into being as a discourse and experience during the Second World War. People did speak of stress before then, of course, but only in the 1940s did it become an explicit topic for research. Only then did it enter the public arena and progressively get absorbed by the general public as a lesson derived from the medical and psychological sciences. (2) In the first half of the twentieth century, something like stress existed. That was an "age of anxiety," during which psychological perspectives and professions developed in response to medical and spiritual distresses that Victorian medical assumptions could not explain. This period was transitional also, because its solutions to the difficulties of the day created new problems, which efforts such as psychosomatics tried to rectify, and which only the systems thinking of the post–1945 period have "solved." (3) The third step carries us into the nineteenth century, from the period beginning around 1830. There we encounter an "age of strain." With strain, the inner reactions of the individual dominated the picture, for strain belonged to the self of bourgeois culture. Strain marked the epiphany of the engineering mentality in medicine, but unlike stress it indicated primarily the dangers of depletion of scarce inner (physiological and psychological) resources, a bankruptcy in the face of a struggle for survival and success. (4) The final step takes us to the threshold beyond which our assumptions find little echo. We will peer across it into the eighteenth century and inquire into the kind of world that knew no stresses, anxieties, or strains of our sort. While we will find some fragments that seemingly anticipate the development of engineered grief, primarily what we find is a radically different discourse, one that I call "med-ical-moral" in contrast to the engineering discourse that strain inaugurated. Throughout this backward scanning, social practices and contexts will be on the horizon of our gaze, in order to keep the investigation from becoming an exercise in the history of ideas. I would rather call it a cultural-historical inquiry into psychosocial experience.

THE WAR OF THE WORLDS

> Much farther to the North, five miles or more, he saw the two television relay towers—gigantic red and white skeletons of steel, like a pair of Martian monsters stranded on the brink of the world.
>   —Edward Abbey, *The Brave Cowboy*[2]

During the dark days surrounding the Second World War, the notion of stress emerged from the background of collective perception and discourse. The ground was ready to produce such a growth. To recall the temper of the time: In the fall of 1938, after the war scare abated with Chamberlain's appeasement of Hitler, a Halloween radio broadcast caused widespread panic in the United States. The Mercury Theatre had dramatized an adaptation of H. G. Welles's *The War of the Worlds*. Thousands had believed that the play was a news broadcast and had fled their homes. For these people, Martians had really invaded. In the play itself, the hero Pierson meets an artilleryman who cynically observes:

Well, it isn't all of us that are made for wild beasts, and that's what it's got to be.... All these little office workers that used to live in these houses—they'd be no good. They haven't any stuff in 'em. They just used to run off to work. I've seen hundreds of 'em, running wild to catch their commuters' train in the morning for fear that they'd get canned if they didn't....The Martians will be a godsend for those guys. Nice roomy cages, good food, careful breeding, no worries.[3]

The artilleryman is a survivor, perhaps the first such, an appellation now synonymous with Everyman. His motive for enduring hardship is biological: "Life...that's what! I want to live. And so do you! We're not going to be exterminated. And I don't mean to be caught, either, and tamed, and fattened, and bred like an ox." He puts the issue squarely: The war of the worlds is about life, its survival, and the technological domination of life.

Shortly after the panic, social psychologist Hadley Cantril interviewed people who had taken the play literally, publishing his results in *The Invasion from Mars*. He wrote that the event "shows us how the common man reacts in a time of stress and strain." Among his findings was a personality trait common to many who panicked:

The individual is unable to rely on his own resources to see him through. He feels relatively helpless and believes his own best efforts at better adjustment are insufficient. This means, furthermore, that the individual believes his life and his fate are very largely dependent on some forces outside himself—on chance, on economic conditions far beyond his control or on the whim of some supernatural being.[4]

This personality trait—or better, this perception of the world as alien and beyond influence or control—is the very one that the artilleryman saw in the office workers scurrying for their trains. The Martian invasion was daily life writ large. Let us say that the broadcast was a cultural dream, even a recurrent dream, since the play is periodically replayed and its fiftieth anniversary was widely celebrated. The dream announced that a new regime had arrived, a rule of Martians. Although the world war overtook the dream of a war of the worlds, the Martian invasion prefigured a cultural epoch in which Martians dwell among us. Or taking the dream logic further, it announced that we had become Martians. The dream asks: Will our humanity submit to this alien power?

As for the man-eating aliens, despite their technological superiority, they suffered a humiliating biological defeat: "they were killed by the putrefactive and disease bacteria against which their systems were unprepared, ... slain after all man's defenses had failed."[5] The permutations of the dream open intriguing prospects here. Suffice it to say that this cultural dream says something about disease as well as war. The dream has as its domain life conceived as war. Fifty years later, our sensibilities are such that every child would be amazed at the Martians' naivete. How could they not have known that alien environments are hostile and will overpower their immune system? Perhaps we have adapted.

THE EMERGENCE OF THE DISCOURSE ON STRESS (1935–1955)

Before the war, no one spoke of stress; after it, increasingly, everyone did. This statement, true though it be, needs qualification. There was interest in stress before the war, but little focal interest. Stress inhabited the periphery of the scientific gaze, and it had not the cliche value it now possesses. This qualification likewise needs qualification. Before the war stress lived at the edge of the discourse it now dominates, yet in moving to the fore it altered its nature. What is at issue in this chapter is this altered nature—stress in its manifest form. We begin by considering the context of its emergence, as that has marked stress with its brand.

Stress had no one source. In various forms it appeared in a number of fields around the same time. The writers of the history of stress cite several early laboratory and clinical sources: Cannon's work on homeostasis, Selye's on the general adaptation syndrome, Harold G. Wolff's experiments in psychosomatics, Dunbar's systematic organization of psychosomatics, and the clinical studies of combat neurosis by military psychiatrists. To this list can be added the later epidemiological investigations of Holmes and Rahe and the development of the psychology of coping. The historians of stress agree that stress emerged in the late 1930s and the early 1940s. By the 1950s this research found a common ground in a systems approach to health and disease. The new importance of stress was reflected in its inclusion in various indices: *Psychological Abstracts* (1942), *Biological Abstracts* (1949), and *Index Medicus* (1950).[6]

Despite the variety of its sources and the lack of consensus on its nature, there are certain essential aspects of stress. First is a question expressed in protean ways and without which stress cannot be said to exist for contemporary consciousness: How much stress can a being take before it breaks? This question arises from an interest so native to the contemporary mind that it is impossible to imagine its absence, namely the desire to know, to test, and to extend the limits of adaptation. This interest aims at expanding the human potential to dwell and thrive in increasingly alien domains. Hence, the emphasis on attack and defense in stress discourse, on the traumatic and hostile nature of the world, and on defensive measures to cope with it. Second, there is the coinage *eustress*, the level of stress necessary for well-being. Finally, there is the notion that stress is ultimately manageable.

No one talked about stress before the war. What difference did the war make for our perceptions of the hardships of life? Historians of stress describe the researches that began at the time as if the war were merely the occasion for the development of a scientific concept. But what if the war were the contingency that gave stress its distinctive character? What if combat hammered perceptions such that combat experience is the type for all stresses? And what if the war—and the Cold War and the regional conflicts that came in its wake—so changed the world that stress belongs to a qualitatively different world from that of the preceding decades? To address these questions, we begin with what writers on stress in the aftermath of World War II saw as the lessons of the war. Then we will ask if these lessons resounded in the discourse and practices concerning stress.

LESSONS OF GLOBAL WARFARE

World War II was not just another war, not even a repetition of World War I. Medical commentators of the time reckoned with its unprecedented nature. It was truly global and fully mechanized. It obliterated the distinction between civilian and soldier, in part because air power permitted death to fall from the skies, and in part because of the character of strategic planning. In this latter respect, it continued a development of the first World War: "In modern warfare, there is no knightly comradeship. The objective is often to deprive the enemy of his basic instrument of violence, his army."[7] The aim was biological: mass extermination, a Martian approach. Individual heroism exists in such a conflict, but it is subordinated to the complex management of large numbers of soldiers and machines. A relatively small number actually fight, the rest acting as support for the combat units. Those that fight often do so from afar.

Roy R. Grinker and John P. Spiegel were American Army Air Force psychiatrists who treated aviators suffering from various mental disorders. Grinker was a neurologist-turned-psychiatrist who had been analyzed by Freud in the 1930s; Spiegel had been Grinker's student. Their 1945 *Men under Stress* was a landmark. Grinker wrote later that a major lesson of the war presented in this book was "the reactions of the mind and body under sudden and severe stress."[8] Spiegel, 25 years afterward, recalled:

Our theoretical views were based principally on psychoanalysis, which had always held the social environment at a respectable distance. We were forced to deal with the environment because we ourselves experienced it as a source of stress and because we hoped to be able to influence military policy in the areas of prevention and therapy.[9]

There were three specific lessons of the war. First stress had become a factor to be reckoned with in human life. Second, the world exerts such stresses as to break the shell of the psyche; this conclusion appears in Spiegel's reminiscence. Prior to World War II, psychiatry got by without having to deal with the environment, but the world could no longer be held at bay. Third, it became necessary to reckon theoretically with the hostility of the outer world in a new way. These lessons imply that stress was already in the air: the perceptions of the military medical personnel were prepared to perceive stress when they faced it. To borrow a term from William James, they preperceived the situation in terms of stress. To elucidate this preperception, we digress into a vision of Walter B. Cannon.

CANNON'S VISION

In a 1935 essay, Cannon, the renowned physiologist who had developed the concept of homeostasis, had, as Moses had the Promised Land, previewed the stress field:

The chance of gaining insight into the strength and endurance of stabilizing factors of the organism, and thus into its ability to resist the operation of disturbing forces, makes it worth while to enquire where the limits lie beyond which stresses overwhelm these corrective factors and significantly alter the steady state of the internal environment.[10]

Clarifying, he added that *significantly alter* means that which "lessens the efficiency of the organism." Cannon noted that "no intentional effort seems to have been directed toward the invention of means of measuring the critical stresses which various conditions might place upon the regulators of homeostasis."[11] The responses of pilots to flight at high altitudes had been conducted during World War I, and Cannon reviewed those results. Anoxemia (an abnormal decrease in the blood's oxygen content) occurs at high altitudes, but the organisms (human beings) "break" at widely differing heights. Psychological factors contribute to the variable level of human endurance at rarefied atmospheres. Cannon concluded his address with a vision:

A vast territory, enticing for biological and medical exploration, would be disclosed. We should have to learn how steady are the steady states and where the critical stress is found, not only in normal individuals, but also in individuals at various developmental epochs and during various disorders. . . . Indeed, the whole gamut of human diseases might be studied from this point of view.[12]

When Cannon envisioned this future, he conjured the image of airmen high above in a genuinely hostile environment. Indeed, only when the environment became so hostile, so alien to human flesh, could the question of "stabilizing forces" resisting the "disturbing forces" come into question. The plight of pilots challenged thinking to imagine stress.

The territory Cannon spied lay as much behind the eye as before it. Cannon's enormously influential work helped shape the terms in which medical personnel perceived. They preperceived the functional efficiency of the organism, the elastic limits of its functioning, and the maintenance of equilibrium within the body despite a fluctuating environment.

THE LIMITS OF ENDURANCE: TESTING, TRAINING, AND MORALE

The demands of the war pushed all participants to their limits. This in itself was no novelty of World War II, but air warfare was. Aviators dealt not only with the threats to life and limb that war always brings, they also had to rely on the soundness of their aircraft and reckon with the industrial-like pattern of bombing missions. As one physician observed: "military life . . . is essentially industry plus additional stresses."[13] Thus, military life was "normal" life pushed to its limits.

One result of the new industrial conditions of warfare was an emphasis on management, in particular the effort to estimate the limits of endurance in what came to be called "stress testing." These exercises in human engineering sought to determine the functional efficiency of individual performance under pressure. The psychologist G. L. Freeman devised a test in which subjects performed discrimination tasks while being distracted. Grinker and Spiegel used a "stress tolerance test" to see if patients had become emotionally strong enough to return to duty. While testing someone's mettle is hardly novel, the scientific design of standardized tests to do so was. The tests were often viewed as analogues of engineering tests.

This lesson of the war remains with us. Stress cannot be thought of without also thinking of the testing of limits of efficient, rational behavior. There now exists an entire industry that assesses the material of applicants and employees to see not only if they are competent but also if their personalities are suitable to the stress level of the job. Moreover, excessive levels of stress, even mental stress, ground many a legal claim in workers' compensation cases and support defense claims in criminal trials.[14]

Training to increase endurance was a second consequence of the war's insights into stress. Harold Palmer, a British military psychiatrist, wrote, "If a man is well trained and has high morale, he will continue to tolerate cumulative strain not only well past the breaking point of the average man but also well past his own innate stability."[15] Training meant both training to do one's job correctly and "basic training." It also meant "battle inoculation," a plan the British and Americans introduced in 1942: the conditioning of soldiers to the sights and sounds of live ammunition. A British psychiatric consultant, T. F. Main, advised the Director of Military Training that

the important condition for the use of explosives during training was that small "doses" should be used first so that the men might become adjusted to the experience, and that the intensity should then gradually be increased, so that finally the men should not react unduly to dangerous maximal explosions.[16]

Note the Martian connotation of *inoculation*, a biological term employed to designate the process of adjusting men to a terrifying environment.

The intention of this successful program of conditioning was to enhance morale, since that was the basis for performance on the battlefield. "Man-management" produced morale and prevented "breakdown under actual battle conditions."[17] Morale building (a World War II term[18]) strengthened the military in an essential way, for as Ahrenfeldt noted in a widely held view, "In modern war, victory depended not so much on the number killed as on the number demoralized."[19] Morale facilitated performance by fortifying the inner being of the soldier: He fights because he wants to. If morale were high, then the mind and heart were committed to battle, with the result that the soldier did not fight merely from fear of punishment.

Concern for stress thus reinforced the necessity to pay attention to morale. As Palmer wrote, "The Army psychiatrist is concerned not only with the soldier's capacity to fight but also with his willingness to fight. Although the general concept of psychoneurotic conflict is applicable to psychiatric casualties, the critical factor in two-thirds of the cases is morale."[20] Good morale mobilized the soldier to face the stresses of war. Grinker and Spiegel clearly understood that morale was in the psychiatrist's purview:

The soldier who attempts to run away or avoid combat when morale is good is psychologically ill and should be dealt with through medical procedures. If psychiatric evaluation demonstrates that there is a weak sense of duty, that the individual is consciously attempting to evade combat stress ... the disposition of the case is usually through administrative and disciplinary methods.[21]

This latter group aside, psychiatric consultants had suggestions for building morale, the details of which need not detain us. The essential point is that morale, which can be improved by effective management, steels the individual to face stress. World War II saw the emergence of systematic efforts by psychiatry and psychology to shape the personalities of the soldiers and improve their efficiency and productivity. The notion of stress figured into this effort, playing a role in the determination of limits of endurance, in training to increase those limits, in the assessment of disability produced by the psychological conditions of modern warfare, and finally in the molding of good morale, which is essential to life in an alien environment.

LIVING IN AN ALIEN ENVIRONMENT

The military context for the emergence of stress expressed an adversarial relation between the individual and the world. Whether aloft in a bomber or back at base, the airman had no dwelling place. If *stress* designated only such extreme situations, as it had formerly done, it would have posed no special problem. But it has been generalized to embrace all of life's experiences, beckoning us always to be vigilant against the outside which threatens to attack. The key terms of this vigilant relation between an individual and the world run throughout the early physiological and psychiatric literature and continue to dominate our sensibilities.

What is stress as described in the early writings? Little was it defined, and it had not yet been subjected to attempts to operationalize its meaning. The "stress of war" was already part of the vernacular, but in the psychiatric literature it had also the character of a metaphor borrowed from engineering. Stress was something "outer" that forced adaptation, a kind of hostile force impinging on the ego or the organism. Even in the psychoanalytic writings of Grinker and Spiegel, who wrote of the stress of inner drives and conflicts, stress was external to the ego. John Whitehorn provided word associations: "stimulus–trauma–stress."[22] Joost Meerloo equated it with danger, fear, conflict, anxiety. In contrast to *strain*, which in the nineteenth century denoted internal damage, *stress* signified a dangerous state of the outer and other. Stress causes strain, as World War II psychiatrists knew. The accent on stress meant a break with the medical habit of finding the source of disease within the body (as had been the case since the rise of the "medical gaze" in the early nineteenth century[23]). As Spiegel recalled, he and Grinker were "forced to deal with the environment"[24] because they themselves experienced it as stressful.

This new assessment of the outer world belongs not only to *stress* but also to Selye's neologism *stressor*. Selye wrote that because of unfamiliarity with the English language, he misapplied the term *stress* to the physiological re-action of the body to noxious stimuli, and so he coined *stressor* to refer to the external agents themselves.[25] Reflecting on stress research, Jerome Kagan writes that "the current popularity of the concept of stressor reflects a profound shift in the community's mood regarding the causes of human unhappiness."[26] Kagan relates the shift to political and social developments, especially in the 1960s, during which time environmental factors were increasingly appreciated as causes of social problems, rather than factors of heredity and character, internal to individuals: "by the mid-1960s, the external events that had been viewed as only the potential beginning of a sequence that might generate dysphoric affect and disorganized behavior had become the primary causal agents."[27] This change in emphasis had been present since the 1940s in the discourse on stress: "men with little predisposition to break-down may finally develop severe symptoms under great stress,"[28] wrote three military psychiatrists in a preliminary study of the effects of the war on airmen. What distinguishes the 1940s from today is the level of stress that "causes" breakdown: Now virtually any level is pathogenic.

Nothing captures the alien nature of the world, and hence the novelty of the experience of stress, better than air warfare. London, Dresden, and Hiroshima—cities become emblems of the modern world—felt the full force of the mechanized destruction that had come into being in the twentieth century. The study of stress began, however, not with the populations subjected to aerial warfare, but with the bomber and fighter plane crews. It is impossible, on a literal level, to gauge the psychological significance of the inception of stress in the study of airmen, but with an eye and an ear for metaphor we can discern its genealogy. Brigadier General Eugen Reinartz, of the United States Army, concluded that relative to other branches of the military, "the stresses and strains incident to aviation, and their effect on the psychic constitution of those engaged in this branch of the military service are probably greater."[29] General Reinartz made an important observation in this address, a remark that should steer attention to the underlying character of the stressful nature of air warfare. "The instant one leaves the ground," he wrote, "this [self-preservative] instinct is brought into play, as the individual is then projected into a new medium and the sustentation of which he has been accustomed, by reason of being a terrestrial animal, is removed."[30] Aviation is stressful primarily because it ungrounds us, lifts us up into an environment that cannot sustain human life. In other words, the flesh shakes with fear when projected into the air, for we are human—that is, of the earth. Given what we found in our phenomenology, the emblematic character of air combat is not surprising. Those airmen were literally where we all are now at least psychologically and socially: groundless, and supplied with life-support systems to compensate us as we fly through alien and hostile territory, reading a grid for guidance.

Air war, or more simply, air travel was both the literal and the metaphorical context of stress. As the literal event, technological advance made possible a previously unexperienceable situation. A generation later we can hardly appreciate the novelty that these men faced. Today air travel has been refined and rarely does one actually experience being in the air. Commercial aircraft insulate passengers against the hostile environment of 35,000 feet. As Schivelbusch shows with respect to the development of comfortable railroads, air travelers are spectators of the space through which they fly.[31] Air travel is largely a visual experience, not a haptic one. We are saved from some of the stresses of the air by this disembodiment. Our consciousness is fully airborne; such was not yet the case in 1943:

In World War II airmen had few creature comforts when aloft: Prolonged muscular tension [because of cramped quarters] and lack of sleep are not the only sources of physical stress. Combat crews of heavy bombers have to withstand extremely low temperatures at high altitudes.... At high altitudes, a less frequent but more fatal physical menace than extreme cold is oxygen-lack.[32]

These conditions exist as the base of the dangers incident to combat itself. The men must depend upon their aircraft to see them safely through. The crews identified with their aircraft, as Grinker and Spiegel observed:

the flying characteristics of heavy, four engine or two engine bomber type aircraft are those of steadiness, lack of maneuverability, reliability and great power over a long distance.... The fliers in such groups, especially the pilots, tend to fit in with these characteristics. They are usually older, more mature, steadier and less willing to take risks and indulge in maneuvers than fighter pilots.[33]

The men became airmen, incorporating through habituation the plane into their bodily selves. This identification with the machine constituted a metamorphosis of the flesh: Like strange moths, men in the twentieth century have, by insulating themselves from the world in cocoons of instrumentation and comfort, emerged as winged beings. Stress occurs when one inhabits an inhospitable world by virtue of prostheses that make it livable.

We are all airmen. We occupy a space in modern society only to the extent that we support ourselves with the techniques of a rationalized consciousness (air being a symbol of consciousness). Being up here is stressful: We quiver at the prospect of falling.[34]

The airmen's stresses thus display the nature of stress. To be under stress is to be groundless, to have life sustained by machines, to survive by means of a complex network or system that can be operated only through one's own participation. In other words, stress is a shorthand character for a radical reshaping of the human condition, a reshaping enabled by technological achievements. During the war, Hudson Hoagland, working in the physiology of the "stress 17-ketosteroids," addressed himself to this meaning of stress:

In recent years with the development of aviation man has desired to be free in an environment for which his evolutionary history could not possibly have fitted him. In high-speed airplanes he is assailed by new and formidable stresses. Living as he does at the bottom of a sea of air supplying a continuous and plentiful amount of oxygen he has been unprepared by evolution to store oxygen in his body.... He must adjust to severe and unaccustomed accelerations and rapid changes of atmospheric pressures which, together with the peculiar emotional stresses of modern aviation, may be exacting in the extreme.... [I]t is the task of aviation medicine to devise means of preventing the stresses of flight from interfering too greatly with our homeostatic mechanisms.[35]

Stress accompanies a desire to be no longer tied to the limitations of corporeal existence on the earth. In other senses, this desire for transcendence is not new, insofar as aspirations for immortality and excesses of hubris are perennial. What is novel is its achievement in physical terms. The "adventures in biological engineering" Hoagland celebrated have come to pass. The desire for transcendence through knowledge and technique has a decisive voice in the discourse on stress. The tacit drive for transcendence in this discourse acts like the bed and banks of a river, directing the flow of thought and deliberation, so that when we perceive the stresses of a situation we are led in part to a desire to escape the limitations of corporeality by means of knowledge and technique. We, like Daedalus, "engineer" a response so that we can endure what otherwise would be intolerable.

Airmen altered not only combat but also the perception of earth and sky, distance and nearness, safety and danger. The groundlessness that emerged as stress was reflected in these changed perceptions. The emotional atmosphere since the war has been charged with fear of war and death from the air. In the late 1940s and early 1950s, when the world was war weary, when the Cold War began, and when the Iron Curtain dropped across Europe, suspicion and anxiety infected everyday life. An early memory of my own is of an air raid drill. I was five at the time (1953), growing up in New Jersey. As I stepped out of our apartment building onto the sidewalk, I was jerked back by a stranger. Then I became aware of the sirens blaring, saw the cars frozen in their tracks on the busy avenue and the empty sidewalks. I learned that this was practice, in case we were attacked. Several years later, a Nike Ajax missile at a coastal defense base blew up, killing several men, dropping plaster on our heads at school, and sending a piece of missile into the empty sandbox in a friend's backyard. These events helped to form an image of air and sky. They dramatically accentuated what we soaked in from the movies, television, and the stories of our fathers and uncles who had fought in the war. As the 1950s progressed, the airborne experience became commonplace, and rocket travel materialized. We grew up knowing that the important things take to the skies, that people can live up there.

As a child, I had not yet heard of stress, but in the adult imagination stress was already linked with death from the air. The *New York Times Magazine* presented Selye's general adaptation syndrome to the laity on December 16, 1951. In describing its first or alarm stage, an analogy appears: "The alarm reaction is like the scream of a siren that warns the inhabitants of a city of impending attack by bombers."[36] The precision of this image supplements the more prosaic account of the bodily response to stress in terms of mobilization and defense. Twenty-five years later, it comes as a shock to realize that we alone, of all the generations, take this image of the air raid for granted. We are no longer terrestrial animals.

The sense of emergency played a decisive role in forming the stress mentality. The stress mentality's accents on adaptation and transcendence in the face of imminent danger made it easy to interpret the loss and grief produced by stress's ungrounding as breakdowns that can be corrected or, failing that, eliminated by removing the people who cannot take it, or by making minor adjustments to routine. Stress engineers grief by remaining silent about what we lose in taking flight. Who has time for grief, when there's a job to be done, when the stakes are so high? This attitude, appropriate to military mobilizations, has become our customary way of being.

THE STRESS ON SYSTEMS

The new ungrounded style of life has taken a toll on cherished beliefs about our individuality. As Grinker and Spiegel commented, "The spirit of self-sacrifice, so characteristic of the combat personality, is at the heart of good morale and is not so easily achieved in a cultural group so traditionally individualistic and self-assertive as the American."[37]

To face stress successfully, the individual needed to merge with the group. The self-reliant, pioneering, self-made person needed to become a team player. The image of what Grinker and Spiegel called the "hypothetical American," "a lover of liberty and independence," a master of his own destiny, "essentially optimistic," who yet has ties of loyalty to his community, expressed the ideal of peacetime democratic society. When trained to be a soldier, "the independent American became submissive to authority and dependent upon the group."[38] The "regression" to dependence, which should have afforded security in combat, often failed under the stress of war, and the returning soldier carried with him "an unquenchable need for love and support."[39] Grinker and Spiegel expressed the fear that these men, who were potentially explosive, might become easy prey for fascist organizations. Because so many soldiers cracked under stress, the war revealed how far we were from being a nation of self-reliant individuals. As a matter of fact, many aspects of society fostered childish dependence. The road ahead, they concluded, required intensive psychiatric treatment for these soldiers. Central to it was to be "a national program based upon a thorough understanding of the problem by every segment of the population." A "host of specialists who are experts in social, economic and political techniques" would be required.[40]

Not only soldiers were in danger. The war, the weapons that had been perfected in it, and the world that had been created by it produced the conditions for mass regression and for unleashing the primitive urges that civilization ordinarily keeps in check. Fascist and communist regimes, the war and the explosion of the atomic bomb made this fear realistic:

These mental reactions are fortified by the world in which we live—a world full of unknown future dangers. "Does the potential enemy have atom bombs?" we ask ourselves. "Can their rockets reach us? Are they preparing for war?"

Dangerous mass-infection of these hidden emotions is spreading. All such questions and rumors keep our attitudes on a primitive level. Hitler's War of Nerves brought about the same reaction.[41]

These events, heralding a time of stress, invite us to ask what has happened to the individual in the postwar period. Despite the ideal of autonomous individuality, individuals today appear increasingly troubled by uncertain boundaries, dependencies, addictions, and narcissism. By way of example, the psychological suffering of our age has less to do with the inner workings of the self than it has to do with defining a self in the first place. Experienced Montessori guides note that whereas in years past (say, 15 years ago), 3–6-year-old children could be introduced immediately to the classroom material; now much time must be devoted first to establishing trust and helping the children identify feelings.[42] Increasingly, the self is "empty" or fragile, making interpersonal relations problematic.[43] The "cultural epidemiology" of the postwar suggests something amiss with individuality.[44]

A BRIEF ARCHEOLOGY OF THE INDIVIDUAL UNDER STRESS

What has happened is that the term *individual* has been redefined. The individual today is a subsystem—i.e., a system within a hierarchical group of more encompassing and encompassed systems. This redefinition took root in the wake of the war and is inseparable from the realization that existence is now under stress. This redefinition of individuality was central to the stress field on what we can call, following Foucault, the archeological level.[45] Congruence on the archeological level facilitated the convergence of disparate disciplines on the subject of stress, and this "meeting of the minds" across a variety of disciplines helped to give stress its great persuasive power as a mode of discourse.

The convergence was upon the experience of emergency. And with emergencies as the commons of the domain of stress, a synthesis of many different approaches to the question of adaptation to dangerous change was possible because an "epistemological field," with stress as its linchpin, emerged at the time. The terms of this synthesis are homeostasis, equilibrium of forces, mobilization of resources, elasticity of material, and systems. Homeostasis of psychological and physiological systems framed the understanding of stress on all levels of adaptation. On the psychiatric side, Freudian ego psychology was dominant. The 1946 psychiatric committee (including Leo Bartemeier, Lawrence Kubie, Karl Menninger, John Romano, and John Whitehorn) report on combat exhaustion discussed the psychological makeup of soldiers in these terms:

it can be assumed that the soldier inducted into the Army is one who had adjusted himself to internal and external stresses with a fair degree of personal comfort and social acceptability, and has shown himself capable of enduring some temporary increases in either the internal or external pressures, or both, without untoward reactions. A working psychic equilibrium is maintained.[46]

The ego, the inner agency that mediates between the forces of the id, the superego, and the external world, is the locus of the equilibrium. As Menninger later explained, the ego functions as a homeostatic mechanism:

The essence of my thesis is that the principle of homeostasis or steady state maintenance can be applied to psychological phenomena and psychoanalytic theory. The functions of the ego in receiving external and internal stimuli and in dealing with them for the best interests of the organism can be viewed as those of a homeostatic effector. The constructive and destructive drives of the organism must be so directed and modified as to permit the maintenance of a level of tension which is both tolerable and conducive to safe, productive, and satisfying living and continued growth.[47]

In this approach, pathology is actually a way of adapting, a distorted equilibrium. Individuality could no longer be a point of departure for psychiatric theory. The Bartemeier committee concluded:

Our mode of psychiatric thought and practice and our general American ideology have been almost exclusively developed on the consideration of the individual.... This point of view has not actually been adequate for the best civilian psychiatric practice, but its inadequacy has been generally overlooked, in part because of the professional difficulty in grasping and utilizing new concepts. It is our impression that a psychiatrist adhering to the exclusively individualistic point of view in psychiatry is quite unable to understand a large proportion of the psychiatric disabilities of the combat soldier.[48]

These passages suggest that at the very time that stress was becoming figural, the image of the person as a rugged individual was suffering eclipse, no longer reflecting the realities of mid-twentieth-century life.

On the biological side, Selye described the GAS, which he first formulated in 1936, in terms of stress and stressors. Stressors came to include psychological and social demands as well. The GAS, like homeostasis, was a "biological equivalent of elasticity,"[49] and was welded to the psychosomatic approach to disease. In the 1954 edition of *Emotions and Bodily Change*, Helen Flanders Dunbar added for the first time a presentation of Selye's work. She wrote that considerations of the "organism-environment as a whole" was becoming integral in biology and physiology.[50]

By the mid-1950s the psychiatric literature had articulated an integrated systems approach to stress. It was, as George Engel wrote, a "unitary concept" of health and disease as phases of life: "Health represents the phase of successful adjustment, disease the phase of failure."[51] The notion of system allowed psychiatrists to assimilate the work of Cannon, Selye, Freud, and others into a conceptual gestalt. This gestalt abandoned the unicausal model of disease that had developed in the previous century and that had expressed the ideology of possessive individualism,[52] that Engel later called the "biomedical model." The new "biopsychosocial model" conceives disease as a disharmony among systems (from the atomic to the ecospheric) and calls for a holistic response by a team of "health care professionals," not so much to conquer disease as to monitor and manage living, as Arney and Bergen have made clear.[53] As "open systems" are self-correcting, goal-directed, and capable of using "information" to make adjustments in equilibrium, the range of possibilities for management expand infinitely.

The systems approach clearly had its medical antecedents in Freudian instinct theory and in Adolf Meyer's psychobiology of the 'teens and twenties, but only in the 1950s did systems theory emerge. Bertalanffy in 1950 wrote that something like systems thinking was showing up in modern physics, biology, medicine, psychology, social science, and philosophy. He identified the vision of systems thinking in these terms:

There exist therefore *general system laws* which apply to any system of a certain type, irrespective of the particular properties of the system or the elements involved. We may say also that there is a structural correspondence or logical homology of systems in which the entities concerned are of a wholly different nature.[54]

Arney and Bergen cite Bertalanffy's paper as one that "revolutionized biological thinking in 1950" and note that he "judged the intellectual climate unreceptive to his ideas during the decades prior to 1950."[55] I cannot account for the epistemological "mutation" that produced a systems approach; however, given the postwar unification of the first and second worlds around the Iron Curtain and the proverbial shrinkage of the earth as airmen increasingly populated it, the motivations existed to shift perceptions from atomistic individuality to a systems view. As Norman Cousins proclaimed in 1945, the old, competitive, isolated modern man is dead.[56]

Not that atomistic individuality has ceased to be a social value—indeed it has been integral to political movements of the postwar period. The emphasis on systems does not reflect so much a consensus as it does a conflict about the relations between the person and society. The "system" carries negative connotations, and Americans have become increasingly mistrustful of large organizations, including government at all levels. At the same time, we have become more dependent upon them. The conflict stems from our ambivalence over this dependence. Another location for this conflict lies in the political tone of interpersonal relationships (in employment, marriage, and education), which coincides with a decline in political activity (voting rates). Systems thinking directs attention to relationships rather than to the entities that relate, dissolving them into systems in their own right. Moreover, a great deal of systems talk is euphemsitic, masking the cutthroat competitiveness that well-managed systems tolerate and often promote. "Enlightened self-interest," for example, is not seen as a demon to be exorcised but as energy to be harmonized.

This systems approach has its primary locus in the epistemological field of contemporary thought. Stress has largely been formulated in relation to systems thinking, since systems thinking emphasizes relationships and stress is a relational term. But while systems thinking proposes a goal of harmony, stress evokes an image of the world as essentially hostile. Survival depends upon adaptation, and adaptation depends upon strength and availability of resources, which are held within relationships. In psychology as in physics, one calculates the ratio of strength of material (whether personality factors or health) relative to the load the material must bear. The individual is the dynamic equilibrium of strength versus load. A calculation of the load relative to resources enables estimation of the outcome of the response to demand. In this scheme, the individual has been reinterpreted. No longer an isolated agent opposing the mindlessness of the masses or the id, the individual now exists by virtue of the energy in the systems that define him. It is now assumed that the world is so inherently stressful that training and boosting morale are lifelong needs. Homeostasis is the metaphor for this perception of the individual.

BREAKDOWNS AND UNREALITIES

> Thus the practical significance of homeostasis—indeed, its very meaning—was transformed yet again. The generation of behavioral scientists that grew to professional maturity just before and during World War II restored an analytic and immediate technology of control.... Behavioral scientists had become engineers of technological artifacts rather than physicians of living organisms.
> —Stephen J. Cross and William R. Albury[57]

By 1955, stress was considered a factor in the etiology of all disease. An organismic approach articulated in terms of systems thinking was fully articulated. This unitary approach views health and disease as varying styles of adaptation, some more conducive to well-being than others. All diseases have multiple causes, including psychological and social causes. As this systems approach has taken root, the responsibility for health maintenance has been placed into the hands of the health care consumer since, as stress studies show, healing forces (the *vis mediatrix naturae*), now called homeostatic mechanisms, lie within. The duty for self-monitoring has been so thoroughly mixed with legitimate and spurious spiritual themes and modes of discourse that it has been difficult for us to know when we are pursuing the Great Liberation and when we are accommodating the "biocracy."[58] This systems view of disease has increasingly come to prevail in the contemporary world and has displaced the specificity theory of the previous century-and-a-half.

This new perceptual style of systems took root, generating the stress research industry. This industry reflects and has helped produce new realities. To some extent—and this is what makes ideological critiques difficult—the new approach mirrored the postwar world more adequately than the individualistic approach it displaced. Let us now turn to the new realities and see what became unreal as stress became real. During the war there were a number of reassessments of diagnoses. Some changes were continuations of insights hatched in the heat of World War I; others saw the light of day only in the second war. Together they reveal changing perceptions of the suffering of loss. These changes continued a trend begun earlier, namely a disembedding of suffering from the body and to a more abstract field, one that includes the body as an objective thing, graspable by the informed gaze of the physician-scientist.

With all perception, the place, position, and nature of the perceiver plays a constituting role in determining what appears. On the level of public reality, this perceiver is best understood in terms of the professional allegiances of the men and women who made the observations about stress. During World War II, psychiatry and psychology played major roles in formulating the nature of medical disorders suffered by soldiers and in formulating the meaning of the terror of combat. By way of illustration, during the war 850,000 American service personnel were hospitalized for psychoneurosis, and 1,000,000 men were rejected for military service because of mental and neurological disorders.[59] Paul Starr writes that "the recognition of psychiatry during the [Second World] war was, quite likely, its greatest achievement." For psychiatry the establishment of the National Institute for Mental Health (NIMH) was an important achievement in the immediate postwar period, because it provided funds for training, research, and treatment. NIMH, whose mandate included "a broad mission to promote mental health as well as to deal with mental illness,"[60] also helped institutionalize the new field of clinical psychology for the same reasons. These two fields, armed with funds and an increasing number of university departments, generated the research on stress over the past generation. The social production of stress has received wide institutional backing in the years since 1949.

For two decades following the war, a psychoanalytic ego psychology dominated the psychiatric community in the United States. This orientation fostered a concern for the ego as the psychic agent of adaptation and mastery of primitive urges. It also cultivated a special emphasis on the etiological role of anxiety, since anxiety, as these psychiatrists knew, could be experienced by patients under any number of disguises. Finally, the orientation implied treatment plans that could include psychotherapy.

The nature of the diseases produced by World War II—not the wounds or the infectious diseases, but the vague ones that affected seemingly healthy men and that looked like cowardice in some military eyes—differed from earlier wars. World War I had its own diagnoses: neurocirculatory asthenia, the effort syndrome, disordered action of the heart, and shellshock. The first war also saw an abundance of neurasthenia and hysteria cases. While these classifications were still familiar in the 1940s, psychiatry largely abandoned them because they emphasized the physical side of the complaint at the expense of the psychological. The new diseases spawned in World War II had roots in the patients' life histories.

World War II produced one major new disorder, operational or battle fatigue (or combat exhaustion). The notion of fatigue harkens back to nineteenth-century thought, for which depletion of nervous force from overwork could produce serious disease. Actually, while fatigue was a genuine problem for the soldier during World War II, it was not considered the major cause of neurosis. Using *fatigue* and *exhaustion* to label these disorders was a face-saving measure. The British psychiatrist John Rees admitted in 1945 that

the use of the term 'exhaustion' as a euphemism for all psychiatric breakdowns in the line has, on the whole, been very successful. Shell shock or even anxiety neurosis have a much more serious implication of illness than the label 'exhaustion.' The man who is sent to the division or corps exhaustion centre and after a few days is able to return to duty goes back with no diagnostic label, even though he recognizes that 'exhaustion' was actually an alternative name for what he knew he had—anxiety that brought him near to the end of his tether.[61]

Grinker and Spiegel made a similar point but noted that the euphemism created confusion because it suggested "that rest is obviously the treatment of choice."[62] They added that to see the situation correctly (in a widely held view): "The question . . . is: How much did his previous personality and how much did the stress he experienced contribute to his reaction?"[63] A combination of the two, stress and predisposition, prevailed in the view of military psychiatrists to account for war-related neuroses.

A psychodynamic explanation for neurosis was hardly new in 1940. Essentially, all adult psychopathologies were understood to have their origin in earliest childhood. This causal account was not abandoned after World War II. Rather, it was supplemented by another that focused on stress. A group of American military psychiatrists, writing in 1943 about operational fatigue, found that "men with little predisposition to breakdown, may finally develop severe symptoms under great stress."[64] As "stress" and "stressor" came to dominate thinking, the external cause of psychiatric disorders did too. In 1945, still transitional to the age of stress, this external perspective had not yet crystallized. For Grinker and Spiegel, "after the initial blow, the pattern is internalized and repetitive according to the previous patterns of personality."[65] By the end of the Vietnam War, by contrast, the external world was seen as the main cause of such disorders (now called PTSS). In the words of one Vietnam-era psychiatrist, "individuals who have lived in a psychotic environment and whose reality was beyond the scope of the ordinary life"[66] are liable to break down. It is indeterminate the extent to which this change (from internal to external) reflects a shift in perceptual style and the extent to which it reflects a difference in the social world.

Medical personnel in the 1940s were aware that the modern, altered conditions of warfare promoted a changed pattern of psychiatric disorders. Psychiatrist Edward Strecker observed in 1944 that World War II "was and is being fought not only on the surface of the earth, but in the skies at oxygen deprivation heights, beneath the sea, in subarctic wastes, on burning desert sands."[67] In World War I, conversion hysteria was the common neurosis, but in World War II anxiety neuroses predominated. Strecker wrote:

clinical manifestations seem to indicate that much deeper human emotional recesses have been penetrated. . . . It seems unlikely that in a few decades the ethical stratum of man's superego should have progressed so rapidly. More likely is it that the calamitous and horrifying situations produced by modern war machines penetrate deeper and more acutely sensitive emotional levels.[68]

Subsequent events proved how perceptive Strecker was. In the age of stress, disease appears related causally to the increasing hostility of the outer world, in which we have become alien airmen. By 1949 already, "stress diseases are looming ever larger in our lives—the duodenal ulcer, the thyrotoxicosis, the non-renal hypertension with its vascular accidents," wrote a British family doctor.[69] The only major change since then is the number of diseases, some of them unknown or rare in 1949, that have been added to the list.

The preceding remarks indicate what was emerging. What now needs addressing is what faded as the age of stress prevailed: Diseases that once embodied psychological suffering in the flesh, especially in the heart, are now seen as increasingly unreal. In the new perception, such embodiment is a misperception called *somatization* (the mislabeling of a psychological symptom as a physical one; for example, complaining of chest pain when the problem is really anxiety). DaCosta's syndrome, neurocirculatory asthenia, the effort syndrome, and neurasthenia were among the diseases that ceased to be accepted as real in the postwar period. Medical personnel did not believe in such diagnoses any longer, and they saw less of them. Whitehorn expressed the new outlook:

We have inherited other related terms and ideas, such as the "irritable heart of the soldier" or "neurocirculatory asthenia"—concepts which we now recognize as having something to do with stress and with limitation of the general reactions of the organism under stress, in contrast to the earlier preoccupation with presumed defects of the heart or the neurocirculatory apparatus.[70]

What had appeared to an earlier generation as a physical disorder now seemed revealed as an emotional response to stress. Grinker and Spiegel wrote that they expected to see these functional heart diseases, "including the so-called 'effort syndrome,' " from accounts of the previous war:

However, true DaCosta's syndrome was not observed. Many patients with anxiety states had tachycardia. . . . In fact, an unstable cardiac rate has been found in most cases of war neuroses. Vague and transient precordial pain and palpitation were complained of by others. However, as an isolated and specific psychosomatic entity, cardiac neuroses were not frequently observed.[71]

All of which indicates a changed reality: Diseases that had been perceived as existing in the body were now perceived as existing in the personality.

Even before the war these functional heart diseases were under suspicion.[72]

Indeed, psychoanalytically oriented medicine viewed them with a jaundiced eye during the First World War.[73] However, they remained widely diagnosed and subject to serious debate through the 1950s. In a major study by a British nonpsychiatrist, physician Paul Wood in 1941 concluded that these cardiac disorders were really "an emotional reactive pattern peculiar to psychopathic personalities and to subjects of almost any form of psychoneurosis."[74] What happens to such patients is that normal physiological reactions to stress become fixated upon as the problem, keeping the real psychological issues at bay. Patients thus "somaticize" their conflicts, construing life difficulties as pain in the heart.[75]

What was the nature of this kind of disease that lost its reality at this time? How did patients experience it? Wood summarized:

a group of symptoms which unduly limit the subject's capacity for effort.... The cardinal symptoms are breathlessness, palpitations, fatigue, left thoracic pain, and dizziness; the cardinal signs are those of functional disturbance of the respiratory, vasomotor, muscular, and sudomotor systems. It is admitted that this definition is concerned entirely with the physical side of the picture, but it is from this aspect that the cases have been viewed by the majority of physicians from 1861 to 1941.[76]

Physicians had viewed the distress through the anatomical image of the body, which had the virtue for these patients of locating the suffering in the same place that they felt it. But this gaze no longer sufficed in the age of stress. Grinker and Spiegel gave a single example in *Men under Stress* of "palpitation and precordial distress without cardiac disease":

A 30 year old clerk spent three years overseas under the jurisdiction of officers who were poor leaders, inefficient and hostile to their men. Living conditions were not good and opportunities for diversion infrequent. During this period the patient, who had never been ill or had cardiac symptoms, became conscious of his heart.

After several interviews he was able to reconstruct the relation of his heart symptoms to external events. When terribly annoyed with his officers or after some particularly unfair treatment, he developed precordial distress.[77]

The clerk's problems had nothing to do with his heart.

Nothing to do with his heart? But wasn't the patient's pent-up rage at unfair treatment a heart dis-ease? Apparently not. What the psychiatrist avoided was locating the problem in the anatomical heart. The rage had no business in the heart-as-pump. Caughey had warned about

the physician who is unable or unwilling to consider his patient as something more than an isolated mechanical unit. An individual who has noticed some cardiac symptom during a time of physical or mental strain, and has become anxious about his condition, may have his fears accentuated by an excessively careful physical examination of the heart.[78]

The rage belongs to the patient's total reaction to a difficult situation and not primarily to the anatomical organ. That organ may be in common speech the locus of love and anger, but such loose talk cannot be tolerated in medical science. The feelings felt there, in one's chest, belong in this instance to the psychological realm and are the purview of the psychiatrist and psychologist, not of the cardiologist.

For all its limitations, the earlier medical perception that the pain really signaled a cardiac or at least a physical condition honored the individual's lived experience of suffering felt there in the chest. The older view seriously misconstrued it in terms of murmurs and enlargements, of course. But the newer view of stress and systems creates its own artifacts: It transforms the pain into a discourse of pent-up rage, predispositions from personal history, anxiety, and somaticization. If the older view construed the heart through the stethoscope, the newer view did so through a complex web of theory, competing professions, and institutions.

Neurocirculatory asthenia and its kin were shimmering realities at best. They had mixed pedigrees, but what they shared in formulation was a difference from earlier discourses on the "same" diseases—overstrain of the heart, nervous prostration, etc.—that saw the culprit as the physical organ's depletion or weakness. Neurocirculatory asthenia and the effort syndrome were, as we shall see, already attempts to turn attention away from the heart. But they did so ambiguously, and this ambiguity haunted them until their demise in the 1950s. These diagnoses assumed some physiological deficiency in the patient, some compromise in functional efficiency, without assuming an anatomical defect as had Victorian physicians. They coexisted with that of psychoneurosis, which competed with them for dominance. During the lull between the wars, the psychological and physiological realms were professionally separate; no unifying vision bound them together. The reconstruction of these "heart" disorders after the Second World War in terms of psychological subsystems of the person made it possible to accommodate the anatomical image of the body with the psychological image of the person. From then on, one had to know what "level" one was addressing, which subsystem one intended to monitor and correct. The body that the patient felt he had loses in this synthesis its being as a substantial entity.

The discourse on stress threw tangible, felt bodily experiences up into the air of systems. The stresses of war, that might otherwise have been called the griefs of war, thus received a framework that focused on harnessing manpower for responding to emergencies, especially those emergencies of hostility. Stress names a modern form of grief. We now understand the context of its emergence and the symbolic dimensions it embraces: It came into being in the context of the military emergency of the Second World War and its symbolic landscape is being in the air.

Stress emerged from the background of medical perception as the world plunged into total warfare. The world that took form after the war was increasingly alien, inhospitable to human life as it used to be lived. Correlative to this inhospitality, "we" became airmen, who like the Martians from the *War of the Worlds* relied completely on life-support systems for survival and who were subject to disease from living in this alien landscape. *Stress* names the experience of living in such a world. It also names the realization that human beings are elastic: With testing, training and morale-building, we can learn to endure and even thrive in this groundless space. With this world comes also a new vision of systems instead of atomistic individuals, systems instead of bodies.

NOTES

1. Michel Foucault, *The Order of Things: An Archeology of the Human Sciences* (New York: Vintage Books, 1970), and *The History of Sexuality*, Part I: *Introduction* (New York: Pantheon, 1978).

2. Edward Abbey, *The Brave Cowboy* (1956; reprint, Albuquerque: University of New Mexico Press, 1977), p. 260.

3. Howard Koch, scriptwriter of "The War of the Worlds," in Hadley Cantril, *The Invasion from Mars: A Study in the Psychology of Panic* (1940; reprint, New York: Harper Torchbooks, 1966), p. 38.

4. Cantril, *The Invasion from Mars*, p. 138. The preceding quotation is from p. xi.

5. Koch, "The War of the Worlds," p. 41.

6. Lawrence Hinkle, "The concept of 'stress' in the biological and social sciences," *International Journal of Psychiatry in Medicine* 5, no. 4 (1974), 335–357; John Mason, "A historical view of the stress field," *Journal of Human Stress* 1, no. 1 (March 1975), 6–12; Hans Selye, *The Stress of Life* (New York: McGraw-Hill, 1975). Reviewing the various indices, one finds, in general, no citations before 1950, when suddenly they multiply. The pattern also exists in *Current List of Medical Literature*; volumes 18 and 19 (1950) contain a total of 14 listings under "stress," while earlier volumes contain none.

7. Richard Rubenstein, *The Cunning of History: The Holocaust and the American Future* (New York: Harper Colophon, 1975), p. 8.

8. Roy R. Grinker, *Psychosomatic Research* (New York: Norton, 1953), p. 64.

9. John Spiegel, "Transactional theory and social change," in Daniel Offer and Daniel Freedman, eds., *Modern Psychiatry and Clinical Research: Essays in Honor of Roy R. Grinker* (New York: Basic Books, 1972), p. 18.

10. Walter B. Cannon, "Stresses and strains of homeostasis," *American Journal of the Medical Sciences* 189 (1935), 7.

11. Ibid., pp. 9–10.

12. Ibid., pp. 13–14.

13. E. F. Skinner "Psychological stresses in industry," *Practitioner* 53 (1944), 37–44.

14. See Donald DeCarlo, "Stress in the workplace—An assessment of the problem," *Insurance Review* (May/June 1985), 2–7; Philip R. Voluck and Herbert Abramson, "How to avoid stress-related disability claims," *Personnel Journal* (May 1987), 95–98; John M. Ivancevich, Michael T. Matteson, and Edward Prichards, "Who's liable for stress on the job?" *Harvard Business Review* (March–April 1985), 60–72;

Olov Ostberg and Carina Nilsson, "Emerging technology and stress," in C. L. Cooper and M. J. Smith, eds., *Job Stress and Blue Collar Work* (New York: Wiley, 1985), pp. 149–69; David Kalish, "Straight for the gut," *Marketing and Media Decisions* 23 (July 1988), 26.

15. H. Palmer "Military psychiatric casualties: Experience with 12,000 cases," *Lancet* 1945, no. 2, 456.

16. Quoted in Robert Ahrenfeldt, *Psychiatry in the British Army in the Second World War* (New York: Columbia University Press, 1958), p. 202.

17. Ibid., p. 198.

18. *Oxford English Dictionary*, 2nd ed. (Oxford: Clarendon Press, 1989). *Morale* acquired the meaning of "esprit de corps" only in the nineteenth century. Previously it meant "moral."

19. Ibid.

20. Palmer, "Military psychiatric casualties," p. 494.

21. Roy R. Grinker and John Spiegel, *Men under Stress* (Philadelphia: Blakiston, 1945), pp. 69–70.

22. John Whitehorn, "Introduction and survey of the problems of stress," in *Symposium on Stress, 16–18 March 1953* (Washington: Walter Reed Army Medical Center, Army Medical Service Graduate School, 1953), p. 2.

23. For the beginnings of the medical gaze, see Michel Foucault, *The Birth of the Clinic* (New York: Vintage Books, 1975).

24. See note 9.

25. Hans Selye, *The Stress of Life*, rev. ed. (New York: McGraw-Hill, 1976), p. 51.

26. Jerome Kagan, "Stress and coping in early development," in Norman Garmezy and Michael Ruter, eds., *Stress, Coping, and Development in Children* (Baltimore: Johns Hopkins University Press, 1983), p. 193.

27. Ibid., p. 193.

28. Donald W. Hastings, David G. Wright, and Bernard C. Glueck, *Psychiatric Experiences of the Eighth Air Force, First Year of Combat (July 4, 1942–July 4, 1943)* (New York: Josiah Macy, Jr. Foundation, 1944), p. 93.

29. Eugen Reinartz, "Psychiatry in aviation," in F. J. Sladen, ed., *Psychiatry and the War* (Springfield, IL and Baltimore: Charles C. Thomas, 1943), p. 276.

30. Ibid., p. 267.

31. Wolfgang Schivelbusch, *The Railway Journey: Trains and Travel in the Nineteenth Century* (Oxford: Basil Blackwell, 1979).

32. Grinker and Spiegel, *Men under Stress*, p. 31.

33. Ibid., p. 27.

34. Yet like the Adam of Gnostic myth, we are erotically drawn to the earth, as we are to the image of the earth seen from the moon.

35. Hudson Hoagland, "Adventures in Biological Engineering," *Science* 100 (1944), 63–64.

36. Waldemar Kaempffert, "Cortisone and ACTH: An assay," *New York Times Magazine*, December 16, 1951, p. 30. See also the editorial "Psychosomatics," *New England Journal of Medicine* 232 (1945), 545: "It has required for the population at large a second world war and a popular pictorial magazine to acquaint them with the actuality of psychosomatics."

37. Grinker and Spiegel, *Men under stress*, p. 45.

38. Ibid., p. 447.

39. Ibid., p. 449.

40. Ibid., p. 460.

41. Joost A. M. Meerloo, *Delusion and Mass Delusion* (New York: Nervous and Mental Disease Monographs, 1949), p. 96.

42. Personal communication.

43. See Philip Cushman, "Why the self is empty: Toward a historically situated psychology," *American Psychologist* 45 (1990), 599–611.

44. David Michael Levin, in D. M. Levin, ed., *Pathologies of the Modern Self* (New York: New York University Press, 1987).

45. By "archeological level," Foucault refers to underlying assumptions, rules of discourse, and concept patterns that appear, during a given historical epoch, in otherwise diverse knowledge fields. With stress, on the archeological level, the self is no longer a social atom.

46. Leo H. Bartemeier, Lawrence S. Kubie, Karl M. Menninger, et al., "Combat exhaustion," *Journal of Nervous and Mental Diseases* 104 (October and November 1946), 364.

47. Karl Menninger, "Regulatory devices of the ego under major stress," in *A Psychiatrist's World: The Selected Papers of Karl Menninger*, ed. Bernard H. Hall (New York: Viking Press, 1959), p. 515.

48. Bartemeier et al., "Combat exhaustion," p. 371.

49. Whitehorn, "Introduction and survey," p. 7.

50. Helen Flanders Dunbar, *Emotions and Bodily Changes*, 4th ed. (New York: Columbia University Press, 1954), p. 745.

51. George Engel, "Behavioral adjustment and the concept of health and disease," in Roy R. Grinker, ed., *Mid-Century Psychiatry* (Springfield, IL: Charles C. Thomas, 1953), p. 33.

52. J. Comaroff, "Medicine: Symbol and ideology," in P. Wright and A. Treacher, eds., *The Problem of Medical Knowledge* (Edinburgh: Edinburgh University Press), 49–68.

53. William Arney and Bernard Bergen, *Medicine and the Management of Living: Taming the Last Great Beast* (Chicago: University of Chicago Press, 1984).

54. Ludwig von Bertalanffy, "An outline of general systems theory," *British Journal of the Philosophy of Science* 1 (1950), 138–39.

55. Arney and Bergen, *Medicine and the Management of Living*, p. 71.

56. Norman Cousins, *Modern Man Is Dead* (New York: Random House, 1945).

57. Stephen J. Cross and William R. Albury, "Walter B. Cannon, J. Henderson, and the Organic Analogy," *Osiris* 3, 2nd series (1987), 191.

58. Cannon's word: See Walter B. Cannon, "Biocracy: Does the human body contain the secret of economic stabilization?" *The Technology Review* 35, no. 6 (March 1933), 203–206, 227. See also ibid.

59. Paul Starr, *The Social Transformation of American Medicine* (New York: Basic Books, 1982), p. 344. The quotation that follows is from p. 344.

60. Ernest Hilgard, *Psychology in America: A Historical Survey* (Austin: Harcourt Brace Jovanovich, 1987), p. 634.

61. John Rees, *The Shaping of Psychiatry by War* (New York: Norton, 1945), p. 115.

62. Grinker and Spiegel, *Men under Stress*, p. 209.

63. Ibid., pp. 212–13.

64. Hastings, et al. *Psychiatric Experiences*, p. 93.

65. Grinker and Spiegel, *Men under Stress*, p. 348.

66. Henry Krystal, "Psychoanalytic views on human emotional damage," in B. A. Van der Kolk, *Post-Traumatic Stress Disorders: Psychological and Biological Sequelae* (Washington, DC: American Psychiatric Association, 1984), p 22.

67. Edward Strecker, "War psychiatry and its influence upon postwar psychiatry and upon civilization," *Journal of Nervous and Mental Diseases* 101 (May 1945), 403.

68. Ibid., p. 403.

69. R. J. Perring, "Family doctor," *Lancet* 1949, no. 2, 1166.

70. Whitehorn, "Introduction and survey," p. 4.

71. Roy R. Grinker and John P. Spiegel, *War Neuroses*, rev. ed. (Philadelphia: Blakiston, 1945), p. 22.

72. See J. L. Caughey, "Cardiovascular neurosis—A review," *Psychosomatic Medicine* 1, no. 2 (April 1939), 311–24.

73. W.H.R. Rivers, "War neurosis and military training," *Mental Hygiene* 2, no. 4 (1918), 513–33; see Millais Culpin, "Disordered action of the heart," *British Medical Journal*, 1918, no. ii, 395: "the syndrome known as DAH [disordered action of the heart], which now incapacitates thousands of men, is a manifestation of emotional disturbance and not a result of infection. . . . I dislike the word 'neurosis,' but would admit its application to symptoms, including DAH, caused by interference from emotional causes at this lower level of the central nervous system.

"The practical importance of this view is immediate. The original cause of emotion may have vanished; but when a man believes he is suffering from 'heart disease' a fresh source is opened out from which he derives new fears. His fears maintain the symptoms and the symptoms maintain the fears."

74. Paul Wood, "DaCosta's syndrome," *British Medical Journal*, 1941, no. i, 849.

75. See William Menninger, "Modern concepts of war neuroses," *Bulletin of the Menninger Clinic* 10 (1946), 157.

76. Wood, "DaCosta's syndrome," p. 767.

77. Grinker and Spiegel, *Men under Stress*, p. 272.

78. Caughey, "Cardiovascular neurosis," p. 320.

4

Preparing the Groundless

Under the name of stress, engineered grief emerged from the pain of the Second World War. To discover the immediate predecessor to stress, we turn to the first half of the twentieth century, which saw the First World War, relativity theory, and quantum mechanics, modernism in art and literature, the Great Depression, and fascist and socialist revolutions—a time which prepared the groundless domain that we now occupy. What we find are understandings of energy, limits, and the flesh that were transitional between the Victorian period and our own. We also find an engineering mentality embodied in medical language undergoing a transformation from the nineteenth-century preoccupation with scarcity to a twentieth-century anxiety over abundance. Finally, we notice in the early part of our century the preparation of a systems view that organizes our present response to loss of the familiar.

HIDDEN RESERVES OF POWER

> Much excited by possibility of adrenalin activation explaining second wind.
>
> —W. B. Cannon[1]

Into a book devoted largely to the results of physiological research, Cannon poured stories of knights and athletes as well as those of blood and urine tests. He evoked a college football game with its influx of the fans to town,

its songs, its pep rallies, its electric excitement in the air, its tens of thousands
in the stands to cheer their heroes on. His football story calls to mind a more
innocent time before drug scandals and urine tests became as important as
the game itself. Enter the physiologist, fully appreciative of the enthusiasm
of the players:

In the dressing room before a critical contest I have seen a "gridiron warrior," ready
in canvas suit, cleated shoes, and leather helmet, sitting grimly on a bench, his fist
clenched, his jaws tight, and his face the grayish color of clay. He performed wonderfully when the game began, and after it was over there was a large percentage of
sugar in his urine! Probably no sport requires a more sustained and extreme display
of neuro-muscular effort than American football. And from the foregoing description
of the conditions that surround the contests it is easy to realize that they conspire to
arouse in the players excitements which would bring forth very efficiently the bodily
reserves for use in the fierce struggle which the game requires.[2]

Not only sugar, either. His research had shown that the hormone adrenalin,
"when freely liberated in the blood, not only aids in bringing out sugar from
the liver's store of glycogen, but also has a remarkable influence in quickly
restoring to fatigued muscles ... the same readiness for response which they
had when fresh."[3] The liberation of this hormone unleashes our powers,
enabling performance at a high level of physiological efficiency; thereby we
exceed the limits we had hitherto believed we possessed.

Cannon's work in this area reflected the tenor of the epoch which, roughly
speaking, spanned the years 1905–1945. It was like all epochs fraught with
conflicting formulations, yet it distinguished itself from the age of stress which
followed it and the preceding age of strain in its essentially optimistic assessment of human energy and limits. I shall call it, to borrow Auden's term,
the age of anxiety, because anxiety had then become (and largely remains)
indicative not of dissipation but of pent-up energy, of a boiling under pressure, dangerous if not tapped or channeled.[4] Anxiety and the energy it man-
ifests mirrored the transformation taking place in other aspects of social life:
the development of automobile and air travel, the diffusion of electricity
throughout society, and the beginnings of an economy in which consumption
displaced production and savings as the path to well-being.

I do not wish to evoke a zeitgeist, but rather the attitudes and orientations
in the domain within medicine and psychology that is concerned with questions of the engineering of human performance. This "age," to give it a high-
sounding name, is continuous with the succeeding one in many respects. The
discontinuities center, briefly, on the lessons of mass death. The age of stress
knows the terrible consequences of unleashing human and natural potential
energy; hence in part our grief. The age of anxiety, the Waste Land generation, tasted it to be sure, yet withal believed in the fruits of progress.

"Laboratory medicine" increasingly gained an important place in the En-
glish-speaking world in the early twentieth century. Removed from the clin-

ical setting as the primary source of new knowledge, medical perception altered in the laboratory. Physiological function, not anatomical structure, became figural in the understanding of disease. Function is temporal, structure spatial, and this shift in medical perception indicated a broader epistemological change which concentrated upon dynamics and processes. Back in the 1870s, the German Ottomar Rosenbach, among others, had already made the move and, as Ackerknecht notes, "he coined such useful notions as that of the 'latent reserve force' of organs."[5] Interest in function flowered in many domains in the new century. One need think only of developments in painting, poetry, physics, philosophy, and music to discover that "becoming" and not "being" was the core interest. All was in evolution, if not revolution.

The engineering approach to the body, which exists in mature form in modern stress theory, was a going concern in the early years of the twentieth century. "What are the limits of human faculty in various directions?" asked William James, the great philosopher and psychologist of the period. While James meant the question broadly, it admits of answers from engineering. With the notions of function and latent reserve force, the question of limits had a fitting context.

Samuel J. Meltzer, a friend of Cannon's and a research physiologist, on delivering the Harvey Society Lecture in 1906, drew on an engineering concept and asked:

Are the structures and the functions of the living animal body provided with such factors of safety [as engineers design into structures they build]? As far as I know, that question has never yet been clearly raised, and certainly was never made the subject of a direct investigation.[6]

The question resembles the one Cannon later asked in 1935. Cannon of course knew Meltzer's question, since he quotes him in *The Wisdom of the Body*. But the difference between the times in which the questions were asked is noteworthy. Cannon's "call" was heard, indeed was already being heard, in Selye's laboratory, in psychosomatic consultations and speculations, and on psychoanalytic couches. Meltzer could complain, however, that a bias existed against the notion of factors of safety in animal design. The animal economy had been reassessed between the time of Meltzer's complaint (1907) and Cannon's call (1935). Meltzer was looking with "laboratory eyes" and perceived reserves in the body that many of his clinically oriented contemporaries could not see. Medical assumptions hitherto had regarded animal economy as niggardly, as a hoarding of meager stores of energy, as fearful of wastage. Reviewing the record of physiological inquiry, however, Meltzer found the body "uneconomical" in design. The major organs have ample reserves, and energy abounds: "with regard to the function of supply of tissue and energy . . . nature meant it should be governed by the same principle of affluence which governs the entire construction of the animal for the safety of its life and the perpetuation of its species."[7] As the psyche has a powerful reservoir of libido, so the organism has ample power.

Reserve force or factors of safety appeared everywhere in the body to those who looked with "laboratory eyes." Two examples will illustrate this point. J. George Adami, the British physiologist, observed that reserve force may be "the keystone to adaptation, and, in brief, of the evolution of the race."[8] Adami cited an example of rabbits living normally after having had three-quarters of their livers removed: "In other words one-quarter of that organ suffices to satisfy the needs of the organism, or, . . . under normal conditions the liver cells are working only at one-quarter of their capacity."[9] James Mackenzie, the general practitioner from Burnley who led the way to ex-perimental medicine in Britain, explained the reserve force of the heart by noting that "only a portion of the muscle cells participates in each contraction of the ventricles. . . . [W]hen effort is made a much larger proportion takes part in the contraction."[10] Mackenzie had pursued the measure of the heart's reserve power because he had been interested in the "efficiency of the heart" in conditions of both rest and effort. The implication is that the healthy heart is indeed efficient.[11] Physicians and physiologists, such as Mackenzie, Adami, Meltzer, and Cannon saw the body as having abundant resources to deal with emergencies.

Both Adami and Mackenzie considered the cell to be the unit for phys-iological analysis. The cell had been perceived, since Virchow in the mid-nineteenth century, as the building block of the body. Adami defined the cell's function as "a machine for the evolution of energy."[12] Reserve force is thus ultimately the energy reserve of the cells that is not needed for ordinary performance.[13] The metaphor of machine in Adami's definition connects the body as energy producer with industrial production.[14] Physiological activity was work done by the cells and the organs. Reserve force, albeit "uneco-nomical," pointed to the great (and as yet untapped) potential of the body.

JAMES'S VISION

Two of William James's most charming essays are "The Energies of Men" (1907) and "The Gospel of Relaxation" (1899). Point and counterpoint, they voice the best of the epoch. In "The Energies of Men," James commented on fatigue. Usually it serves as a barrier to further effort. However, if we "push through the obstruction" the following occurs:

The fatigue gets worse up to a certain critical point, when gradually or suddenly it passes away, and we are fresher than before. We have evidently tapped a level of new energy, masked until then by the fatigue-obstacle usually obeyed. There may be layer after layer of this experience. A third and a fourth "wind" may supervene."[15]

He asked in this essay the critical questions which guide the search for limits: "What are the limits of human faculty in various directions?" "By what diversity of means, in the differing types of human beings, may the faculties be stimulated to their best results?" Acknowledging the "triviality" of these questions, what he meant to suggest is that they be taken up "*as a methodical programme of scientific inquiry.*"[16] The programmatic character of the inquiry is the critical thing, as James emphasized.

James's practical tips I leave to the reader to enjoy; the essay has much to commend it. But to illustrate the difference between James's epoch and our own, regard what he said about city versus country life:

The rapid rate of life, the number of decisions in an hour, the many things to keep account of, in a busy city man's or woman's life, seems monstrous to a country brother. He doesn't see how we live at all. A day in New York or Chicago fills him with terror. The danger and noise make it appear like permanent earthquake. But *settle* him there, and in a year or two he will have caught the pulsebeat. He will vibrate to the city's rhythms; and if he only succeeds in his avocation, whatever that may be, he will find a joy in all the hurry and the tension, . . . and get as much out of himself in any week as he ever did in ten weeks in the country.[17]

The observations ring true. We, however, are less sanguine than James was in this passage, as witnessed by a recent study correlating a quickened pace of life to coronary heart disease,[18] and the ambivalence we experience being in the whirlwind of daily life.

A former student of James, Cannon found "The Energies of Men" stimulating his own thought. He regarded his own work on the adrenal medulla as giving "physiological support for the views Professor James expressed" in that essay.[19] Adrenalin helped cause "extraordinary feats of strength and greatly increased endurance of men under stress of emotional excitement."[20] Publicity for Cannon's *Bodily Changes in Pain, Hunger, Fear and Rage* (1915) through newspaper accounts resulted in "the word *adrenalin* slipp[ing] into the mainstream of everyday speech as a metaphor for energy."[21] Today people under stress *feel* adrenalin rushing into their bloodstream as they become energized. The metaphor has become literalized as a feeling that connotes the evocation of energy reserves that our bodies produce and we consume.

James also preached a gospel of relaxation. He noted that the difference between American and European physiognomies becomes apparent to Americans when they return home from abroad. They "find a wild-eyed look upon their compatriot's faces, either of too desperate eagerness and anxiety or of too intense responsiveness and good-will."[22] This intensity tends to make us nervous, and neither overwork nor climate, both considered causes of "American nervousness" in the nineteenth century, cause the nervous collapses so prominent on our shores, he claimed. Rather the cause lies in "those absurd feelings of hurry and having no time, in that breathlessness and tension, that anxiety of feature and that solicitude for results, that lack of inner harmony and ease, in short, by which with us the work is so apt to be accompanied."[23]

He attributed these characteristics to "the over-active conscience" of his countrymen, especially in New England. Guilt drives us to fritter away our energies in trivialities and produces nervous maladies. Scruples of conscience make us too self-conscious and too inhibited. It takes effort to inhibit, hence our potential dissipates itself in restraint rather than in positive activity. His solution: The formation of new habits which would free us from "egoistic preoccupation about results."[24] James advises the production-oriented Protestant conscience to relax and enjoy the process, the flow. What signals this analysis as characteristic of its age is the claim that *inhibition* rather than *overwork* causes nervous strain. Constraining energy, not spending energy, wears us down.

ENERGY AND ANXIETY

James's reading of the discontents of civilization reveals one of the conflicts of a period confident of civilization's powers. The desire to work and to overwork remained, and it was coupled by a sense of confidence in having ample power for whatever needed doing. It was a period, too, when nineteenth-century individualism met twentieth-century social planning. In the progressive era in the United States (1900–1920), a marked reevaluation of the fictions of "the autonomous economic man, the autonomous possessor of property rights, the autonomous man of character"[25] occurred. In many fields of discourse, including social reform, economics, education, politics, and philosophy, ideals of interdependence and cooperation appeared, as did the conclusion that "the notion of a separate and independent ego is an illusion."[26] Robert Wiebe argues that the period from 1877 to 1920 witnessed the transformation of American society from a collection of more or less independent towns and regions into a tightly knit unity, with consequent loss of local control. With the rise of the new professions and middle class in the new industrial urban centers came a bureaucratic mentality that sought to manage this unprecedented and confusing social scene. The bureaucrats applied "scientific method" to social issues:

They pictured a society of ceaselessly interacting members and concentrated upon adjustments within it. Although they included rules and principles of human behavior, these necessarily had an indeterminate quality because perpetual interaction was itself indeterminate. . . . A society in flux always contained that irreducible element of contingency, and predictability really meant probability. Thus the rules, resembling orientations much more than laws, stressed techniques of constant watchfulness and mechanisms of continuous management.[27]

The bureaucratic mind dwelt upon process, procedure, and implementation of plans for the purpose of social "engineering," to use a metaphor new during this period. With an eye for social dynamics, the bureaucrats attempted to harmonize the explosive social situation.

Thus the sense that hidden reserves of energies existed and awaited exploitation went hand-in-hand with a "guidance system" to conduct the exploitation. The notion of mental conflict is best understood within this context. Whereas in the nineteenth century anxiety was viewed largely in terms of exhaustion, in the early twentieth century depth psychology, then on the ascendent, viewed anxiety as a signal of inner conflict. The primary conflict was considered as existing between unconscious drives on the one hand, and the demands of the external world, the ego as the conscious personality, and the inner representatives of parental authority on the other. The power to harness or otherwise deflect instinctual drives made social progress possible by delaying immediate gratification with the promise of great gratification after work on the external world was achieved, but at the price of an ever-increasing level of neurosis.[28] Anxiety, the chief symptom of neurosis, was the measure of the level of advancement of civilization. Anxiety is produced in the process of harnessing an individual's excess energy. And anxiety causes neuroses, because in harnessing excess energies we are stifling our instinctual drives. As we stifle our drives, we become more civilized because we become more attuned to the demands of the external world. Thus was the work ethic transposed into the key of the scientific view of human vitality.

Within depth psychology there were divergent theories about conflict, but they had in common the ideas that an energetics of the human psyche was possible, that the sources of psychic energy lay in the unconscious, that the energy of the unconscious was greater than consciousness generally realized, and that the healthy channeling of psychic energy was the main issue in therapy. Hence the stress on conflict and not, as in an earlier day, on exhaustion and rest. For all practical purposes, the unconscious had a limitless supply of energy, yet this limitless supply could not be simply tapped. Freud viewed our condition as tragic: Psychic energy was duplex, Eros and Thanatos, in his final formulation, which meant that war always raged within us. Inner struggle was essential and not accidental to the human soul. Others, like Reich, influenced by Marx, saw conflict as expressive of capitalist society, not as innate to the human being. For Jung, psychic energy had multiple points of origin in the collective unconscious, and he variously named and numbered basic instincts. This very multiplicity both ensured and diffused strife in the soul, although with Jung's notion of the Self as the archetype of unity conflict had a goal of harmony. The upshot from the perspective of depth psychology is that in the human psyche conflict reigned and anxiety was its epiphany.

The unconscious was seen through a lens made in part by Darwin. Depending on the angle from which one looked, different aspects of the unconscious emerged. From one point of view, the unconscious slowed social progress. William Alanson White, a leading American psychiatrist, psychoanalyst, and promoter of mental hygiene, described how the unconscious blocked progress in terms that resonate with the conflict at the heart of stress. He emphasized the infantile and selfish nature of the unconscious, to which stands opposed the necessity for adjustment to social reality. Psychological conflict occurs when an individual avoids reckoning with the outer world because of an unconscious desire to be secure. When "we find the individual resisting the demands of reality that would project him into the great region of the unknown, again we find him reacting to *the instinct for the familiar— the safety motive.*"[29] White specifically defined this unconscious tendency in relation to selfishness: unconscious wishes "desire the greatest possible development of the individual . . . whereas progress can only take place by sacrificing something of this desire."[30] The self-satisfying creatures who cannot progress in this way include the insane, criminals, the feeble-minded, paupers, prostitutes, etc. What each group needs, what society needs, is "mental hygiene": compassionate understanding of their "mental enfeeblement" and "social inadequacy," programs designed to treat their problems "on the level of scientific interest (love) which will be able to see the facts in their real setting," programs which would respect the need for "individual treatment."[31]

If White saw the unconscious as in need of social planning, M. D. Eder, a British physician and psychotherapist saw its potential:

I have spoken of the unconscious as something archaic and crude, but I now want to correct that by adding that the unconscious is also creative and elaborative. A cross-section, so to say, of any mind at any given moment would reveal not only the past but the germs of the future—the potentialities to become realities with time. The psyche never is, but is always becoming—changing; there is ever an onward thrust.[32]

This attitude, called liberationist by Fred Matthews, "sees truth, beauty, and goodness in the creative energy of the repressed unconscious, and the arrival of heaven on earth when the social censorship internalized in the superego is eliminated."[33] The contrasting views, exemplified by White and Eder, show the ambivalence with which the unconscious was considered.

The "unconscious" was but one name for the "secondary personality," which early twentieth-century observers of the soul noticed. Psychical researchers (who for a time competed with psychoanalysts and others for prominence in the new field of psychology),[34] and theosophists described a "subliminal self," whose potential the surface personality had yet to realize. This casting of our inner energy reservoir as a "higher self" was as in tune with the American spirit of the epoch as was White's cautionary view. Anita and Michael Fellman discuss the reformulation of American medical advice after the end of the nineteenth century:

the will persisted as a central device, but now it could become, with the discovery of the unconscious, part of an abundant individual energy source, sometimes liberating, sometimes frightening, linked to a singularly ambiguous, dynamic society. . . . In general, images of social abundance and the potential of finding collective means to overcome problems tilted the balance of possible gains and losses in the early twentieth century as compared with the *fin de siecle*.[35]

Overly tense Americans saw potential in their anxieties, and as electricity snaked into the cities, automobiles chugged on the streets, and the Wright brothers conquered the skies, the prospects were rosy that James's question about the limits of human faculties would be answered: The sky's the limit.

ENGINEERING AND ECONOMIC METAPHORS

Considerations of reserve force, untapped potential, and efficiency belong to a widely held engineering mentality that was in place in medical perception in the early twentieth century. Engineering had achieved a high social status in the United States and Great Britain, and metaphors drawn from that field carried persuasive weight. Fledgling American psychologists, for example, began calling themselves "human engineers," and their metaphorical comparisons, including that between intelligence tests and engineering tests of materials, helped convince military leaders in 1917 that psychologists were important to the war effort.[36] Physicians, especially those who sought to develop medicine as a scientific enterprise, regularly employed engineering terms and concepts. Coupled with engineering metaphors were economic metaphors. Wealth, like strength of material, implies power, and engineering concerns were as they are today closely allied to business: "the engineer is a businessman, for engineering is business and business is engineering."[37] These two kinds of metaphors shaped the understanding of reserve force and hidden energy in the body.

Since it is at the limits of endurance that attitudes toward the body and the psyche show themselves most directly, we turn to the effects of "stress and strain," especially on the nervous and circulatory systems, where stress and strain produced their most evident effects.

First, the emphasis on reserve force altered perception of a disease of the nervous system. For a 40-year period beginning in 1880, neurasthenia had been the principle disease resulting from overstrain of the nervous system, and produced in turn myriad other disorders. Literally "nerve weakness," neurasthenia was discovered/invented by the American physician George M. Beard in 1868, and named a widespread ailment on both sides of the Atlantic. British physicians began writing about it during the 1880s, several years after the Americans noticed it.[38] Neurasthenia had many synonyms, including *nervousness, nervous exhaustion, nervous prostration*, and *nervous breakdown*. The causes of neurasthenia varied, but the immediate cause was exhaustion of nerve energy. In the discussion of the etiology of neurasthenia lay the engineering and economic metaphors. Guthrie Rankin wrote in 1903 that the "nervous capital" one has inherited can "break down under the stress of work and worry," especially when life is lived at "high pressure." In a typical explanation, Rankin stated that weariness, the major symptom, results from depletion of nervous resources.

Almost anything could be a source of "wear and tear," "tension" or "stress": competitive exams, railway journeys, the daily press, etc.[39] The explanation was that daily life takes its toll on the nervous system, that events tax its store of force, a force necessary for the maintenance of tone in all the body's organs. In nineteenth-century medicine, with its view of nerve force as a scarce resource, exhaustion was a perpetual threat, and the principle treatment for neurasthenia was rest.

Clifford Allbutt, a leading British physician in the second half of the century, held a calm view on this as on other topics. In an influential article in *Contemporary Review*, he declared that the nervous system is not weakened or exhausted by use; rather, that by nature it is active. He disagreed with the popular opinion that the nineteenth century was "a century of stress and unsatisfied desires."[40] Existence had changed, he affirmed, but our difficulties laid in our moral weakness. People had to become self-directed adults, for external sources of authority had withered. People needed inner strength and freely chosen forms of association. Much of the complaints about nervous exhaustion were, he wrote, excuses masking moral lassitude.

Not that Allbutt denied that neurasthenia existed. What he objected to was the indulgent misuse of the diagnosis. In "Neurasthenia," a review essay in his *System of Medicine*, Allbutt gave a standard medical account of the disease. The higher centers of the brain become exhausted of their energy more easily than the inferior centers of action in the brainstem, and fatigue of the higher centers lay at the cause of neurasthenia. More in the European fashion than the American, Allbutt saw the tendency to the depletion of the "potential energy" of these nerve centers as biologically inherited (whereas Americans, such as Beard, emphasized the role of climate and pace of life in their models.)[41] A man's worry over business or a young woman's constant care of her invalid parent produced mental stress of the kind that induced neurasthenia. In his account, Allbutt, the careful stylist, made free use of the metaphors of engineering and economics. Some people have less potential energy in their nerve centers, and so are "indigent" and prone to "bankruptcy" (neurasthenia). While the majority of metaphors in this essay are financial, they do mix with those of "energy" and "force," reflecting the engineer's sense of the mechanical.

Perhaps because neurasthenia could not be measured by medical instruments, economic rather than engineering metaphors appear more frequently in the discourse on neurasthenia. However, when we consider medical anxiety over the effects of exertion on the heart and circulatory system, made visible to the medical gaze through the stethoscope and autopsy, we see that engineering metaphors abound. Earlier medical perceptions that overwork and mental anxiety could damage the healthy heart fell victim to World War I, as did neurasthenia. With both neurasthenia and functional heart diseases, *strain* had been the key word in the Victorian period. In the first decade of the new century, however, strain as the engineering metaphor implying depletion was displaced. In the first edition of his *System of Medicine* (1896), Allbutt contributed "Mechanical Strain of the Heart." When the essay appeared in the second edition of 1909, it was retitled "Over-stress of the Heart." The name change signaled the new century's optimistic assessment of power and strength, since stress implies a conquerable tension, but strain implies an exhaustion, a weakness. Significantly, Allbutt, who turned to physiology for "a discipline and a preciser terminology," and who had a keen sense for *le mot juste*, criticized the earlier usage of *overstrain*:

we must define the word *strain*, so freely yet so loosely used by many writers. In an earlier essay I used the title "Over-strain," which is, of course, absurd; over-stress is an intelligible term, but all strain is over-strain. Over-stress may end in strain, or it may not; it may produce only a transient harm, no more than a passing fatigue. But the harm of a strain is perhaps always permanent; ... some alteration of texture probably remains, slight and partial as it may be.[42]

The terminological change embodied Allbutt's contention that the heart can be strained, but not as easily as had been thought. He wrote that after 30 years "of close observation of heart-stress, ... the importance of muscular effort as a factor in cardiac injury has been much exaggerated. In the sound adult organism the effects of physical stress upon the heart are promptly counteracted by equilibrating machinery."[43] In part, the reassessment of the equilibrating machinery prompted the shift from strain to stress as the key metaphor in medical discourse on effort and energy.

A discourse on stress took form as the medical community began to grow optimistic about the limits of the heart's ability to work under pressure. Allbutt referred to the "margin of safety," which physicians were coming to appreciate:

Within the past few years ... devotion to athletics, occupation with the chemistry of the body, the appointment of medical officers of schools, and other such changes have enlarged our opportunities. ... The immediate result of these opportunities has been ... to open the eyes of the physician more fully to the vast range of cardiac accommodation, and to make him hesitate in pronouncing too readily upon cardiac strain.[44]

Allbutt's statement clearly spelled out the medical context of this epoch-specific change of perception of the heart's power. *Strain* gave way to *stress* as physicians began to focus not on dangers of overwork but on the possibilities—to use an anachronism—for empowerment. Significant in this quotation is the implication that as medical power expanded, so did the heart's.

The range of the engineering discourse extended beyond overstrain of the heart. Hypertension, arteriosclerosis, and angina pectoris were but three examples of "engineered" ailments. Hypertension played an important role in the spread of the engineering mentality in medicine, since its discernment was wholly dependent on an understanding of hydraulics and on the development of instrumentation.[45] Allbutt in 1895 was one of the first to describe essential hypertension (which he called hyperpiesia). Using Allbutt as exemplar, we see the range of the mentality. In an 1898 tour of the United States, he lectured on a variety of topics, including "cardiac physics, diseases of the arteries, senile arterial plethora or hyperpiesia, . . . and angina pectoris. . . . A lecture given on 'Mechanical Strain of the Heart' "[46] was among the topics he addressed. This string of topics has as its common thread engineering interests in the matter of the body.

By the first decade of the twentieth century, the engineering mentality and its discourse on stress were fully established in the medical community. All of life's trials were comprehended in engineering terms. Writing about the cause of essential hypertension in 1903, Allbutt included "mental stress and grief."[47] While the term "mental strain" was a common term already, the easy move from cardiac physics to worry, all in the same terminology, is striking. In *Diseases of the Arteries, Including Angina Pectoris*, Allbutt devoted much attention to the strengths of blood vessels and to the effects upon them of raised blood pressure. He noted that anxiety does raise blood pressure, yet he thought that the "wear and tear" of worry and competition was an unimportant etiological factor.[48] Allbutt's fellow regius professor, William Osler, wrote about diseases of the arteries in the same year (1915), with the same engineering terminology. In discussing the etiology of arteriosclerosis, he deemed physical stress important, and also that "the incessant strain and anxiety of public life or of business may lead to degeneration of the blood vessels." The arteries considered as tubes differ in "the capacity to resist the ordinary stresses of life," especially since we run "at high pressure nowadays."[49] The framing of modern life in engineering terms was already sedimented in language by 1915, these passages illustrating the extent to which engineering considerations permeated medical thinking, and the diversity of the regions of existence embraced by this discourse.

Even more telling in this regard was the listing of the causes of arteriosclerosis in Osler's *The Principles and Practice of Medicine*, "possibly the most widely used textbook of the early twentieth century."[50] In the sixth edition of 1905, the "stress and strain of modern life" was included for the first time among the causes of arteriosclerosis. The ninth edition (1923) stated the case in these terms: "Stress and strain.—There are men in the fifth decade who have not had syphilis or gout, who have eaten and drunk with discretion, and in whom none of the ordinary factors are present—men in whom arteriosclerosis seems to come on as a direct result of a high-pressure life."[51] By the end of the first decade of this century, then, all matters of the heart had come under the sway of engineering.

The engineering mentality's comprehensiveness lay in its view of health and disease in terms of equilibrium. While the germ theory made great strides in the late nineteenth century, physicians such as Allbutt did not neglect the larger picture of the organism and the patient. Allbutt said that diseases were not entities but "the living body itself in a peculiar state." Physicians should strive to recall the body to its healthy equilibrium: "Like all systems of force, the human body, when disturbed tends to recover equilibrium, and it is for modern medicine to show how this tendency may be detected and set free to act without hindrance."[52] Seen from an engineering framework, the equilibrium of health is a balance of forces. This view, traceable to Claude Bernard on the one hand and to thermodynamics on the other, was rooted in an effort to explain vital properties in physicalistic terms. It originated in an anti-vitalistic effort in the nineteenth century and was championed by Bernard.[53] The emergence of a discourse on stress in a mature form around 1905 signaled the triumph of the anti-vitalists. The development of endocrinology—the "new humoralism," (secretin was discovered in 1902)—proved to be the keystone in the construction of the "engineered body" of the twentieth century, insofar as it made for a more comprehensive grasp of the body in terms of its stresses. Cannon's and Selye's work indicated how the engineering mentality would be applied in the new century. Whereas the nineteenth century saw mechanical strain in the tissues and organs, the new focus was upon a more complex play of forces, measurable chemically and psychologically. Ackerknecht notes how Selye's work in the 1930s gave "new impetus to" endocrinology—Selye, whose work brought stress from background to foreground in the post–World War II era.

ENGINEERING AND LIMITS

The implication of this mentality is that the self is engineer of the body. Osler's 1910 lectures on angina pectoris included this figure of the engineer as the character of the self in relation to his body:

The ordinary high-pressure business or professional man may find relief, or even cure, in the simple process of slowing the engines, reducing the speed from the 25 knots of a *Lusitania* to the 10 knots of a "black Bilboa tramp." The difficulty is to induce a man of this type to lessen "the race, an' rack, an' strain."[54]

In the "new cardiology" of the twentieth century, the figure of speech remained but the advice differed: "I put it to you that physical exertion is mainly a matter of will-power. Some men have the will to drive the engine harder than others."[55] Our century has demonstrated that the will to drive the engine leads to efforts to redesign it. Indeed, the first heart surgery and the first artificial body part implant concerned the mitral valve, so subject to overstrain in the nineteenth century. We have become, as Freud noted in *Civilization and its Discontents*, "prosthetic beings."[56]

What were the limits of reserve force in the new epoch? This question, alive at the time, came to the fore during World War I when a potpourri of odd ailments turned an apparently disproportionate number of soldiers into invalids. The military response was at first discipline: the men were cowards. But the no-man's land between the trenches of that static war, where young men were machine-gunned and gassed and bombed, reflected diseases that puzzled the medical community. The *Lancet* on March 18, 1916 described these diseases as belonging themselves in a "neutral zone, a no-man's land ... which really defies definition."[57] It is to these diseases we turn to comprehend the meaning of the limits of human energy in this epoch of anxiety.

MEDICAL ANOMALIES

> "A soldier is a machine for work ... and the capacity of the machine can only be determined by certain tests."
>
> —Sir William Osler[58]

Soldier's Heart

"Soldier's heart" named a condition first described as "irritable heart" by the American physician Jacob DaCosta during the American Civil War. Its primary symptoms were palpitations, breathlessness, and easy fatigue upon effort. During the second half of the nineteenth century, irritable heart was widely diagnosed and treated with rest cures. Early in the twentieth century, with the rise of the "new school" of cardiology championed by James Mackenzie, the disease's existence was questioned. As Joel Howell writes, in World War I soldier's heart caught the eye of the new school, "following the August 1914 retreat from Mons, which saw many soldiers sent back to England with chest pains, dyspepsia, palpitations on exertion and tachycardia. It eventually became the third leading cause of discharge from the British Army during the war."[59]

The diagnosis of soldier's heart implied that the heart itself was injured as a result of exertion or overstrain. The diagnosis was made with the aid of a stethoscope, which could detect heart murmurs, and with the aid of palpitation, to detect cardiac dilatation and hypertrophy, both considered dangerous. The new cardiologists questioned both the reliability of these methods and the significance of the findings.[60] Anatomical change had hitherto meant disease, but in the new mode of medical perception, such changes were of less consequence than "functional efficiency." Mackenzie later wrote:

That dilatation can be produced in a healthy heart as a result of overstrain, more particularly among the young and athletic, is a belief widely held. This is a view for which there is no justification. For more than a quarter of a century large numbers of young people who play games strenuously and were employed in laborious occupations were continually observed, and during that time not one individual showed heart dilatation as a result of over-exertion.[61]

With a sense that the heart had "enormous endurance and resources almost illimitable,"[62] with the shifting perception from anatomical structure to physiological function, and with the locus of investigation centering on experimentation in the laboratory rather than on clinical observation, soldier's heart as an observed condition began to whither like a plant denied its sustenance.

Soldier's heart was a casualty of the First World War. Mackenzie indicated that "the healthy heart in the young can exhibit murmurs and variations in rate and rhythm, which are perfectly physiological in origin and indicative neither of disease nor of impairment."[63] What physicians had considered to be heart disease was in fact not a cardiac problem at all. After examining 400 cases, Mackenzie concluded that 90 percent suffered from "general exhaustion," not from " 'valvular disease of the heart,' 'disordered action of the heart,' or 'dilatation.' "[64] Subsequent research by military physicians, British and American, confirmed Mackenzie's findings and helped solidify the new perceptions of the heart.

The meaning of the shift in perception toward the phenomena of soldier's heart becomes clear by looking at a debate between Mackenzie and Allbutt on the significance of cardiac murmurs. Allbutt, like Mackenzie, doubted that effort ordinarily injured the healthy young heart, but in other respects he was of the old school. Adolphe Abrahams, cardiologist, long distance runner, and later medical consultant to British Olympic teams, had stated the new position colorfully in early 1917: "Now so long as the heart does its work properly what does a little music in its mechanism matter?"[65] By testing the patient's response to effort, Mackenzie argued, the physician could ascertain the meaning of a murmur. Long experience had taught that signs which the old school deemed diagnostic of heart disease were compatible with long and active life. Allbutt responded to Mackenzie by stating that murmurs indicate something amiss in the hydraulics of blood flow. The effects of murmurs were cumulative:

A young myocardium is capable of miracles, but it is not safe to argue that, so long as the heart is doing its work, even in response to an extraordinary call or test, this waste of energy may be neglected, and the murmur pardoned for its 'innocence.' Internal stresses have a habit of slow multiplication.[66]

He cited an example of valvular disease "attributed to rowing in [a] college boat," whose "mere murmur" preceded the man's sudden death at age 55.

The contention of the old school was that effort caused structural damage to the healthy heart by forcing it beyond its elastic limits. Accordingly, the major form of treatment was rest. Dissenters within the old school, such as Allbutt, viewed the overprescription of rest with a jaundiced eye, yet even Allbutt never doubted that overstrain could damage the heart. Mackenzie and the new school urged the use of effort diagnostically to determine the efficiency of the heart, and recommended exercise as a major mode of treatment for the class of patients suffering from "heart strain." Anxiety about the limits of exertion fell by the wayside; physiological limits were believed to exceed previous expectations and were to be tested. Mackenzie, Abrahams, and Thomas Lewis (who redefined soldier's heart as "the effort syndrome") had a more confident attitude toward exercise, urging physicians not to let their soldier's heart patients rest. "A priori," wrote Abrahams, "there should be no expectation of the heart failing through pressure of work any more than of a diaphragm becoming fatigued."[67] He even cited his own 16 years of competitive sports as evidence in favor of the body's reserve force. His comments on his own experiences with too much running or rowing directly countered earlier claims by his immediate predecessors and many contemporaries that such strain damages healthy young bodies.[68]

Mackenzie and others tended to perceive soldier's heart as akin to neurasthenia or "general exhaustion."[69] The effort syndrome (or neurocirculatory asthenia, as the Americans called it) resulted from previous infection and the demands of battle. These patients were not to be told that their hearts are diseased as "this knowledge always tends to depress, and to make them extremely amenable to that form of treatment that is the worst for them—rest in bed or the avoidance of exertion."[70] Soldier's heart was becoming redefined as a neurological and psychological disorder. Both sides in the debate appealed to engineering considerations. Allbutt used the engineer as a metaphor for the physician: Like an engineer, a physician determines the load a structure can bear.[71] Without using the metaphor explicitly, Mackenzie framed his task in like terms.[72] But the nature of the interest in the post "strain" days were on the abundance of strength rather than its limits; on function rather than structure; upon the syncopated rhythms of the coming jazz age, when "purrs, barks, and roars" of engines were no cause for alarm. Thus ended the mechanical rhythms of the old school, for whom "a murmur in the machinery" would have sent the "engineer to rouse himself instantly to set things right."[73] The twentieth-century engineers sought to maximize efficiency and potential, where their predecessors had sought to guard against dissipation.

Shell Shock

Shell Shock was the other condition that puzzled the authorities during the Great War and provided a proving ground for the question of limits. Shell shock originated as a slang expression among British troops in late 1914; it first appeared in medical literature in early 1915. In keeping with the physicalistic bias then reigning in medicine, shell shock was at first seen (by F. W. Mott) as neurological damage following exposure to an exploding shell. This picture quickly dissipated, shell shock soon being recognized as a vague label for a variety of complaints from head injury to hysteria. It was later banned at least twice from medical vocabulary,[74] but it nevertheless survived on a popular level, as American veterans of World War II will testify.[75] E. E. Southard, a Boston psychiatrist, however, understood the emotional value of the term even as he acknowledged its denotative short-comings. In 1918, addressing the Massachusetts Medical Society, he grew eloquent as he proclaimed:

Let us drop for the nonce what the term [shell] denotes. Does it not *connote* the war? What better symbol of the great war, by and large, both as war and as the greatest of wars, than the shell—the shell of powder, the shell of fire, the shell of death by gas, the shell of tears, the shell of sneezing that strips the mask for death, the sea torpedo, the aerial torpedo, the mine, the shell of the psychological supergun, the shell that sank the *Lusitania*, and above all, the shell of fear.[76]

Shock too carries emotive power, for it originally referred to a military attack, and has broadened to mean "mechanical and moral agitations and commotions."[77] Despite its imprecision, shell shock names "for us today something of the ultimate physiological and psychological questions which confront the analyst of these conditions."[78] Its symbolic value, expressing the physically and morally shocking events of the war, with its shells of metal and of fear, makes the term invaluable for coming to grips with the experience of the epoch.

Shell shock was thus a cultural phenomenon of great importance. Foreseen by Baudelaire, shock was the foundational human response to the continual revolution of modernity. World War I bitterly epitomized the modern world in this regard, since it was, as Eder noted in 1916, "from the combatant's point of view . . . industrial warfare; from the medical point of view it might be well characterized as nerve warfare."[79] Shocking was the military might sent against enemy positions; shocking too was the relative inability to do anything in response. Cannon characterized twentieth-century warfare in terms of its "dull grind in preparation . . . , the monotonous regularity of subservience, the substitution everywhere of mechanism for muscle, and often the attack on an enemy who lies wholly unseen."[80] The mechanization of warfare converted it into a war of nerves because in part there was nothing physical to do; the valor of the flesh was often made superfluous and some-times even ridiculous and meaningless. A British physician and advocate of psychotherapy, G. Eliot Smith, wrote during the war that "natural fighting, face to face with his antagonist" evokes anger:

But in trench warfare the conditions are different. A man has seldom a personal enemy whom he can see and upon whom he can observe the effects of his attacks. His anger cannot be directed intensely night and day against a trench full of unseen men in the same way in which it can be provoked by an attack upon him by an individual. . . . One natural way is forbidden him in which he might give vent to his pent-up emotion, by rushing out and charging the enemy. He is thus attacked from within and without.[81]

In this kind of situation, shock occurred. We would say stress occurred, the difference in terminology indicating perhaps our inability to be (morally) shocked any longer.

The notion of shell shock included a nineteenth-century medical belief that sudden shock causes disease (as seen in traumatic neurasthenia, railway spine, and hysteria). Shock thus implied a stable, "normal" unshocking backdrop against which the traumatic event stands out; a rupture in life, an intrusion of the unknowable. Shock thereby connoted a stable world and well-defined characters within it. Shell shock names an existential condition of facing the rupture of all that *shell* means: modern warfare, living in a mechanized world that is no-man's land. Like soldier's heart, shell shock carried into the new century some of the perceptions of the fading Victorian period, and represented the confrontation of those old verities with the brave new world.

Again like soldier's heart, shell shock instigated official response. The guiding principle of this response was the "necessity for the rapid restoration of man power."[82] Some cases of shell shock were treated by military measures, with some soldiers executed for cowardice. Others were handled indiscriminately with other medical conditions, leading to "an accumulation of un-progressing cases of shell-shock in the military hospitals."[83] Medical personnel discovered that treatment as close as possible to the front line was effective in returning soldiers to duty. When soldiers were sent to general hospitals and also went untreated psychiatrically, their symptoms became fixed.

For these reasons, receiving centers were set up within five to ten kilometers from the front lines with psychiatrists on duty who saw all sick men as soon as they came back from the front. . . . From 60 to 70% of all such cases were returned from these centers back to the front line trenches within forty-eight hours.[84]

These men basically received rest and food. For those evacuated further back, there were a variety of treatments, including "application of strong faradic currents for one or two hours,"[85] rest, isolation, reeducation, discipline, work, and psychotherapy. As would be true in World War II, brief forms of treatment were preferred, so that even a psychoanalyst like Eder did not find analysis expedient.

The other procedure, established especially by the Americans in light of British experience, was screening at the time of induction to weed out those most likely to succumb to neurotic breakdown. Physicians made "a rapid neuropsychiatric examination of all men. On the basis of a brief conversation and observation during physical examination the recruit was passed, or if unsatisfactory, was deferred for a thorough examination."[86] In these ways, the medical community aided the war effort and improved (so they thought) military efficiency.

Reflecting on changes in psychiatric thinking, John C. Whitehorn later (1955) observed:

It is significant that the extensive use of those terms "trauma" and "stress" in the psychiatric literature can be dated roughly in the periods just after the two World Wars, "trauma" after World War I and "stress" after World War II....The term "psychological trauma" although it was in use to a limited extent before that war, came into *widespread* psychiatric use during and after World War I because it appeared to supply the necessary explanation for so-called "shell-shock."[87]

What terms such as *trauma* and *stress* enabled was an explanation for symptoms for which actual shocks from shells were not the cause. Moreover, "The general conception of human functioning prevalent at that time was also an important consideration favoring this concept, for by that general conception it was to be expected that the human organism would function in its normal manner unless injured."[88] It remained for the 1970s to see the two terms put together in "posttraumatic stress," a term connoting not so much normal functioning unless injured (World War I *trauma*) nor injury exacerbated by predisposition (World War II *stress*), but the violence of unexperienceable events in the context of social nihilism.

VICTORY FOR PSYCHODYNAMICS

Within the parameters set by medical perceptions in World War I, battle raged within the medical community. While both sides agreed on the aim of manpower preservation, disagreement and even ambiguity about the nature of war neurosis raised the meaning of human limits. The physicalistic bias of the nineteenth century confronted the psychodynamic bias of the twentieth, much as the old and the new cardiologies clashed over the meaning of solider's heart. Allied with the physicalistic perspective were Victorian attitudes about will-power and character: Proper breeding and education made a man master of his fate; "mental" disease arose from degeneracy and was in truth a physical degeneracy.[89] For those with these Victorian biases, the high number of war neuroses resulted from "a class of persons who, by constitution and by their previous life experience, are unfit for military service."[90] But for the psychologically minded:

The war has shown us one indisputable fact, that a psychoneurosis may be produced in almost anyone if only his environment be made "difficult" enough for him. It has warned us that the pessimistic, helpless appeal to heredity, so common in the case of insanity, must go the same way as its lugubrious homologue which formerly did duty in the case of tuberculosis.[91]

Shell shock proved to be the undoing of the older, physicalistic biases. As Bogacz describes the workings of the Committee of Enquiry into "Shell-Shock" and its cultural context, the witnesses who appeared before it

failed to convince [the committee whose members were inclined toward the older biases] that shell-shock was all a matter of morale, discipline and especially character. ... Shell-shock could not be tamed, it could not be safely attributed solely to misfits, mental degenerates or weak men of the lower orders; rather it was an impervious leveler of classes. For a generation raised to believe in the exercise of the will, it represented a signal defeat: even the strongest man could fall victim to it.[92]

Shell shock did not fit into any existing medical category. Not only that, it did not fit existing social categories. Will, character, and breeding did not suffice to explain the responses of men to psychic trauma. No-man's land was an existential condition between the old certainties of the nineteenth century and the certainty-less assurances of the post–1945 period. Shell shock served to give psychoneurosis and psychology significant social and cultural positions.

The military response to shell shock illustrates a point made by Paul Starr that "the means of control in the military have shifted from authoritarian and coercive techniques to more subtle, psychological manipulation. The acute needs for control in the military have made it a proving ground for the psychological professions."[93] Both the British and the Americans, the latter with the guidance of Thomas Salmon, a physician who had by 1917 been involved with the National Committee for Mental Hygiene for five years, realized that the best way to deal with cases of shell shock was to keep them as close to the lines as possible, after having screened out misfits at induction centers. While some of these lessons were forgotten within the military by 1940, the prestige of the psychological professions was not. The older military attitude, which could see only cowardice in "neurosis" was clearly anachronistic, but it had the merit of viewing the soldier as a moral agent. Is not part of the shock of being in no-man's land precisely that the perception of the soldier as a moral agent became inappropriate?

Soldier's heart and shell shock thus present a surprising picture. As soldier's heart became reframed as the effort syndrome, older fears about exertion fell by the wayside. The effort syndrome taught that action in the form of exercise was the key to recovery. With shell shock, older beliefs about will-power and heredity were shocked, and with this came recognition of the limits of human endurance in the face of depersonalized warfare. But these limits were not imposed by a scarce supply of nerve force; rather they were the effects of sustained emotional conflict. The existence of war neuroses indicated that men become psychologically and physically exhausted, despite their powerful emotional reserves, when they cannot act.[94]

Both shell shock and the effort syndrome said something about action.

What was the matter with action at that time? It was becoming groundless, in the sense of having lost its basis in traditions of meaning. The symbolic or ritual aspects of human behavior, which connect us to the past and promise a future, which shine into the eternal, were not perceived. Thinkers such as Cannon had seen that modern warfare (despite its horror and valor) does not engage men viscerally as had nonmechanized combat. What the poets Pound and Owen saw was that modern warfare, modern life in general, did not engage men spiritually. Both the flesh and the spirit were missing. Action without a ground in meaning and without the direct involvement of flesh produced diseases of exhaustion and shock. These insights reveal a dark truth behind our commonplaces of the archaic body and the exile, which are distorted ways of acknowledging that we cannot act: Because we cannot grieve for what we have lost, we have no place to be the setting for action. For to grieve means to preserve a thread of continuity between past and future, to extract gold from the lead of loss. With no possibility of this preservation or extraction, we are left without the past to ground us, without a future to beckon us. We arrive nowhere, like refugees cut off from the past and stranded in an internment camp; unlike such refugees, who mourn their estrangement, in our zeal for the future we are self-exiled, repudiating a past that no longer means anything.

In the gap left by the absence of flesh and spirit appeared the psychological professions, not as the cause of the absence but as the effect, as Jung noted in the 1930s:

And as for ideals, the Christian church, the brotherhood of man, international social democracy and the "solidarity" of economic interests have all failed to stand the baptism of fire—the test of reality. . . . I believe I am not exaggerating when I say that modern man has suffered an almost fatal shock, psychologically speaking, as a result has fallen into profound uncertainty.[95]

In this gap, this mood of uncertainity, "a spiritual need has produced in our time our 'discovery' of psychology."[96] This discovery happened quite concretely in the case of the two diseases we have been discussing. The effort syndrome was seen as akin to neurasthenia, a disorder of exhaustion. But by the end of the war, neurasthenia was under attack by psychoanalytically oriented physicians as too physicalistic an explanation. Psychoneurosis was beginning to replace neurasthenia as the diagnosis of choice, although the lag between insight and full acceptance was decades. Similarly, shell shock was seen as a psychological disorder soon after the neurological explanation proved untenable. The move was to the psychological domain; the motives were the loss of the familiar grounds of action.

I conclude that shell shock and the effort syndrome were disorders of grief, the kind of grief we have discovered to be the heart of stress.[97] I also conclude that the response to these diseases by military medicine and psychiatry prefigured the engineering of this modern grief by the attempt to reduce the disabling consequences of the shock and fatigue of modern warfare. The establishment of a psychodynamic perspective enabled soldiers and civilians to cope with the world.

It would be misleading to think that the originators of the new psychologies themselves escaped the distress that they saw in their patients. Peter Homans claims that psychoanalysis has its social origins in the crisis of secularization in the late nineteenth and early twentieth centuries, when it both responded to and replaced the loss of cultural and religious traditions in the lives of early analysts. His thesis in a nutshell is that

structural social change weakened people's ties first to the traditional common culture and then, later, to the national common culture, creating a kind of progressive shared desacralization or decathexis of it. The result was an increased, pain-laden mandate for some to introspect into the inner world which had become even more loosened from control-producing internalizations.[98]

The emerging psychological disciplines and institutions thus grew from the groundless ground that loss of tradition, loss of the flesh, and loss of the spirit had left. This new ground was predominantly an inner, anxious ground during the period of transition to the world of stress.

THE PROFESSIONS AND THEIR AGENDAS

Theoretical disputes occur in social, political, and economic arenas as well as in the mind and heart. And just as World War II "made" clinical psychology and modern mental health care, so World War I made psychology and psychiatry. The war found these groups already moving in the direction of soldifying their status in the early years of the century.[99]

Psychiatry came into its own in this century when it emerged from "institutional isolation" between 1910 and 1914. Nineteenth-century psychiatry had been confined to asylums, which were largely custodial facilities. (Even in 1930, three-fourths of the psychiatrists worked in state institutions, but the picture was changing.) Douglas Thom, a psychiatrist active in the American war effort in 1917, reminisced in 1942 that "the last war contributed more to psychiatry than psychiatry did to the war. I mean that the last war gave psychiatry a certain professional standing which has continued, and after the war it was found that various foundations and organizations recognized psychiatry as a branch of medicine worthy of support."[100]

Thom's assessment stands. Psychiatry benefited from and helped stimulate the therapeutic ethic characteristic of this century. But to see how World War I changed psychiatry, mention of the National Committee for Mental Hygiene is necessary. Founded in 1908 by Clifford Beers, author of the autobiographical *A Mind That Found Itself*, the National Committee collected statistics on mental illness, exposed existing deplorable conditions, vigorously promoted public education, and lobbied Congress for legislation. In 1912, Thomas W. Salmon was appointed its first medical director. Under Salmon's guidance, the National Committee helped the Army establish psychiatric facilities and gather personnel in 1917. Salmon established guidelines for the handling of American shell shock cases.

The mental hygiene movement was thus part of the cultural background for the reassessment of the nature of illness and the promotion of social engineering after the war. The mental hygiene movement also provided one of the matrices (the one that seeks to fix all suffering through science) for the development of the mentality that stress represents. After the war, the reach of psychiatry expanded. Elmer E. Southard, for example, whose metaphorical reading of shell shock has been discussed above, pioneered psychiatric social work with Mary C. Jarrett (the first director of Smith College's training school in psychiatric social work in 1918). Their book, *Kingdom of Evils*, spells out the far-reaching vision and grasp of the mental hygiene mentality.

As with psychiatry, so with psychology. Efforts to establish psychology as a science and profession date back to the 1880s. By 1917, the American Psychological Association was 25 years old, and there were as many psychologists in the United States as in Germany, France, and England combined.[101] But during the prewar years, psychology struggled to assert itself as a viable profession. The situation had changed by the early 1920s, the war playing a crucial role in the difference. "Psychology probably benefitted more from the war than the war effort did from psychology," JoAnn Brown writes in her study of the role of engineering and medical metaphors in psychology's early days. While psychology is peripheral to the concerns of this chapter, at least regarding soldier's heart and shell shock, what is noteworthy is precisely this use of engineering and medical rhetoric by psychologists to stake their claims. A discourse of efficiency, of intellect as a scarce resource, of children as raw material already had currency in educational circles, with psychologists devising the tests to gauge the quantity of these things. James McKeen Cattell in 1904 had argued, "It would under existing conditions be intolerable to erect a building without regard to the quality and strength of materials; yet we often do much this thing in selecting men for their work and adjusting them to it."[102] American psychologists were active in the military effort from the day war was declared, measuring intelligence and evaluating aptitude for military occupations. Whether or not the Army used the tests as psychologists wanted, and whether or not the results of the tests were "scientific,"[103] testing spread after the war to schools and industry. Robert Yerkes declared in his presidential address to the American Psychological Association in 1923 that psychology had become "the science of human engineering."[104] Psychologists, who later would have an impact on the formulation of the construct of stress, participated in the attitude of the epoch insofar as they defined their usefulness to society in terms of social engineering and efficiency, and "proved" their social utility by their participation in the war effort.

The upshot is that throughout this epoch, professional groups formed, gathered both attention and money, and became the touchstones of physical and mental health. Perceptions of reserve force, unconscious conflict, and extendable limits had institutional domains in society via psychology and psychiatry. As Illich argues, such institutions became the purveyors of resources that their clientele "needed." What patients needed, along these lines, was access to their latent powers for purposes of "the conquering of our environment."[105]

SPLITTING THE FLESH

> To me, possibly from personal prejudice, the recent introspective and confessional methods are odious.... Let us beware lest the resentment of the laity against "spiritual direction," against the curious inquisition of the priest into the casuistical paths of naughtiness, may be turned against ourselves.
>
> —Clifford Allbut, "On Neurasthenia"

What was lost on the battlefields of Europe in addition to those men who charged across no-man's land or who, huddled in muddy trenches, were blasted and gassed, was a certain perception of the body. Another entity took its place. As James and Cannon had recognized, modern warfare left little play for physical and martial prowess. Sheer courage remained; it always does. But fear of random death, fear of the shell, the shock of industrialized warfare that made Gallipoli only a bleak parody of Troy, gave rise to a psychologized body. What happened in Europe was a precursor of the splitting of the atom, which took place in 1942, unleashing hidden reserves beyond our wildest dreams. What happened in no-man's land, a groundless terrain, more lunar than terrestrial, was a splitting of the flesh.

In part the split had already occurred and in part it has happened only more recently, at least on the popular level. In medical perception its fissure can be discerned in the fate of soldier's heart, neurasthenia, shell shock, and neurocirculatory asthenia. Initially, each was perceived as a physical disease, the consequence of anatomical breakdown. As the story is usually told in whiggish interpretation, nineteenth-century medicine's physicalistic bias was corrected by the realization of the pathogenic effects of chronic emotional arousal.[106] In light of the dynamic view (i.e., chronic emotional arousal), these diseases became redefined as catch-all terms for psychoneuroses. Each in turn was seen as too vague to be useful for medical purposes, and the old etiology and preferred mode of treatment were superceded by others. Typically, each disease was not read out of existence: it was declared rare and too often misdiagnosed. For example, C. Stanford Read argued in 1918 that true neurasthenia was an uncommon disease; anxiety neurosis was the more common and correct diagnosis in most cases of so-called neurasthenia. Thomas Lewis argued that the name "soldier's heart" ought to be abandoned, since it implied a heart dysfunction where none existed; rather, "the dominant etiological factor in the clinical histories of soldiers complaining of the 'effort syndrome' is infection of one kind or another."[107] Cardiologist Lewis still sought an organic cause of the effort syndrome. But the final word, if such exists, on these conditions was from Edward Weiss in 1952, who observed that neurasthenia, the effort syndrome, and neurocirculatory asthenia (NCA) were really anxiety neuroses:

A person trained in psychodynamics listening to the story of the patient with NCA discovers (1) that the symptoms are those of psychoneurosis...;(5) discussing this [life history] material brings out meaningful behavior on the part of the patient; and (6) dealing with this material has psychotherapeutic value.[108]

Weiss discloses a twofold context for redefining these diseases. First, proper training enables the physician to hear the dynamics of the story. The new diagnosis rests upon the ground of new theory and its institutional supports. Here, psychiatry is that institution, which provides the training in perception: Weiss drew attention to the contrast between the psychiatrist who discerns anxiety neurosis and the internist who discerns NCA. The point here is that professional and theoretical allegiances form and inform the image through which the percept makes sense. Second, institutional background also shapes perception of the results of medical intervention. Weiss wrote that psychodynamic treatment helps patients. But it is worth noting part of what he means by "help": "NCA appeared on the horizon about the time that 'shell-shock' was at the height of its popularity. It seems to me just as bad a name because it is based on a misconception and perpetuates invalidism."[109] Invalidism is bad, of course, and any label that tends to make patients dwell on their presumed physical inferiorities will disable them, whereas (apparently) *neurosis* is a benign label. The shift to a psychodynamic framework supposedly minimized these side-effects, focusing patients' attention on their emotional lives and not on the physical manifestations of their emotions. Avoiding invalidism means then, for all four conditions under discussion (soldier's heart, neurasthenia, the effort syndrome, and NCA), avoiding "somaticization."[110]

As with gifts from Zeus, the shift to psychodynamics was a mixed blessing. On the one hand, it relativized the mechanical image of the body that had dominated medical perception. As Merleau-Ponty wrote, the value of Freud was that he rediscovered the symbolic body, what Merleau-Ponty came to call the flesh. On the other hand, the shift has made the body increasingly marginal by "vaporizing" its ailments. The apotheosis of this trend was in systems theory, which began to take form between 1918 and 1950. By focusing on the "whole" of a person's life and the key role anxiety plays in generating the "somaticized" symptoms (fatigue, jumpiness, palpitations, breathlessness, etc.), the meaning of the patient's existence rises above the flesh into a realm of discourse amenable to psychotherapeutic intervention. It is as if the flesh became word and ceased to dwell among us.[111]

But only in part did the flesh become word under the spell of psychodynamics. Mechanistic interpretations persisted alongside psychodynamic ones, and the two often competed for turf. Some diseases, like tuberculosis and syphilis, were comprehended by the anatomical gaze, while others, such as soldier's heart and neurasthenia, became psychologized. This double vision of the body left no place for meaning in the flesh itself, which is irreducibly physical and meaningful.

This situation proved untenable. The work of Cannon, Adolf Meyer, Flanders Dunbar, Franz Alexander, and others from 1910 through the Second World War sought to forge a "psychobiology" (Meyer) and a "psychosomatic medicine," which became established in the United States in the 1930s.[112] Outside medicine, this period saw the rise of the phenomenology of the body, which likewise criticized the "Cartesian split" in the Western understanding of the body.[113]

Let us conclude by returning to Allbutt's admonition, which serves as epigram to this section. His mistrust of the "incitement to discourse" did express a Victorian prejudice against waste ("most men discover for themselves that if good work is to be done coitus must be economized," he wrote[114]); it did express a valuation of character based on the will ("the very loss of self-control which we seek to repair"[115]); it did express the physicalistic bias of the medicine of his time. Nevertheless, Allbutt's warning, long unheeded, has proven true. "Spiritual direction" has fused with medicine in our day, as the tendency to replace external controls with inner ones has advanced in the social order. Self-regulation of health has become a fundamental virtue of the late twentieth century. Body for Allbutt's time connoted limitation, but the epoch of anxiety that displaced the Victorian ear dispensed with body as limitation, in principle if not in practice. Body as limit remains for us a problematic. Total mobilization (of manpower and inner power) is now possible because energy lies hidden, waiting to be tapped, because reserve force and factors of safety exist, and because the new methods in psychology, psychiatry, and management guarantee efficient and quicker deployment of personnel and second wind (taking the body politic and body physiologic together). The body, as formerly felt, became increasingly a mirage, a mistake of perception. Limits were meant to be tested. The flesh has been converted into a discourse amenable to systems thinking and means–end analysis: What the x-ray and CAT scan leave invisible, psychological instruments probe and uncover.

CONCLUSION

This period appears as transitional between the nineteenth century and the post-World War II period. Its arguments were still with the nineteenth century and that century's views of the autonomous individual. The splitting of the flesh did overcome the limitations of mechanistic theory of disease, but that older theory served the man of character and will, the nineteenth century's self-made man, well. He could figure out where his machinery was running afoul, and attempt to correct it. With the detonation of the ideal of the nineteenth-century productive will-to-power came the beginnings of the individual as potential energy. As the twentieth century progressed, as the old Protestant ethic receded in an age of consumption, secularized and psychologized explanations displaced religious accounts of the springs of human action.[116] The Great War epitomized this new age. The old boundaries of body and mind continued to exist, but were now entrenched and pathological, and between them a no-man's land appeared on which flourished or at least survived a new mode of existence, made memorable as *The Waste Land* generation. No-man's land, pure product of the industrial age, the war theater of the absurd, marked the place where men of an earlier age met their demise. They could not survive there. The situation shocked them. They appeared to suffer from strain or mechanical breakdown, but they did not. They became Remarque's lost souls. They could not act, for there was little to do physically, and in any case they saw no spiritual reason to act. But they were too anxious to grieve for their loss of the flesh and the spirit. Instead, they turned inward, looking to psychology as to a refuge in a time of despair. People of this character type (prefigured by Gogol's Akaky Akakievich in "The Overcoat," and called the Organization Man more recently) found within themselves, in the face of this neurosis, the power to endure. Some learned to adapt. They learned that to reckon with no-man's land, fluidity was all. The fascist mind realized first how to dwell on the groundless space between the trenches: Lightning warfare, air war, evocation of the primitive in cathedrals of pure light. Face up to the fact that we have become aliens. The age of anxiety, with its shocks and traumas, prepared the groundless for us all.

NOTES

1. Quoted in Saul Benison, A. Clifford Barger, Elin L. Wolfe, *Walter B. Cannon: The Life and Times of a Young Scientist* (Cambridge: Belknap Press, 1987), p. 292.
2. Walter B. Cannon, *The Wisdom of the Body* (New York: Norton, 1932), p. 231.
3. Ibid, p. 204.
4. See Walter B. Cannon, "The Stimulation of Adrenal Secretion by Emotional Excitement," *Journal of the American Medical Association* 56 (1911), 742, for a discussion of this. See also studies on the relationship between repression of affect and

the etiology of disease in K. Pelletier, *Mind as Healer, Mind as Slayer* (New York: Dell, 1977). For a critique of this view, see Susan Sontag, *Illness as Metaphor* (New York: Vintage, 1978).

5. Erwin H. Ackerknecht, *A Short History of Medicine*, rev. ed. (Baltimore: Johns Hopkins University Press, 1982), pp. 172–73.

6. S. J. Meltzer, "Factors of Safety in the Animal Economy," *Science*, 25 (January–June 1907), 482.

7. Ibid., p. 498.

8. J. George Adami, *The Principles of Pathology*, Vol. I: *General Pathology* (Philadelphia and New York: Lea & Febiger, 1908), p. 92.

9. Ibid, p. 91.

10. James Mackenzie, *Diseases of the Heart*, 4th ed. (London: Humphrey Milford, Oxford University Press, 1925), p. 31.

11. This usage of *efficiency* was novel to his generation. *Efficiency* used to refer primarily to "operative agents" or causes. In the nineteenth century the word began to mean "fitness or power to accomplish; ... adequate power, effectiveness, efficacy," which corresponds to Mackenzie's usage. But by late in the century, in engineering circles it meant "the ratio of useful work performed to the total energy expended" (*Oxford English Dictionary*).

12. Adami, *Principles of Pathology*, Vol. I, p. 85.

13. For further contemporary references to reserve force, see William Osler, *The Principles and Practice of Medicine*, 4th ed. (New York: D. Appleton, 1901); T. Clifford Allbutt, "The physician and the pathologist on heart failure," *British Medical Journal*, 1912, no. i, 653; 862; H. B. Anderson, "Strain as a factor in cardio-aortic lesions," *British Medical Journal*, 1905, no. ii, 840–45.

14. See Oswei Temkin, "Metaphors of human biology," in *Science and Civilization*, ed. R. Stauffer (Madison: University of Wisconsin Press, 1949), 169–96.

15. William James, "The energies of men," in *Essays in Faith and Morals* (New York: Longmans, Green, 1943), p. 216.

16. Ibid., p. 220.

17. Ibid., pp. 222–23. From the perspective of Linder's book *The Harried Leisure Class* (New York: Columbia University Press, 1970), James's observations are true indeed. James wrote that the country fellow especially could increase the productivity of his time insofar as his farming was largely unmechanized.

18. Robert Levine, "The pace of life," *Psychology Today* 23 (October 1989), 42–46.

19. Walter B. Cannon, quoted in Saul Benison, A. Clifford Barger, and Elin L. Wolfe, *The Life and Times of a Young Scientist* (Cambridge: Harvard University Press, 1987), p. 317.

20. Benison et al., *Walter B. Cannon*, 317.

21. Ibid., p. 321.

22. William James, "The gospel of relaxation," in R. B. Perry, ed., *Essays on Faith and Morals* (Cleveland: World Publishing, 1962), p. 245.

23. Ibid., p. 249.

24. Ibid., p. 253.

25. Daniel T. Rodgers, "In search of progressivism," *Reviews in American History* 10 (December 1982), 125.

26. C. H. Cooley, cited in ibid., p. 125.

27. Robert Wiebe, *Search for Order 1877–1920* (New York: Hill & Wang, 1967), p. 145.

28. A view found in Sigmund Freud, *Civilization and Its Discontents*, trans. James Strachey (New York: W. W. Norton, 1961) and, outside depth psychology, in Emile Durkheim, *Suicide: A Study in Sociology* (New York: Free Press, 1951). See also Stjepan Mestrovic and Barry Glassner, "A Durkheimian hypothesis on stress," *Social Science and Medicine* 17, no. 18 (1983), 1315–27.

29. William Alanson White, *The Principles of Mental Hygiene* (New York: Macmillan, 1917), p. 44.

30. Ibid., p. 38.

31. Ibid., p. 201. We see in White's formulation the secular equivalent of older moral admonitions. See Fred Matthews, "In defense of common sense: Mental hygiene as ideology and mentality in twentieth-century America," *Prospects* 4 (1979), 502, for the continuity between "nineteenth-century moral philosophy and twentieth-century writings on mental hygiene." The difference between them includes "the change from religious and epistemological to scientific framework" (p. 503).

32. M. D. Eder, "The psycho-pathology of the war neuroses," *Lancet*, 1916, no. 2, 267.

33. Matthews, "In defense of common sense," p. 461.

34. See John Cerullo, *The Secularization of the Soul: Psychical Research in Modern Britain* (Philadelphia: Institute for the Study of Human Issues, 1982) for the competition between psychoanalysis and spiritualism in the period 1890–1910.

35. Anita Clair Fellman and Michael Fellman, *Making Sense of Self: Medical Advice Literature in Late Nineteenth Century America* (Philadelphia: University of Pennsylvania Press, 1981), p. 137.

36. JoAnn Brown, *The Semantics of Profession: Metaphor and Power in the History of Psychological Testing, 1890–1929*. Ph.D. Dissertation (Madison: University of Wisconsin, 1985), pp. 178–207.

37. Quoted in ibid., p. 149.

38. See, for example, S. S. Alford, "Defective nerve-power as a primary cause of disease, with its special relation to dipsomania," *British Medical Journal*, 1881, no. 1, 591–93; A. Clark, "Some observations concerning what is called neurasthenia," *Lancet*, 1886, no. 1, 1; F. Clark, "Some remarks on nervous exhaustion and on vasomotor action," *Journal of Anatomy and Physiology* (London) 18 (1883–84), 239–256; T. S. Dowse, *On Brain and Nerve Exhaustion, "Neurasthenia,"* rev. ed. (London, 1887); D. DeB. Hovell, *On Some Conditions of Neurasthenia* (London, 1886); W. H. Kesteven, *Work and Worry from a Medical Point of View* (London, 1884); J. Strahan, "Puzzling conditions of the heart and other organs dependent on neurasthenia," *British Medical Journal*, 1885, no. ii, 435–37; Edwin Wooton, "Nervous exhaustion," *Knowledge* 7 (Jan.–June 1885), 435–36; 500–502; 519–20.

39. "Nerves and Nervelessness," *Eclectic Magazine* 69, no. 122 (February 1894), 278–281.

40. T. Clifford Allbutt, "Nervous disease and modern life," *Contemporary Review* 67 (1895), 210.

41. See George Drinka, *The Birth of Neurosis: Myth, Malady, and the Victorians* (New York: Simon & Schuster, 1984), for a comparison of European and American medical opinions about the etiology of neurasthenia.

42. T. Clifford Allbutt, "Over-stress of the heart," in C. Allbutt and Humphry

Davy Rolleston, eds., *A System of Medicine*, Vol. 6: *Diseases of the Heart and Blood-Vessels*, 2nd ed. (London: Macmillan, 1909), p. 208.

43. Ibid., p. 250.

44. Ibid., p. 198.

45. Mahomed developed the first useful sphygmomanometer in 1876, giving impetus to the study of raised blood pressure. See Stanley Joel Reiser, *Medicine and the Reign of Technology* (Cambridge: University Press, 1978).

46. Humphry Davy Rolleston, *The Right Honorable Sir Thomas Clifford Allbutt: A Memoir* (London: Macmillan, 1929), p. 137.

47. T. Clifford Allbutt, letter to Sir Hermann Weber, quoted in ibid., p. 154.

48. T. Clifford Allbutt, *Diseases of the Arteries, Including Angina Pectoris* (London: Macmillan, 1915), Vol. I, p. 238.

49. William Osler, "Diseases of the arteries," in William Osler and Thomas McCrae, eds., *Modern Medicine, Its Theory and Practice*, Vol. IV: *Diseases of the Circulatory System*, 2nd ed. (Philadelphia: Lea & Fabiger, 1915), p. 453.

50. C. Lawrence, "Moderns and ancients: The 'new cardiology' in Britain 1880–1930," in W. F. Bynum, C. Lawrence, and V. Nutton, eds., *The Emergence of Modern Cardiology, Medical History*, Supplement No. 5 (1985), 5.

51. William Osler, *The Principles and Practice of Medicine*, 9th ed. (New York: Appleton, 1923), p. 835.

52. T. Clifford Allbutt, "The Progress of the Art of Medicine," *Lancet* 1870, no. 2, 38. See T. Clifford Allbutt, "Medicine and the people: A Review of some latter-day tracts," *British Medical Journal*, 1919, no. ii, 763, for the same views 49 years later.

53. The interpretation of health as balance and the assessment of the "wisdom of the body" to restore balance has a fascinating history. In the modern period it may be traceable to van Helmont. Claude Bernard's *Introduction à l'étude de la médicine experimentale* employed the "concept of the fixity of the *milieu interieur* primarily . . . as the epistemological rationale for upholding determinism in physiology against vitalism on the one hand and mechanism on the other. The human domination of nature through scientific experimentation is a theme throughout the *Introduction*." [From Stephen J. Cross and William R. Albury, "Walter B. Cannon, L. J. Henderson, and the organic analogy," *Osiris*, 2nd series, 3 (1987), 175–76.] For van Helmont see P. H. Niebyl, *Venesection and the Concept of the Foreign* (New Haven: Yale University Press, 1969).

54. William Osler, "Lectures on angina pectoris," *Lancet*, 1910, no. 2, 974.

55. Adolphe Abrahams, " 'Soldier's heart,' " *Lancet*, 1917, no. 1, 443.

56. Freud, *Civilization and Its Discontents*. See also John O'Neill, *Five Bodies: The Human Shape of Modern Society* (Ithaca, NY: Cornell University Press, 1985).

57. "Neurasthenia and shell shock," *Lancet*, 1916, no. 1, 627.

58. William Osler, "Graduated exercise in prognosis," *Lancet*, 1918, no. 1, 231.

59. Joel Howell, " 'Soldier's heart': The redefinition of heart disease and specialty formation in early twentieth-century Great Britain," in Bynum, Lawrence, and Nutton, p. 37. See also Pickering, *Creative Malady* (New York: Delta, 1974), pp. 29–31, for a critique of soldier's heart.

60. Dr. J. W. Linnell recalled that Mackenzie "even went to the length on one occasion of saying, as regards hearts, that at times he wondered whether *on the balance* the discovery of the stethoscope had not done as much harm as it had done good,

when he thought of the hundreds and thousands of people all over the world who, by its use, had been unncessarily condemned to lives of invalidism." Quoted in A. Mair, *Sir James Mackenzie M.D. 1853–1925, General Practitioner* (Edinburgh: Churchill Livingstone, 1973), pp. 242–43.

61. James Mackenzie and James Orr, *Principles of Diagnosis and Treatment in Heart Affections*, 3rd ed. (London: Oxford University Press, 1926), pp. 165–66.

62. Allbutt, "Overstress of the heart," p. 197.

63. James Mackenzie, "The recruit's heart: A memorandum for medical examiners," *British Medical Journal*, 1915, no. ii, 563.

64. James Mackenzie, "Soldier's heart," *British Medical Journal*, 1916, no. i, 118.

65. Abrahams, "Soldier's heart," 444.

66. T. Clifford Allbutt, "The Lumleian lectures and medical research: 'Innocent Murmurs,'" *Lancet*, 1917, no. 2, 172.

67. Abrahams, "Soldier's heart," p. 443.

68. Ibid., p. 443. He commented that if he had consulted a physician, he would have become an invalid.

69. Ibid., p. 444; Mackenzie, "Soldier's heart," 119.

70. Mackenzie, "Soldier's heart," 119.

71. Allbutt, "The Lumleian lectures and medical research," 172, 405.

72. "The State in its hour of necessity has called upon the medical profession to undertake the recruiting of impaired individuals for military work," wrote James Mackenzie (*Lancet*, 1917, no. 2, 253). Howell writes, "The same set of symptoms that was renamed the 'effort syndrome' in Great Britain was called 'neurocirculatory asthenia' in the United States," in "'Soldier's heart': The redefinition of heart disease and specialty formation in early twentieth-century Great Britain," in W. F. Bynum et al., eds., *The Emergence of Modern Cardiology*, 43–44. The treatment for neurocirculatory asthenia was rest.

73. Allbutt, "The Lumleian lectures and medical research," 172.

74. Extracts from "Report of the War Office Committee of Enquiry on shell shock" (1922) in E. Miller, ed., *The Neuroses in War* (New York: Macmillan, 1940), p. 220, and D. Denny-Brown, "Shell-shock and effects and high explosives," in Roy D. Halloran and Paul I. Yakolev, eds., *Collected Lectures of the 7th Postgraduate Seminar in Neurology and Psychiatry, including a Review Course in Military Neuropsychiatry, Oct. 3, 1941–April 10, 1942* (Waltham, MA: Metropolitan State Hospital, 1942), p. 110.

75. One former infantryman told me how after a day and night of bombardment on Guadalcanal, one GI jumped up screaming. The narrator and a buddy tackled him to keep to keep him from being shot. "He was shell-shocked, because of the shelling we'd taken."

76. E. E. Southard, "Shell Shock and After," *Boston Medical and Surgical Journal* 79, no. 3 (18 July 1918), 80.

77. Ibid., p. 81.

78. Ibid., p. 83.

79. M. D. Eder, "The psycho-pathology of the war neuroses," *Lancet*, 1916, no. 2, 264.

80. Walter B. Cannon, *Bodily Changes in Pain, Hunger, Fear and Rage* (New York: Norton, 1929), p. 385.

81. G. Eliot Smith and T. H. Pear, *Shell Shock and Its Lessons* (Manchester: University Press, 1917), pp. 9–10.

82. Eric Wittkower and J. P. Spillane, "A survey of the literature of neuroses in war," in Emanuel Miller, ed., *The Neuroses in War*, (New York: Macmillan, 1944), p. 24.

83. "Report of the War Office Committee," p. 213. See Ted Bogacz, "War neurosis and cultural change in England, 1914–22: The work of the War Office Committee of Enquiry into 'Shell-Shock,' " *Journal of Contemporary History* 24, no. 2 (April 1989), 228 for a discussion of military versus medical handling of shell shock.

84. Douglas A. Thom, "War neuroses. Experiences of 1914–1918. Lessons for the current emergency," in Roy D. Halloran and Paul I. Yakolev, eds., *Collected Lectures of the 7th Postgraduate Seminar in Neurology and Psychiatry*, p. 103.

85. Wittkower and Spillane, "A survey of the literature," p. 26.

86. Ibid., p. 23.

87. John C. Whitehorn, *Psychiatric Education and Progress: The Salmon Lectures of the New York Academy of Medicine, November 30, 1955* (Springfield, IL: Charles C. Thomas, 1957), p. 33.

88. Ibid., 33.

89. Bogacz notes that British medicine tended to diagnose neurasthenia in officers, who then received a rest cure, and hysteria in enlisted men, who often were subjected to punitive measures ("War neurosis," p. 255, note 71).

90. I. B. Muirhead, "Shock and the soldier," *Lancet* 1916, no. 1, 1021.

91. Smith and Pear, *Shell Shock*, pp. 87–88.

92. Bogacz, "War neurosis," pp. 247–48.

93. Paul Starr, *The Social Transformation of American Medicine* (New York: Basic, 1982), p. 344.

94. Paul Schilder, *Medical Psychology* (New York: Wiley, 1953), p. 232, gives the basic approach: "Neurosis comes about only when outlet for the revived primitive drive is also barred, and it must find symbolic substitute-gratification."

95. C. G. Jung, "The spiritual problem of modern man," in *Modern Man in Search of a Soul* (New York: Harvest/HBJ Book, n.d.), p. 200.

96. Ibid., p. 201.

97. See Peter Homans, *The Ability to Mourn: Disillusionment and the Social Origins of Psychoanalysis* (Chicago: University of Chicago Press, 1989), p. 226: "Concern with grief as a causative factor in the genesis of mental conflict and suffering received an important impetus during the war, chiefly from the treatment of so-called shell-shocked soldiers. . . . These aperçus and hunches were not, however, pursued at length."

98. Ibid., p. 229. In this passage he is discussing the shift from early psychoanalytic emphasis on the instincts and Oedipal conflicts to British object relations theory. In the latter, the place of loss and grief is more prominent.

99. See Daniel T. Rodgers, "In search of Progressivism," *Reviews in American History* 10 (December 1982), 118.

100. Thom, "War neuroses," p. 96.

101. Thomas M. Camfield, "The professionalization of American psychology," *Journal of the History of the Behavioral Sciences* 9 (1973), 74.

102. James McKeen Cattell, quoted in Brown, p. 172.

103. See I. Samelson, "World War I intelligence testing and the development of psychology," *Journal of the History of the Behavioral Sciences* 13, no. 3 (1977), 280 on this point.

104. Robert Yerkes, quoted in Ibid., p. 275.

105. William A. White, "Extending the field of conscious control" (1919), quoted in Fred Matthews, "In defense of common sense," *Prospects 4* (1979), 493.

106. See Cannon "The Stimulation of adrenal secretion," and Helen Flanders Dunbar, *Emotions and Bodily Changes: A Survey of Literature on Psychosomatic Inter-relationships 1910–1953*, 4th ed. (New York: Columbia University Press, 1954) for the extensive literature.

107. Thomas Lewis, *The soldier's heart and the effort syndrome* (New York: Paul B. Hoeber, 1919), p. 33.

108. Edward Weiss and O. Spurgeon English, *Psychosomatic Medicine*, (Philadelphia: Saunders, 1952), p. 151.

109. Ibid., p. 152.

110. For discussion of this concept, see William Menninger, "Psychosomatic medicine: Somatization reactions." *Psychosomatic Medicine* 9 (1947), 92–97.

111. See Michel Foucault, *The History of Sexuality*, Part I: *Introduction* (New York: Pantheon, 1978), for the relation between sexuality and discourse in the modern period.

112. See Eric Wittkower, "Historical perspective of contemporary psychosomatic medicine," *International Journal of Psychiatry in Medicine* 5, no. 4 (1974), 309–19.

113. Briefly, by "Cartesian split" I mean the division of the human being into two substances, body and mind, which are entirely different and somehow related. For Descartes, the mind was a nonspatial "thinking thing," and the body, all material things, was a nonthinking "extended thing." For phenomenological critiques of such duralism and for a reinterpretation of the essence of the human body, see Erwin Strauss, *The Primary World of Senses: A Vindication of Sensory Experience* (New York: Free Press, 1963); Jean-Paul Sartre, *Being and Nothingness: An Essay on Phenomenological Ontology* (New York: Philosophical Library, 1956); and Maurice Merleau-Ponty, *Phenomenology of Perception* (New York: Humanities Press, 1962).

114. Clifford Allbutt, "Neurasthenia," in *A System of Medicine*, ed. C. Allbutt and Humphrey Davy Rolleston, Vol. 8: *Diseases of the Brain and Mental Disease* (London: Macmillan, 1910), p. 761.

115. Ibid., 760.

116. See Donald Meyer, *The Positive Thinkers: Religion as Pop Psychology from Mary Baker Eddy to Oral Roberts*, reissue (New York: Pantheon, 1980).

5

"This Strange Disease of Modern Life": The Dangers of Strain

A solution of the mysteries of organic life in the simpler and not less
beautiful laws of inanimate matter.

—George Robinson[1]

In industrial societies organized athletic events have become popular quasi-
rituals. Sport carries meaning beyond the physical conditioning and glory it
affords participants and the entertainment it promises spectators. In Victorian
England, athletic prowess was held to develop and make manifest the virtues
of English character, sporting events being occasions for honor, manliness,
and national pride. So when the eminent surgeon and social reformer F. C.
Skey wrote to the *Times* in October 1867 that the university boat races
damaged the health of the young contestants, he raised a furor that echoed
well into the next century.[2]

Skey claimed that the annual races on the Thames subjected the oarsmen
to unreasonable physical strain:

The young men enter the boat apparently in the condition of vigorous health. Having
accomplished their arduous task, they are thoroughly exhausted, and, as I have been
informed by eye-witnesses of their condition, they have been on occasion so reduced
in strength as to be unable to rise from their seats.[3]

Skey stated that muscular fitness, visible to the eye, did not necessarily
mean that the youth was constitutionally fit. Only a physician could determine
that. Because the boat race taxed endurance more than muscular strength,

the internal organs were subject to harm. Great effort, such as rowing and running, "exhaust" the "physical force" of the athlete; there is great "expenditure of the muscular power." Even training for the race "is an aggravation by its draught oft repeated, both on the circulation and on the nervous system."[4]

Skey's letter "startled London," according to Robert Farquharson, then medical officer at Rugby.[5] "Broad Blue," one respondent to Skey, argued that training prevented the problems Skey feared. If an athlete trained, then the following dynamics prevailed during the race: After the initial exertion, "second wind" occurred, followed by a stage of "gradual weariness, as the muscles tire, and the renovating supplies of the commissariat of the body become drained too. When the supply can no longer equal the demand the power fails, and the frame ceases or slackens action." Strain was an effect of exertion on the organs, especially upon the "bellows" and the "forcing-pump," as he called the lungs and heart. But strain did not harm a trained athlete, who "recovers strength even if he has expended his stock in trade." The writer, evidently a nonmedical man familiar with the training of athletes, disagreed with Skey on specifics (especially on second wind) but shared his perceptions of the body under strain.[6]

In a leading article of October 15, 1867, the *Times* responded to Skey. It noted the possibility of "heart complaint" and "exhaustion of the nervous system" as a result of "over-exertion" but stated that the statistics which might help determine such an outcome did not exist. With Skey, the *Times* noted that "animal vigor" or strength of muscle differs from "constitutional vigor," and that lack of attention to the difference could be costly:

So long as a man thrives upon training in respect of appetite, sleep, or spirits, and especially if he scarcely loses weight under the discipline, it is naturally inferred that he is just the right material for an University boat crew. And yet an examination by a skillful physician might show that he is really spending out of the very capital of his health and sensibly diminishing his chances of longevity.[7]

The "capital" of health is limited in supply, such that even apparent health may belie the overdraft that will reveal itself only in later years. Prudence dictated, stated the *Times*, that an oarsman should have "the state of his lungs and heart" determined by a physician. Yet, the article concluded, the races should continue despite the danger: "It is not by so niggardly an economy of nerves that noble races acquire or preserve their vigor. Let us teach our youth by all means the value of their own health, but let us beware of quenching their emulation, lest we foster ... degeneration."[8] This discourse reflected the attitude that exercise without strain was as possible as expenditure without depletion of capital. The discourse also reflected a capitalist orientation toward health as well as wealth, coupled with fears of racial degeneration and emasculation caused by the premature depletion of vitality in youth.[9]

Skey's rejoinder of October 21 clarified what he meant by strain. Rowing is good exercise; indeed, "inasmuch as the act of rowing involves so large a proportion of the entire muscular system, it may be said to be superior to most other forms in this—that it attains its object without strain." Strain was not effort but "waste of power," or excessive effort. Power, moreover, was limited in quantity: Skey doubted the existence of a second wind.[10]

"No topic more occupied the Victorian mind"[11] than health, and Skey's letter tapped the anxiety concerning it. Health involved wholeness (a sound mind in a sound body), and the pursuit of one's calling with great vigor. The symbol of the healthy man as the "player as gentleman-hero"[12] was embodied precisely in the youths whose strain worried Skey. Health, as a central value in Victorian times, provided the context for a discourse on strain—interwoven with metaphors from finance and mechanics. Health, wealth, masculinity, nationalism, and power provided the unsaid in much of the talk about strain and overstrain in nineteenth century Anglo-American medicine.

In the months and years following Skey's letter, the British medical community showed considerable interest in overstrain.[13] Skey's letter did not create this interest, but the furor over it shows that at least the *Times*'s readers perceived the body in terms of the material and financial foundations of industrial society. The metaphors were common currency. Farquharson observed: "running has always struck me as a doubtful form of athletics, from the great amount of strain thrown upon the circulating system. . . . The recent death, from aneurysm, of Richard Manks, England's greatest hero in this department, had a significant bearing on this point."[14]

In 1869, Morgan concluded that rowing did not cause serious health problems; and the *Lancet*, in reviewing Morgan's book, clearly stated the basic issue—and understanding of—strain as a serious matter:

Amongst more civilized nations it early comes to be recognized that neglect of due exercise of the body rapidly leads to deterioration of the race. . . . So long as riding, rowing, and athletics continue to be practiced among us, we shall retain, that which we have long held, a leading place in physical, in moral, and in intellectual endowments among the nations of Europe.[15]

This attitude makes evident the motives for the intensity of the debate over strain: The dangers both of strain and of fearing to risk it.

TRANSITION AND COMPETITION

Benjamin Disraeli depicted in 1844 the transformations that had taken place in Britain:

During five-and-twenty years every influence that can develop the energies and resources of a nation had been acting with concentrated stimulation on the British Isles.

National peril and national glory; the perpetual menace of invasion, the continual triumph of conquest; the most extensive foreign commerce that was ever conducted by a single nation; an illimitable currency; an internal trade supported by swarming millions, whom manufactures and inclosure-bills summoned into existence; above all, the supreme control obtained by man over mechanic power, these are some of the causes of that rapid advance of material civilization in England to which the annals of the world can afford no parallel.[16]

The changes can be summed up in an expression fresh on the tongue in the 1840s: "high pressure." It referred of course to the force of steam in steam engines; it had also come to signify both the force and urgency of "speed, work, business, conditions of life." Harry Coningsby, the protagonist of Disraeli's novel *Coningsby*, meets Mr. G. O. A. Head in Manchester, the new city of the new age. With a verbal head of steam, Mr. Head observes to Harry: "You see, we have all of us a great respect for the town. . . . And it has some first-rate institutions. There's the Manchester Bank. That's a noble institution, full of commercial enterprise; understands the age, sir; high-pressure to the backbone."[17] Before Mr. Head bids young Coningsby adieu, he informs him of train schedules, with times noted to the minute, a sign of the style of life lived at high pressure. "High pressure" connoted upward striving, business, speed, punctuality, and "a state of nervous tension," as satirized by George Gissing late in the century.[18]

This metaphor—bringing together a machine with a way of living and even an ideal type of character—orients us to that aspect of the medical world at issue. A novel set of social and personal questions faced the Victorian world, including new diseases and medical perceptions. Coupled with these questions were new ways of addressing them which had taken root in medical perception. Herein lay the precursors of "stress."

As to the questions: Walter Houghton, in presenting the concerns of the generation of 1830, remarks that the Victorians were well aware that they lived in a transitional age between the medieval (the term was a nineteenth-century neologism) and the modern. The railroads and the Reform Act (1832) signaled, as had the French Revolution, new and accelerating mobility. With mobility came competitiveness and a new awareness of the class character of society. This uprootedness had its parallel in intellectual and moral spheres. Houghton notes that John Stuart Mill "described the age as one in which the opinion that religious belief was necessary for moral and social purposes was universal, and yet real belief was feeble and precarious— a situation well calculated to arouse anxiety."[19] The enthusiasm of high pressure had its counterpoint in the ennui and shock over the prospects that society was losing its transcendent background and support. This disappearance showed, for example, in poetry: By the end of the nineteenth century, the blue canopy above our heads ceased to be the visibility of unseen divinity and became the sky of industry (and industrial pollution) and of science.[20]

At the time, social and economic competition was altering the structure of the medical community. As Ruskin observed in 1851:

The very removal of the massy bars which once separated one class of society from another, has rendered it tenfold more shameful in foolish people's *i.e.*, in most people's eyes, to remain in the lower grades of it, than ever it was before. . . . Now that a man may make money, and rise in the world, and associate himself, unreproached, with people once far above him . . . it becomes a veritable shame to him to remain in the state he was born in, and everybody thinks it is his *duty* to try to be a "gentleman."[21]

It is fair to say that many medical men and their patients shared this sense of duty. Once a relatively humble occupation, medicine throughout this period made great strides in upward mobility as reform-minded physicians pressed for professional hegemony over hospital administration and assumed at least the appearance of scientific rigor.[22]

In this period of fundamental transition, the rhetoric of loss, as part of the stress discourse, took root. As Houghton describes one side of an ambiguous relation to the past, the Victorians' sense of "triumph over nature" and over tradition "attested to their immeasurable superiority to their forefathers."[23] Progress, not loss, was the order of the day, and many were the Mr. G. O. A. Heads in that day. With notions of progress flourishing, people focused on the idea that they were progressing by abandoning old customs and beliefs. There were few who considered that great losses were being incurred while society hurried toward perceived prosperity. Notions flourished that bound together physiological and national progress. Social Darwinism, as popularized by Thomas Huxley and Herbert Spencer, is an obvious expression of the generally accepted notion that "today's" person was superior to "yesterday's."

But such ideas circulated even before Darwin. The physician Robert Verity, for example, drawing on Vico's sense of history and on Newtonian mechanics, addressed the history of physiology. Verity said that the evolution of the race and hence the superiority of the British rested upon the growing delicacy of the English nervous system. "Delicacy" of nerves, already a sign of "neurosis" for Robert Whytt in the preceding century, had in the nineteenth century an ambivalent meaning. For Verity it meant greater sensitivity and refinement; for others it stood for degeneracy. Delicacy was a sign of the advance of civilization. Peasants and others with thickened calluses were not delicate, sensitive, and refined. Delicate people, subject to vapors and hypochondria since the eighteenth century, suffered from the higher life they were leading. Hence the ambivalence: Delicacy of nerves represented evolution of the nervous system and racial superiority; yet it also represented degeneracy subsequent to luxurious living.

The growing predominance of the "nervous temperament," which delicacy produced, became after mid-century tied to concepts of energy and entropy.

Nervous people, more responsive to stimuli, are more easily shocked or strained, more readily depleted of their nerve force and hence inclined to nervous prostration or neurasthenia. "Heat death," imagined as the end of the cosmos, found its embodiment in weary pilgrims slouching toward spas. The concept of energy when applied to the body did not replace the earlier notion of the nervous temperament, but blended with it in various ways. As the storm over the university boat races illustrates, the various inscriptions traced into the bodies of the young men—delicacy of constitution, progress of nation and race, masculinity, energy, capital, and engineering—produced neither a simple nor a univocal text. The boat races displayed the competitive spirit necessary for social and economic progress. Simultaneously, the symptoms they produced revealed the dangers of progress: The finest young Englishmen were potentially ruined for life by the overstrain from striving for victory. Delicacy and overstrain marked the appearance of the suffering of the loss of the old in the straining after the new.

ENGINEERING AS MENTALITY AND DISCOURSE

> For what wears out the life of mortal men?
> 'Tis that from change to change their being rolls; 'Tis
> that repeated shocks, again, again,
>   Exhaust the energy of strongest souls
>   And numb the elastic powers.
> Till having used our nerves with bliss and teen,
>   And tired upon a thousand schemes our wit,
>   To the just-pausing Genius we remit
> Our worn-out life, and are—what we have been.
>   —Matthew Arnold, "The Scholar Gypsy"

Who was exempt from this law of life? In Arnold's poem of 1853 only the Scholar Gypsy himself because, among other reasons:

> O born in days when wits were fresh and clear,
>   And life ran gaily as the sparkling Thames,
>   Before this strange disease of modern life,
> With its sick hurry, its divided aims,
>   Its heads o'ertaxed, its palsied hearts, was rife—

The metaphors that Arnold employed to display "this strange disease of modern life" resonate with the discourses of the sciences of the day. Though he spoke of the energy of the soul, in the next breath he evoked the nerves. *Energy* and *elastic powers* and even *wear* were terms going "from change to change" in the 1850s. The older connotations of these words were being supplemented by scientific engineering ones, which made the language of this passage apt for the symptoms Arnold correctly discerned: "sick hurry," "divided aims," (later called "unconscious conflict" or "divided existence"), "heads o'ertaxed," and "palsied hearts."[24] It was precisely around the date of this poem that an engineering discourse took root in medicine, and the four topics Arnold catalogues (hurry, divided aims, heads overtaxed, and hearts palsied) were those to which the engineering discourse was addressed. The poet in what may be seen as a homeopathic remedy employed the terms of the sickness to describe and rectify it.

Nineteenth-century physicians could come to perceive the body in engineering terms only if such a mentality already existed. By an engineering mentality I mean the questioning after materials' ability to work and to bear pressures and tensions, the resulting knowledge to be applied to construction projects. Engineering in this sense became established during the eighteenth and nineteenth centuries. In 1798, "the first book on strength of material by Girard was published."[25] Cauchy established the modern theory of stress in 1823. But an engineering mentality resides in more than theoretical understandings. It thrives as a mode of thought and action whereby modern states and industries see only the rational nature of each and every phenomenon in the world, be it the course of a river, the construction of bridges and roads, or the behavior of employees. The engineering mentality is above all practical.

In the first half of the nineteenth century, British engineers were consolidating their status as professionals and improving their social status.[26] When industry developed, engineering flourished, especially with the building of railways in the 1830s. Porter and Clifton write that "in mid-Victorian England engineering rode on the crest of triumphant industrial and civil achievements."[27] But formal education in engineering lagged. Timoshenko writes that British engineers, successful in experimentation and application, were deficient in education when compared to their French and German counterparts.[28] Professional organizations, the receipt of titles, and large fees for consultants preceded the solidification of educational standards.

Only when engineering "arrived" did its vocabulary become uniform. The standardization of the terminology of strain and stress fixes the date when one can say that an engineering discourse existed, a discourse that medicine could employ. In neither Samuel Johnson's (1775) nor Noah Webster's (1828) dictionaries had the words *stress* or *strain* formal scientific meanings. But related terms, such as *elastic, pressure*, and *tension*, for example, had. Only in the 1850s did *stress* and *strain* receive their present scientific meanings. The credit goes to William Macquern Rankine (1820–1872), who defined *strain* in 1850:

Although the word strain is used in ordinary language indiscriminately to denote relative molecular displacement, and the force by which it is produced, . . . I shall . . .

use it . . . in the restricted sense of relative displacement of particles, whether consisting in dilatation, condensation, or distortion.[29]

Rankine defined *stress* in 1855, the year he received a chair in engineering at Glasgow University:

The word "stress" will be used to denote the force, or combination of forces, which such molecules exert in tending to recover its free condition, and which, for a state of equilibrium, is equal and opposite to the combination of external forces applied to it.[30]

Rankine's definitions were innovations.[31] His textbook, *A Manual of Applied Mechanics*, "is important in the history of elasticity, for it was among the first to bring the theory of elasticity in a scientific form before engineering students."[32] Rankine's definition of *stress* was "sanctioned" by William Thompson (Lord Kelvin) and Peter Guthrie Tait in their *Treatise on Natural Philosophy* (1867).[33]

Thus, only at mid-century did the engineering profession appropriate a specialized vocabulary (at least the terms that concern this topic). It was then that medical practitioners lifted the key words (such as *strain*) from the vernacular to use in their field. A discourse on strain could not have occurred in medicine before that date. Indeed, it appeared only in the succeeding decades.

Evidence abounds that within the medical community eyes and ears were attuned to engineering and the sciences. For example, the *Lancet* reported in 1832 on a lecture entitled "Elasticity and Bearing Properties of Cast Iron." In the report is included the observation that a "curious prehensile elastic hook, adopted as a substitute in case of amputated forearm" was exhibited at Mr. Cottam's lecture.[34] Medical interest in engineering matters exhibited itself also in the linkage between public health reform, in which engineering feats played a key role, and the reform of medical practice. In commenting on a bill before Parliament "for the better Drainage and Improvement of Buildings in large towns and villages," the *Lancet* observed in 1841: "we are convinced that medical reform is the basis of all sanitary reform."[35] Thus, even before strain emerged as a medical topic, engineering theory and application interested physicians. Moreover, some of the physicians relevant to the topic of strain, notably Clifford Allbutt, Benjamin Ward Richardson, and James Mackenzie, developed new clinical instruments or new uses for old ones. While the medical profession had ambiguously adopted scientific aspirations at mid-century, increasingly its advancement was tied to science.[36] These illustrations indicate that by the second half of the nineteenth century, an engineering mentality existed, and that physicians were receptive to it.

STRAIN AND THE TISSUES OF THE BODY

A second aspect of the science of the strength of materials relevant to this study is experimentation with bodily tissues. Robert Hooke had tested "springy bodies," such as "Metal, Wood, Stones, baked Earths, Hair, Horns, Silk, Bones, Sinews, Glass and the like" in the late seventeenth century.[37] Studies conducted in the eighteenth and early nineteenth centuries examined the cohesion of various tissues under the stress of weight, and the tendency of blood vessels to rupture when distended. Stephen Hales's experiments on blood pressure were published in 1734; Bevan in 1826 wrote "On the strength of bone."[38] The physician George Robinson performed a series of experiments in the 1840s on blood pressure with instruments of his own design to show "ordinary hydrodynamic principles" at work in the body's economy.[39] In 1846 Bishop addressed elastic properties of the body from a clinical perspective, and Wertheim lectured on the elasticity and cohesion of the tissues of the human body.[40] Wertheim extracted tissues from cadavers of both sexes and of various ages, and he tested bones, tendons, muscles, nerves, arteries, and veins. In the same year, Wilhelm Weber published an article on muscle elasticity.[41] A controversy ensued "upon the exact form taken by the stress–strain relation for organic tissues," with articles appearing in the 1850s and '60s.

The experiments discussed above show when and how the elastic limits of the body were first systematically tested. Wertheim considered tissues the constituent elements of the body. The prominence of tissues had begun with the work of Xavier Bichat and the rise of pathological anatomy in the eighteenth century. As Foucault argued in *The Birth of the Clinic*, the shift in medical perception toward tissues and anatomical location of disease coincided with the physician's rising dominance over the patient; the physician could now gaze through the body to the disease rather than engaging the patient in conversation about it.[42] Wertheim's work on tissues required autopsy; it also necessitated perceiving the flesh as decomposable into tissue, i.e., into materials which resembled glass and metal, other objects of Wertheim's research. The question of these early experiments—How much load can the body take before breaking apart?—was emblematic of all concern with strain and stress. Thus, one result of Bichat's discovery that tissues were the elements of the body was an inquiry into the strength of these materials. The inquiry configured the relationship between body and world as one between tissue and load, thus furthering the identification of the body with the new industrial machinery and materials.

THE "OLD CARDIOLOGY"

These inquiries reckoned with the body in the same manner that engineers tested building materials. By mid-century, the heart and blood vessels had come under similar scrutiny. There was "a readiness to perceive" the strength and elastic limits of the heart.[43] In Britain at that time medical practitioners carried out the greater part of physiological research. But while a handful of physicians (such as Allbutt) were scientifically minded, not all were. The medical community strove for social prestige, but prestige was not tied then to at least the appearance of scientific acumen.[44] This condition in particular helps account for the slow growth of the engineering mentality and the discourse on strain. Resistance to an engineering perception surfaced, in one instance, with an angry response to a proposal to publish in the *Lancet* a series of lectures on the principles of mechanics applied to physiology. Those lectures were not published; however, a later series by Carlo Matteucci were. The *Lancet* recounted:

It was with a view to contribute to the spread of a taste for general science amongst our students and practitioners, that we proposed to publish the extended course of lectures on natural philosophy, by Dr. Muller, of Freiburg. Numerous correspondents, however, demurred to the occupation of a professional journal by the general branches of physical science. Pathology and physiology, therapeutics, diagnosis, and clinical medicine, surgery and midwifery, were thought more germane . . . than mechanics, hydrostatics, hydraulics, and pneumatics; and our readers preferred a knowledge of the heart, the brain, the nerves, the stomach, and the uterus, to the best disquisitions on the wheel and axle, the screw, the wedge, and the balance.

In Matteucci's lectures, however, the editorial continued, he carefully distinguished between "the *physics* of physiology, pathology, and practice," and "those phenomena which are strictly vital."[45] This editorial illustrates the profound change in perception that the engineering mentality required.

In fact, only when "laboratory medicine"[46] become dominant did engineering considerations and discourse prevail in British medicine. Allbutt noted in 1909 that "to go with physiology as far as we can is not only to tread so far on relatively firm ground, but also to provide a discipline and a preciser terminology."[47] But the practitioner of 1847 had only the methods of percussion and auscultation with which to discover the signs of the heart. And in the late 1800s these two methods were still the royal road to discerning heart overstrain.

When physicians of this period studied the heart, they were chiefly concerned with its anatomical structure. In this "old cardiology,"[48] valvular diseases dominated. Medical men preperceived anatomical lesions in their patients when they palpated the chest and listened with the stethoscope. The patient's body was a space of tissues of limited strength, and the application of external force or of internal power of will could strain the tissue, instituting disease. Overstrain of the heart was thus a disease belonging to a period when the perceptual mindset for engineering matters existed, yet before the laboratory was firmly established as the sanctuary of medicine. When the laboratory became medicine's sanctuary, functional efficiency replaced anatomical integrity as the touchstone in diagnosis. The roots of the discourse on strain resided in the old cardiology.

THE WORK OF THE HEART

Interest in strain had another source at least as important as that of strength of bodily tissues. Beginning in the 1840s, with the doctrines of conservation of energy and entropy, physiological studies sought to measure the amount of work done by the body as a product of energy consumption. Before Helmholtz's work on thermodynamics, a mechanistic and static image of the body had prevailed, but after Helmholtz, the perception of the body as a heat engine, as the locus of energy transformations, yielded a dynamic image of the body.[49] *Energy* resonated in economic, financial, and psychological discourse as well, with each domain influencing the understanding of energy in the others.[50] By mid-century, "the belief arose that physiology was but a special case of 'the physics of celloids and the chemistry of the proteids.' "[51]

In the study of digestion and respiration as forms of energy transformation, the heart as pump played a central role. By 1870, investigations of the work of the heart were influencing medical perception. Allbutt wrote in that year that "mechanical causation of heart disease" from great and sustained effort was a novel topic. He had previously noted, "More haste, worse speed, is as true of heart work as of any other, and it seems clear that the hurried labour of the overtasked heart is not compensatory, but is mere blindness and bewilderment."[52]

The career of Samuel Haughton (1821–1897) exemplifies the ferment around the engineering approach to the body. Haughton, ordained a priest in 1847, contributed mathematical physics papers in the 1840s that focused on questions of equilibrium and strength of materials. Concurrently he initiated geological inquiries, and the study of fossils led him to anatomy. He then returned to Trinity College for a medical degree, which he obtained in 1862. He turned next to the mechanics of muscular action and to the reform of medical education at Trinity in his capacity as medical registrar. On religious grounds he opposed the theory of evolution; in his view, the wonders of physiological mechanics manifest the wisdom of the Creator. Haughton represented a type at once conservative and radical, and he succeeded in implanting in his own medical perceptions the engineering perspective.

In 1868 Haughton reported experiments done on "the relation of food to work done by the body," in which he had measured his own urea production during vigorous exercise.[53] He then turned his attention to the work of the heart.[54] Haughton described the Divine Engineer's wise design of the fibers of the heart by comparing them to the rings of a 600-pound gun:

I went down to see this great gun. It consists of eight rings. The first, sixth, and eighth rings were burst, the other five were whole. But a perfect gun would burst so that all the eight rings would give way together, each perishing with its neighbour. And that problem—which engineers have yet failed to solve—is solved in the heart.[55]

The image of the gun, in addition to displaying the engineering mentality applied to the work of the heart, is telling: images of battle and contest run throughout the medical literature on the heart at that time.

Along with energy consumption and strength, "wear and tear" were measurable consequences of the heart's work. Haughton referred to studies of the health of Cornish miners, which had been conducted in the 1860s. After noting that the long ladder climb from the mines "throws a heavy strain . . . upon the muscles of the tired worker," he discussed the effects of this strain on the heart:

His heart, over-stimulated by the rapid exertion of muscular work, beats more and more quickly in its efforts to oxidate the blood in the lungs, and so supply the force required. Local congestion of the lung itself frequently follows, and lays the foundation, so graphically, though sadly described, by the miner at forty years of age, who tells us that "his other works are very good, but that he is beginning to leak in the valves."[56]

Both the miner and the physician shared the perception that the heart was an engine subject to wear and tear from overwork. Moreover, strain was not the only source of the work of the body; normal functioning also entailed work. In Haughton's words: "the whole work done by the muscles, voluntary and involuntary, of a hard-worked laborer will amount to less than *one-sixth* of the work expended in maintaining the temperature at 100°F."[57] In this emerging engineering perspective in medicine, all life activities became perceived as work, as energy consumption, taking place by means of materials with elastic limits and subject to wear and tear.

THE SOCIAL CONSTRUCTION OF OVERSTRAIN OF THE HEART (1840–1870)

The first notice of what later came to be called overstrain of the heart occurred in the 1830s. *Hypertrophy* entered the vocabulary in 1834 in a text on Laennec's work. By the mid–1840s, physicians viewed "violent exercise or strong mental emotion" as a cause of hypertrophy and valvular disease. There are numerous observations of this kind in the medical literature of the time.[58] By the 1850s, the notion that "excessive and continued action of the heart, by straining the valves,"[59] produced hypertrophy and valvular disease, was in textbooks. Nevertheless, when strain became a recognized causal factor in the early 1870s, it appeared to physicians to have been hitherto unnoticed, which suggests that a change in perception coincided with a novel epiphany of the heart. By 1870, the engineering mentality had become sedimented into the medical gaze, which then saw the heart as if for the first time.

Athletes and soldiers were the two groups that roused anxiety. Their ill-health helped to crystallize strain. Studies by British medical men in the 1860s concluded that constriction of the chest by knapsack straps caused heart disease among soldiers, although as Howell indicates, in later decades other causes, all related to training methods were found for valvular disease.[60] In MacLean's 1867 description of valvular diseases among soldiers, he noted that the term *irritable heart* was perhaps the appropriate term.

Irritable heart was the name given to a condition among soldiers that the American Jacob M. DaCosta observed during the Civil War; Alfred Stillé and Henry Hartshorne had, around the same time, also noted this condition "observed among soldiers as the result of prolonged and violent exertion."[61] Understood chiefly as a functional disease, even though it could lead to anatomical changes, it had a variety of symptoms, chiefly shortness of breath, palpitations, indigestion, dizziness, and chest pain.[62] The patient was unable to bear fatigue or exertion. When overstrain became recognized as an etiological factor, irritable heart was largely classified as a consequence of it. In 1875, DaCosta viewed irritable heart as a result of "continued over-action and over-work." He extended his observations to civilian life and described "the effects of cardiac strain upon the muscular walls, valvular apparatus, and great vessels of the heart."[63]

Irritable heart continued to be diagnosed well into the twentieth century, appearing in World War I as soldier's heart. As with the controversy Skey caused, irritable heart expressed a profound anxiety over the effects of effort of muscle and above all of will, in the nineteenth century. Treadwell, an American physician who reviewed disability claims of former Union troops, noted that those with irritable heart had organs less "self-reliant" than the normal heart, thus evoking in a physicalistic way one of the cherished ideals of American character.[64] A twentieth-century psychological bias views this statement as a projection of psychological traits into the heart; but at that time, despite mechanistic theory, the heart still had a moral quality, still embodied the character of a person.

In 1870, when Allbutt demonstrated that strain caused heart disease, he made *strain* figural to the medical gaze. Some physicians, including Farquharson and Allbutt, thought that Skey and others had exaggerated the ill-effects of exertion on youth. Allbutt, however, had no doubt about the damage that strain caused to the hearts and aortas of manual laborers. He was attuned to engineering matters. He invented a short clinical thermometer, pioneered the use of the ophthalmoscope, and introduced "estimation of the blood pressure, with the aid of the sphygmomanometer" into British medical practice.[65] His interests were wide-ranging, but he devoted much research to heart disease and mental illness. Many of Allbutt's patients in Leeds were laborers, and it was with them that he encountered heart disease following strenuous physical activity.

Allbutt wrote that mechanical strain was not generally considered a cause of heart disease in either the young or the old; rheumatism was blamed for it in youth, atheroma in age. He noted that other physicians had previously recognized strain as a factor, but that these observations had not had an impact on general medical opinion regarding the causes of heart disease. His patients, "forge-men, colliers, wharfingers, and other persons exposed to the heavy strain of town labor," suffered from heart diseases; they had been neither ill nor old before over-exerting themselves.[66] While there were complicating factors, the patients of greatest interest were healthy, well-fed, and strong.

The symptom-picture varied, but the following was typical. A 23-year-old shoemaker went on drill as a militiaman:

He found the work much harder than before; his clothes were tight, and the cross-belt and straps of knapsack were very confining. He felt this the more, as the drill took place in part up and down a steep hillside. Many of the men complained of being overdone. He managed to keep up during exercise; but . . . on coming home and removing his knapsack, he was seized with a violent and distressing fit of coughing, which lasted an hour or more. He never had a cough before. When his time was over, he felt very short of breath and oppressed in the chest, which symptoms, before unknown to him, have grown worse.[67]

The framing of the experience occurred with the aid of percussion and auscultation:

On examination in Oct. 1870, the heartbeat is much diffused, rather rapid and excited. The whole heart is much dilated, its dullness extending nearly an inch beyond the sternum, and its sounds are thin and short. There is a systolic murmur heard at the apex, and less loudly over the xiphoid cartilage.

Allbutt's diagnosis was dilatation of the heart which "had resulted in mitral and perhaps tricuspid regurgitation."[68] The explanatory model was as follows: Dilatation occurred when weak muscles of the ventricles did not force out all the blood during systole; because of increased blood flow into the heart's chambers during physical exertion, dilatation progressively worsened. The mitral valve between the left auricle and ventricle and the tricuspid valve between the chambers on the right, then were affected. Blood flowed backward (regurgitation), as indicated by the heart sounds.

The framing of the disorder in engineering terms occurred in the move from the symptoms to the diagnosis. The shoemaker suffered an illness in the non-engineering or vernacular sense; after his visit to the physician he suffered from strain of the heart. Overstrain resulted because his heart was not strong enough to do the work required of it; it had surpassed its elastic limits.

The perception of the body from an engineering standpoint showed itself most clearly in Allbutt's discussion of the aorta:

it has no power of strengthening itself according to circumstances. Its resistance is great; but its activity is nothing, or rather it is nothing more than the recoil of elastic fibre. Strain of such coats as these, so far from bringing gain of strength, brings loss of elasticity and weakness.[69]

Allbutt drew on evidence obtained from pathological as well as physical examination, referring to microscopic analysis of the coats of the aorta, and to signs detected by means of the stethoscope and the sphygmograph. Overstrain, then, in the engineering sense, was a condition perceived through the products of an engineering mentality.

Although the presence of instruments and a readiness to perceive in engineering terms contributed to the construction of overstrain, there were other factors. Allbutt's patients worked primarily in heavy industry and engineering projects. Patients took an engineering perspective toward themselves, construing their experience in the discourse of their occupations.[70] They were perfectly aware that their labor was excessive. In attributing their symptoms to their jobs, they protested injustices at the workplace. Allbutt commented, however, that physicians did not seem to get the message: "If these patients attribute their disease to a particular strain, the note-taker is as likely as not to set aside the story as immaterial."[71] Whereas patients blamed their symptoms on their work, physicians had tended to see constitutional degeneration (rheumatism or atheroma) as the cause. Strain as an etiological factor shifted responsibility from the patient's constitution to his work.

Strain participated in debates over worker health and safety. Indeed, one impetus for the construction of overstrain of the heart was pressure by the coal-worker unions. The Coal Act of 1860 mandated the study of the health of miners. The ensuing reports, especially the image of the Cornish miners having to climb ladders for an hour or more at the end of their shift, were persistently cited in the literature on overstrain.[72] J. Milner Fothergill expressly related strain on the heart to occupational safety:

A general recognition of these facts would lead to some more equable and fair remuneration of the men exposed to disease from mechanical strain. The rate of wages should be such that the man can, if so inclined, make provision for himself when this form of labour must be abandoned, and some easier occupation substituted in its stead, and also for his family when he is taken away, as he almost certainly will be, before he reaches what we term the allotted span of existence.[73]

Similar arguments were made for the health of soldiers and university athletes. In all, strain of effort, understood in terms of the elastic strength of the circulatory system, caused damage that demanded responsible social action.

THE OVERSTRAINED HEART (1870–1920)

Overstrain of the heart thus came into existence as a clinical condition. While debate followed over the extent of damage caused by overstrain and the nature of overstrain—whether sudden effort or prolonged tedious work was more significant—in general the British medical community accepted its existence. When Allbutt addressed the Clinical Society of London on February 28, 1873 on "Overstrain of the Heart and Aorta," the comments of the members illustrate their readiness to perceive the heart as subject to strain. Allbutt summarized his findings by stating that "affections of the heart due to physical strain were by no means rare. They consisted in an obstinate 'irritability' of the organ, and in dilatation of both chambers with or without hypertrophy; and these cases were often very difficult to cure."[74] Allbutt did not think that athletics were a major source of strain. (As the medical journals noted in reporting the lecture, Allbutt, still a young man, was a regular mountain climber.[75]) For Allbutt, the "heavier labor of the working class" caused more injury. This kind of work "was more continuous, and left less time for repair. It was also carried on in spite of fatigue, of diminished health, and imperfect feeding. It is probable, too, that work done *con amore* was less exhausting than the drearier kind of toil."[76] In response to Allbutt, some members of the Clinical Society, including surgeon Arthur Myers, emphasized the dangers of excessive athletics: "it would be better policy to teach moderation, and thus prevent, or at least check, many cases of incipient heart-disease, such as irritability and slight hypertrophy with or without dilatation."[77] The general sentiment was in favor of athletics at the universities, but they urged caution because, as John Ogle observed, "many undergraduates possessed delicate organs."[78] Despite Allbutt's insistence that heavy and boring labor was the chief threat, university athletics was the touchstone for many. Only Robert Farquharson, who later stopped practicing medicine and became a member of Parliament when he obtained his inheritance, appeared to see a tendency toward heart strain in both lower and upper classes. Farquharson thought that among the laboring classes, "concurrent influence of drink, tobacco, bad food, and general insanitary conditions" contributed to heart diseases, and that among the "upper ranks, anxiety of mind, with worry or overwork," predisposed to heart disease.[79] Allbutt responded by stating that nervous causes contributed to irritable heart, thus showing that *strain* connoted *psychological* even as it denoted physical events.

The majority of contributions to the study of overstrain were clinical. Thompson, Richardson, and Fothergill were among those writing on the topic in the early 1870s. In the United States, too, there was interest.[80] DaCosta's 1875 Toner Lectures painted the familiar picture of overstrain: sudden strain or prolonged work can lead to "breaks and tears in the valvular apparatus and great vessels." Moreover, "the same result . . . may happen from extraordinary mental emotion or shock."[81]

Fothergill's essays stressed experimental research in his review of the literature, and engineering discourse was quite prominent. While his own experimental work was limited, he consistently referred to physiological studies. George William Balfour, in his *Clinical Lectures on Diseases of the Heart and Aorta* (1876), criticized neglect of engineering considerations in cases of compensatory hypertrophy of the left ventricle: "too much attention has been bestowed upon what we may call the vital forces, and too little upon the simple mechanical agencies involved in aortic regurgitation."[82] In 1888 overstrain had its experimental confirmation. C. S. Roy and J. G. Adami conducted research on the relation between the work of the heart and physical changes produced by that work. They observed the elastic limits of the heart and the consequences of exceeding them. Summarizing their experiments, they stated:

The work of the heart varies very greatly within physiological limits as a result both of the changes in the arterial pressure and in the amount of blood which reaches the organ.... Increase in the work done, other things being equal, produces diminished completeness of contraction in systole, and therefore an increase in the residual blood in the ventricle. This physiological dilatation of the heart with increased work becomes, when excessive, the cause of failure of the organ from overwork or overstrain, as it is generally called.[83]

They wrote that the mitral valve is where strain produces damage.

Roy and Adami's research succeeded in actualizing strain, in the sense that they artificially produced and observed it. Dogs' hearts, once connected to the instruments, literally drove pistons to which recording devices were attached. Literally as well as figuratively, the heart became an engine. The cardiometer, which enclosed "the living and working heart in what is for all practical purposes a rigid air-tight box," formed a fitting symbol for the condition of overstrain of the heart: a disease of a competitive industrial society, in which the forces of vitality have been placed in the service of running the "machinery." A disease had arisen undetected in the heart: The vital center had become a pump.

The discourse of strain reflected anxiety over the changing character of life. Advances in society had outstripped our physiological organization, which needed to catch up. Richardson wrote:

The animal body, in order to maintain equality of power, and be the equal of the soul within it, must, in the course of the suns, be replaced by an organism more finely moulded ... and more impressionable to cure or to injury through the mind than through the baser body.[84]

Intellectual work, steadily increasing in society, was a danger and a promise. Richardson listed the physical illnesses which resulted from overwork among the professional classes and indicated that such diseases signified superior social standing: "Our uneducated, cloddish populations are . . . the breeders of our abstract insanity, while our educated, ambitious, over-straining, un-tiring, mental workers are the breeders and intensifiers of some of the worst forms of physical maladies."[85] I conclude from these mixed messages that the discourse on strain in mid-Victorian England belonged to a rhetoric of the heroic.

The discourse on strain reflected an engineering approach to the body and its health, but an engineering approach did not imply only a detached concern for elasticity and ability to do work. Strain was a way to speak of matters of the spirit of youth, of nationalistic striving, of complaints about modern life, even of the relation of the heart to love. Recall the passage from Allbutt, cited above, that read: "more haste, worse speed, is as true of heart work as of any other, and it seems clear that the hurried labour of the overtasked heart is not compensatory, but is mere blindness and bewilderment." Though the literal meaning concerns mechanics, the resonances speak of the life of feeling and love. Allbutt, after all, spoke of work done *con amore* as less straining than that done without love. Nineteenth-century medical discourse was in this sense too somaticized, with mechanistic denotations carrying moral and emotional connotations. It was a discourse geared to the aspirations of medical men as experts of the anatomized body. It was a mixed discourse, reflecting scientific, ethnic, and "psychological" values and concerns. It was, in short, a new discourse for new and perennial issues; and it preserved and refigured those issues. Finally, the discourse on strain was an engineering discourse for the expression of heroism; that is, the persistent striving for immortality. The figure of the heart as athlete was the centerpiece in this heroic struggle. But it was a refigured heart: medical perception, informed by engineering concerns, recast the heart as the center of the heroic spirit in the new mold of industrial production. The heart was a muscle that worked. Industrial society realized this conception of the heart.

Anxiety over limits was radically transformed with the end of overstrain of the heart. With a perception of cardiac reserve, exertion became a measure of power, even for the ill. Limits were tested and pushed back. In the emerging discourse on stress, exertion was no cause of heart disease; the new enemy was rest—and consciousness of the heart. Exertion now had diagnostic value, and in principle, power lay waiting in reserve to be tapped. Exertion as strain had been a limit, at best a tempering of character, but always fraught with danger. Exertion as stress, on the other hand, made possible the mining of hidden potential. Only with the disillusionment with modern life, hammered home by two world wars, did exhaustion again become prominent in the discourse on stress.

The perception of the heart under strain was indeed a mosaic. The dom-inant image was that of the wounded athlete, overcome and broken as a result of his efforts to win. Overstrain presented a dis-spiritedness of youth. It was a somaticized form of depression: *somaticized* meaning a psychological disorder felt in the heart. Conversely, it may be only the twentieth century that greatly succeeds in dis-incarnating human existence on a popular level, to the extent that we raise bodily complaints into the air of biopsychosocial systems. The demise of overstrain of the heart, Mackenzie's call to not mention the heart to the soldiers, the coming wave of psychological analysis, all was central to the breakdown of the fragile mosaic that held together the notions of the pre-anatomical heart, and the heart as a pump.

LIFE UNDER STRAIN

> It is dimly felt by society that the reign of bone and muscle is over, and that the reign of brain and nerve is taking its place.
> —T. Clifford Allbutt, "On Brain Forcing"

Nervous or mental strain ranked with overstrain of the heart as a cause for worry a century ago. Indeed the two were often seen as causally related, mental strain or shock leading to heart disease among other ailments. To reckon with these nineteenth-century understandings, we have to abandon our modern perceptions of the body for ones rather visceral. For despite the nineteenth century's mechanistic explanations of nervous and circulatory diseases, an older sense of the body as the flesh of existence remained. This older, more tangible understanding of the flesh existed as a palimpsest with the older script incompletely erased, upon which was printed texts according to Bichat, Darwin, and Helmholtz. At the end of the century, Allbutt noted that his contemporaries complained about their nerves as their grandfathers had about their livers. No mere substitute, this; what bound both complaints together was the extent to which they both referred to the digestive tract. In this constant reference to the gut we find the blend of the older, more fleshy sense of the body, and the newer sense, which is more abstract, mediated through instrumentation and anatomical knowledge.

In the 1890s, Herbert Spencer (1820–1903) in his *Autobiography* reflected on the physiological basis of his character. He began with this observation:

Consciousness forthwith ceases if the current of blood through the brain is stopped. The amounts and kinds of mental action constituting consciousness vary, other things equal, according to the rapidity, the quantity, and the quality, of the blood-supply; and all these vary according to the size and proportions of the sundry organs which unite in preparing blood from food, the organs which circulate it and the organs which purify it from waste products.[86]

This view for Spencer implied, and it was widely held, that nervousness resulted from autointoxication, or the accumulation of waste in the digestive system. Nerve force, which the brain generates, was stronger or weaker depending upon the quality of the blood, which in turn depended on the quality of digestion. Even those, such as Allbutt who disputed this view could nonetheless hold that "the volume of [nerve] force issuing from the brain is largely dependent . . . upon the power of the stomach and allied viscera."[87] The felt connection between eating and thinking, between excreting and thinking, was a vivid one. And this explanatory model makes logical the primary treatments of nervousness and mental strain: "Dr. Diet and Dr. Quiet," to name the famous "Mitchell cure" of the late nineteenth century. Whereas our approaches to these ailments involve medication and psychotherapy, in the late nineteenth century the focus was on building up the blood and providing rest (which promotes, of course, digestion).

Silas Weir Mitchell (1829–1914), the famous American neurologist, developed this cure and published two books with the telling titles *Blood and Fat, and How to Make Them* and *Wear and Tear, or Hints for the Overworked.*[88] The Mitchell cure, widely emulated, was a major treatment style prior to the advent of psychotherapy, which in many senses displaced it. Its essence lay in removing the patient (very often a woman diagnosed with hysteria) from the "harmful sympathy" of her family, bed rest, a diet to build fat (many of the patients were described as emaciated), massage and electrical stimulation of the muscles (passive exercise was held to be no strain on the nervous system), and avoidance of conversation about the symptoms. In light of Foucault's observations about the incitement to discourse on sexuality in the modern world, the Mitchell cure was in this regard premodern, since confessional speech was considered pathological—it encourages the patient to dwell on symptoms and to solicit sympathy. In this sense, the way to the heart of the matter was through the stomach.

Spencer related his character directly to his digestive and circulatory limitations, evoking in the context of mechanistic and thermodynamic concepts allusions to old humoral medicine, as in this passage: "Having all through life had an even flow of spirits, unvaried by either elation or depression, I have usually supposed that I tended towards neither sanguine nor despondent views. . . . I must be constitutionally sanguine."[89] Despite such allusions, the major focus of the discourse on mental strain lay in the notion that the body is a heat engine, with food coming to be seen as fuel for that engine. With a weak circulatory system, the brain has less energy; therefore, egoistic impulses dominate, the force necessary for sympathy being unavailable: "There has not been displayed by me as great an amount of altruistic feeling as was displayed by both [my parents]. One apparent reason is that the cerebral circulation has . . . been throughout my life rendered less vigorous than it should be."[90] What food fueled, as this and other passages suggest, is a character type compatible with nineteenth-century industrialism. Recall the terms in which the *Times* and surgeon Skey expressed their fears for youth: the capital of their health, the dangers of strain on the inner organs. Self-interest comes first; if energy remains, it may be spent as discretionary funds for "charity."

Spencer and others with similar limitations suffered from the ill-effects of overwork and fatigue throughout life. Enormously productive as he was, Spencer felt his restraints keenly and punctuated his work with fishing trips, visits to spas, etc., in the typical fashion. Anson Rabinbach's research into the topic of fatigue in the nineteenth century demonstrates the extent to which strain and fatigue had become enemies at that time: Fatigue "appears as an obstacle, the source of inhibition or resistance, imposed by physiology."[91] Fatigue became the enemy, replacing idleness as the principle vice of industrial society, and the numerous attempts to combat fatigue were in the service of liberating human energy:

In the 1860s and 1870s the metaphors of energy and exhaustion took on a mythic quality. The power attributed to the concept of energy in all spheres of life is the reverse side of the anxiety which haunted the image of exhaustion. The quantification of the body's energies, the isolation and determination of the economies of force in the physical and nervous systems, and ultimately the establishment of a system of equivalences between technological and physical energy all expressed a Promethean idolization of productive force.[92]

Nervous strain developed in this context. The overwork it denoted carried connotations of strength of material and thermodynamics.

Spencer's nervous breakdown occurred in 1855:

This place was Pen-y-Gwyrid—a place of sad memories to me; for it was here that my nervous system finally gave way.... [I]n the absence of all other guests at the hotel, I was alone; and thinking went on during meals and in the evening, as well as while I was at work and while I was walking.... One morning soon after beginning work, there commenced a sensation in my head—not pain, nor heat, nor fullness, nor tension, but simply a sensation, bearable enough but abnormal. The seriousness of the symptom was at once manifest to me. I put away my manuscript and sallied out, fishing-rod in hand, to a mountain tarn in the hills behind the hotel, in pursuance of a resolve to give myself a week's rest; thinking that would suffice.[93]

It did not, health eluding his grasp for the next 48 years. His drama typified that of many of his contemporaries. Where we would be inclined to a psychological explanation for Spencer's situation, he viewed his condition as overwork of the brain and nervous system (the constant thinking). He needed a rest. That Spencer was said to suffer also from overstrain of the heart makes him an exemplar of these conditions so common a century ago.

Did high-pressure life produce nervous strain and breakdown? Was it constant thinking and intellectual work that took its toll on the Spencers of the time? The question was hotly debated. In 1851, William Rathbone Greg, an industrialist/essayist and nonphysician, wrote: "We live sadly too fast. Our existence, in nearly all ranks, is a crush, a struggle, and a strife. Immensely as the field of lucrative employment has been enlarged, it is still too limited for the numbers that crowd into it.... [A]ll groan under the pressure. All who work at all are overworked."[94] He repeated the claim in 1875, in "Life at High Pressure." His lecture resounded widely, receiving comment in the *Lancet* from Samuel Wilks, a physician like Allbutt concerned with advancing the scientific status of medicine. "Are people suffering from overwork?" Wilks asked. "I for one should have no hesitation in saying, No; but, on the contrary, if both sexes be taken, I should say the opposite is nearer the truth, and that more persons are suffering from idleness than from excessive work."[95] Eleven years later, the less eminent physician Robson Roose, writing in the *Fortnightly Review*, seconded Greg's declaration and disputed Wilks's claim.[96] What Wilks and Roose shared, however, were the terms in which they disputed. "The human body is made for work, physical and mental," wrote Wilks, echoed by Roose in nearly identical phrasing. How much work was the point of the dispute, not that work was good or bad in itself. As with overstrain of the heart, so with nervous strain: Differences of opinion centered on the quantity of effort that produced overstrain and breakdown. The engineering perspective is thus embedded in the debate as an undiscussed premise.

Engineering and energy questions underlay much of the concern over nervous and mental strain as it emerged in the quintessential disease of nerve weakness—neurasthenia. First described by the American George Beard in 1869, neurasthenia was widely diagnosed throughout the Western world until the 1920s. (In parts of the Orient, with its different social and medical context, it remains a prevalent diagnosis.) At first it was a disease of the "better classes," but later became recognized throughout society. It was a physical ailment, the result of insufficient nerve force. The causes of the insufficiency were debated, Americans tending to blame climate and progress, Europeans favoring heredity.[97] Treatment proved more uniform: Mitchell's rest cure, electricity, pilgrimages to spas, and the use of hypnosis by Charcot and others.

Beneath the anxiety over neurasthenia was the notion that nervous energy was a scarce commodity and must be carefully husbanded. Rest and diet provided the cure because the overworked and neurasthenic were depleted of their energy. A vast array of symptoms from hay fever to insanity resulted from overdraft of nerve force. As in the discourse on overstrain of the heart, metaphors from commerce mingled freely with those from engineering, reflecting and reinforcing the social organization of work.

In fact, aside from generalizations concerning nerve force and exhaustion, engineering considerations played a subsidiary role to economic metaphors. There was of course the question of strength of material, the notion that neurasthenics had smaller reserves of energy, but such discussions were, by their nature, unspecific. The major differentiation between nerve and heart overstrain was that with the former no instrumentation could detect it. The measurement of fatigue did develop; Rabinbach's study shows the place of such measures in the science of labor. Tests of fatigue were applied to the diagnosis of neurasthenia, and Allbutt found them satisfactory.[98] Fatigability aside, there was no stethoscope to hear the murmurs of tiredness or the brain's work.

The economic metaphors used in the discourse on neurasthenia expressed and reinforced the image of the body as made for work, an image which guided medical treatment. Nervous strain or neurasthenia was a consequence not simply of overwork but of the kind of work more and more common in civilized societies. Beard capitalized on this point in *American Nervousness*. While not all agreed with him that Westerners had become more delicate or refined in nervous structure, or that the speed and complexity of life had increased nervous disorders, it was held that the nature of life was changing radically. Allbutt, no alarmist, saw society progressing from handwork to brain work and from "childhood" to "maturity." Economic and social progress was making a decisive difference in the West. The Enlightenment echoed in his analysis of (for him so-called) modern nervousness:

The forces of social order are no longer external to us. . . . [I]nternal bonds, forces of social cohesion, of mutual help and brotherhood, are drawing us together within ourselves, and are filling the place of external authority as, on the death of the father, a family learns to govern itself in mutual dependence, is happily to be seen also; but meanwhile, in this state of transition, the repulsions and discontents of individuals and the absence of outward control and support will result here and there in anarchy of many kinds, in bewilderments, blight and desolations.[99]

More commonly, physicians attributed modern nervousness to the pace of life. Allbutt's comments, however, probe the issue deeper than did the complaints over speed. External authority—the "father"—had died, leaving the "family" to fend for itself. It was this loss of paternal authority, this transition between medieval and modern, between childhood and maturity, that provided the context for strain. Strain expressed that loss, which took its toll on the heart and the nerves. In an age in which the figure of the orphan was often portrayed, as in Dickens, as the cultural hero, grief over the death of the father, the anxiety of not having someone to tell you what to do, found expression in the diseases of overstrain. Freud's anthropological fairy tale in *Totem and Taboo* gave voice to an anxiety and an explanatory myth of *his* day, not of the dim beginnings of humankind. To be modern is to have lost the "father." Strain results from the striving that this loss and freedom makes possible. It results from the attempt to act heroically in an industrializing world. While we hear today that society is patriarchial, in a profound sense that is simply not true. Yes, biological males predominate in positions of power, but they are not patriarchs. They engender nothing. The psychological and social complaint has been, at least since the time of Allbutt and Freud, that the father is absent. Father as a figure stands for law, distance, kingship, and husbandry: God the Father, Zeus, Agamemnon, Odysseus. Allbutt observed that the death of the father meant that individuals must be self-governing. It also meant that the traditions governing warfare and ambition had crumbled. World War I took place on no-father's land, despite the appeals of propagandists. The ages of strain and stress are fatherless ages.[100]

STRAIN: METAPHOR FOR THE WILL

The discourse on strain in the nineteenth century gave voice to a will to progress economically, socially, and scientifically. This discourse also expresses the anguish and anxiety over the losses that such changes entail. The root metaphor of the discourse on strain is *homo faber*: the heart, the nerves, the body, the man are made for work. How much work, now as then, remains the question, but the tradition that this discourse initiated has never questioned its base assumption.

Strain was superceded by *stress* in the early twentieth century when depletion no longer appeared as the primary danger. Rather, as we have seen, excessive energy and not entropy became the danger; explosion and not heat death the fear. The splitting of the flesh, that is, our alienation from our physical selves, occurred with the emergence of psychoanalysis and its kin (which institutionalized the split). The splitting of the flesh replaced the Victorian "steam engine" perception of the relations between stomach, heart, and brain. With the age of stress, systems thinking has sought to fuse together those products of fission to enable us to cope with energy. Systems thinking raises again the problem of exhaustion brought on by a century of technologically produced destruction.

But the question that presents itself at this juncture concerns what preceded the emergence of the discourse on strain? Can we envision a world without strain or stress? How do we even begin to ask such questions? Do we say: "See, in the eighteenth century, seventeenth, fifth century, they too had their stresses. They coped poorly or well, but they had different social mechanisms and ways of speaking." But if we decline to import our certainties to a past that did not share them, decline to say what they "really meant" but were too ignorant to say, if we acknowledge that the discourse on strain was part of a rupture with the past, as the Victorians themselves acknowledged, then how do we even begin to question the past to find some domain that permits a common ground to acknowledge our common humanity? An overlap of horizons is of vital necessity for us. Our ancestors' ways of meeting what have become for us stresses—that modern form of grief—can give us reflective room to reconsider our certainties and the enslavement that these certainties entail. Call it a desire for a Renaissance. Like Petrarch we can dialogue and correspond with the dead, not for antiquarian purposes, but to address our burdens and cares and sufferings.

To peer further back, to a time before strain, it would help to find a missing link, a transitional moment when the new metaphors replaced something older. John Charles Bucknill and Daniel Tuke, Victorian mad-doctors, discussed briefly the fate of Hugh Miller in their *Manual of Psychological Medicine* (1858). The reference came in a chapter devoted to "Modern Civilization in Its Bearing upon Insanity," a topic that generated much debate last century. Miller was a commoner of the laboring class who came to distinguish himself as a geologist. His major work was *The Old Red Sandstone* (1857), a text devoted to the geological features of an area of Britain. Miller began his text with "advise to young working-men, desirous of bettering their circumstances."[101] He advised them to "seek [happiness] in what is termed study," since "society . . . is in a state of continual flux: some in the upper classes are from time to time going down, and some of you . . . mounting to their places." He noted that "you are jealous of the upper classes. . . . Do not let them get ahead of you in intelligence." Study was the key, since knowledge is power. Such a strategy of self-help led, according to Bucknill and Tuke, to Miller's downfall:

The fatal effects of an overworked brain would not have occurred, had he not substituted head-work for manual labour. "He has not wrought out his way," writes one who knew him well, "from the stone-mason's quarry to so distinguished a position in science and literature, without a life of incessant and wearing mental toil. In fact, he had worked much too hard and constantly; and although a man of sturdy physique, his brain was unable to stand *the stress of his will, and the strain of his perseverance.*"[102]

Miller went insane and killed himself, but the metaphor was created. *Stress* and *strain*, then being defined by Rankine for engineering, were simultaneously being used for a discourse on the will, as a substitute for a discourse on the will, transposing that discourse into the physicalistic language of the anatomized body and of engineering. *Stress* and *strain* in the quotation above refer to the feeling of effort that marks deliberations and actions of the will. The engineering denotations of the terms, given the nature of engineering projects, allowed for the volitional connotations to remain: Engineering expresses the human will. The metaphors sound so natural that by century's end, we find William James using engineering terms to describe the actions of the will and William Osler in the early twentieth century sliding between engineering and moral meanings of strain. In an essay on angina pectoris, for instance, Osler located the pathophysiology in part in "cold, emotion, toxic agents interfering with the orderly action of the peripheral mechanism, increase the tension in the pump walls or in the larger central mains, causing strain, and a type of abnormal contraction enough to excite in the involuntary muscles painful afferent stimuli." Equally it was "the high-pressure life of modern days" that had increased this disease among the robust men of the better classes: "It is not the delicate neurotic person who is prone to angina, but the robust, the vigorous in mind and body, the keen and ambitious man, the indicator of whose engines is always at 'full speed ahead.' "[103] The explanatory model, with the body as a heat engine made for work, grounded the usages of *strain* in both the social and hydrostatic sense, making the metaphor natural to the age. It remains natural to us.

Strain was, then, a constellation of the will, in an age when old certainties were dying like fathers of families. The orphans who remained, robust or delicate, or robust/delicate, struggled to climb the social ladder in a society in flux; they felt overworked, sick at heart, exhausted, lost.

To look backward, to dialogue with our pre-strain ancestors, we have to hear the unnaturalness of the metaphor, attend to its audacity, and learn to hear of effort, ambition, and will in a society that was not undergoing so noticeable or problematic a mutation from medieval to modern times. What was the world like before we became subjected to strains and stresses?

NOTES

1. George Robinson, *Contributions to the Physiology and Pathology of the Circulation of the Blood* (London: Longman, Brown, Green, Longmans & Roberts, 1857), p. 123.

2. F. C. Skey, letter to the *Times* (London), October 10, 1867, p. 9. For the echo, see Adolphe Abrahams, "Physiology of violent exercise in relation to the possibility of strain," *Lancet*, 1928, no. 1, 429–35.

3. Skey, letter to the *Times*, p. 9.

4. Ibid.

5. Robert Farquharson, "The influence of athletic sports on health," *Lancet*, 1870, no. 2, 370.

6. "Broad Blue," letter to the *Times*, (London), October 14, 1867, p. 10.

7. *Times* (London), October 15, 1867, p. 6.

8. Ibid.

9. The ideological framework of this controversy is captured by the following: "From the 1860s there was a new cult of masculinity in the public schools. Thomas Arnold's emphasis on spiritual autonomy and intellectual maturity was increasingly replaced by a new stress on physical characteristics, on the demonstration of pure willpower. Sport . . . took on many of the functions of the rites of passage once reserved to the Latin language, and enshrined the separation of boys from the world of women. The model of the early public school was the monastery. The model of the later public school was definitely military. While women were increasingly associated with weakness and emotion, by 1860 men no longer dared embrace in public or shed tears. . . . And with the new stress on games and militaristic training came undoubted echoes of imperialism and also of race consciousness; the notion that the upper middle classes were a race apart with separate physical possibilities and powers." Jeffrey Weeks, *Sex, Politics, and Society* (New York: Longman, 1981), p. 40.

10. F. C. Skey, letter to the *Times*, October 21, 1867, p. 10.

11. Bruce Haley, *The Healthy Body and Victorian Culture* (Cambridge: Harvard University Press, 1978), p. 261.

12. Ibid., p. 261.

13. For example, the *Lancet* (1869, "Dilatation . . . in a pedestrian," *Lancet*, 1869,

no. 2, 442) reported a case of "Dilatation of right side of the heart in a pedestrian," which was an object lesson against "severe training, and especially running." The patient, aged 50, was a "pedestrian" and "on one occasion he had walked a thousand miles in a thousand consecutive hours."

14. Farquharson, "The influence of athletic sports," p. 371.

15. "The Oxford and Cambridge Boat Race," *Lancet*, 1873, no. 1, 452–53, reviewing Morgan, *University Oars* (1869).

16. Benjamin Disraeli, *The Works of Benjamin Disraeli, Earl of Beaconsfield; Embracing Novels, Romances, Plays, Poems, Biography, Short Stories, and Great Speeches*, Vol. 12: *Coningsby* (London and New York: M. W. Dunne, 1904–1905), pp. 93–94.

17. Ibid., 210.

18. George Gissing, "Life at high pressure," in *Human Odds and Ends: Stories and Sketches* (London: Lawrence & Bullen, 1898), pp. 270–76.

19. Walter Houghton, *The Victorian Frame of Mind, 1830–1870* (New Haven: Yale University Press, 1957), pp. 58–59.

20. Suzanne Nalbantian, *The Symbol of the Soul from Holderlin to Yeats* (New York: Columbia University Press, 1977).

21. Ruskin, "Pre-Raphaelitism," quoted in Houghton, p. 187.

22. See M. Jeanne Peterson, *The Medical Profession in Mid-Victorian London* (Berkeley: University of California Press, 1978), for a study of the social status of medicine and its transformations during this period.

23. Houghton, p. 45.

24. Matthew Arnold, "The Scholar Gypsy," *Poetical Works of Matthew Arnold* (London: Macmillan, 1891). See also J. H. van den Berg, *Divided Existence and Complex Society* (Pittsburgh: Duquesne University Press, 1974).

25. Stephen Timoshenko, *History of Strength of Materials* (New York: McGraw-Hill, 1953), p. 42.

26. R. A. Buchanan, "Gentlemen engineers: The making of a profession," *Victorian Studies* 26, no. 4 (1983), 411.

27. Dale H. Porter and Gloria C. Clifton, "Patronage, professional values, and Victorian public works: Engineering and contracting the Thames Embankment," *Victorian Studies* 31, no. 3 (1988), 330.

28. Timoshenko, *History of Strength of Materials*, p. 123.

29. William J. M. Rankine, *Miscellaneous Scientific Papers* (1881), p. 68, quoted in the *Oxford English Dictionary*.

30. Ibid, p. 120.

31. Isaac Todhunter, *A History of the Theory of Elasticity and of the Strength of Materials*, ed. Karl Pearson (1886; reprint, New York: Dover, 1960), Vol. 2, Part I, p. 316.

32. Ibid, Part I, p. 316.

33. Ibid, Part II, p. 447.

34. "Elasticity and bearing properties of cast iron," *Lancet*, 1831–32, no. 2, 187.

35. "Lord Normanby's Drainage Bill," *Lancet*, 1840–41, no. 2, 17.

36. See Peterson, p. 173. Allbutt in 1888 "urged that the study of mathematics and physics was one of the chief needs in the education of young physicians, who proposed to devote themselves to original research." (Report of discussion following C. S. Roy and J. G. Adami, "Remarks of failure of the heart from overstrain," *British Medical Journal*, 1888, ii, no. 1326.)

Another chapter in the development of the engineering approach in medicine belongs to the story of medical technology. Muirhead in 1869 "used a Thompson siphon recorder, devised by William Thompson to record signals passing through the Atlantic cable, which had been laid in 1866. Muirhead himself became a successful telegraph engineer," writes J. Burnett ("The origins of the electrocardiograph as a clinical instrument," in W. F. Bynum, C. Lawrence, and V. Nutton, eds., *The Emergence of Modern Cardiology, Medical History*, Supplement No. 5 (London: Wellcome Institute for the History of Medicine, 1985), p. 60). The sphygmograph of Marey (1860), the sphygmomanometer of von Basch (1876), and other instruments further drew the body into the orbit of technical investigation. This trend gathered momentum as the century ended.

37. Robert Hooke, *De potentia restitutiva* (1678), quoted in Todhunter, *A History of the Theory of Elasticity*, Vol. 1, p. 5.

38. Bevan wrote, "A substance like bone, so universally abounding, possessing such great strength, and considerable flexibility, ought to be restored to its proper place in the scale of bodies, applicable to so many purposes in the arts." *On the Strength of Bone*, quoted in Todhunter, *A History of the Theory of Elasticity*, Vol. I, p. 190.

39. Robinson, *Contributions to the Physiology*, p. 190.

40. John Bishop, "On the causes, pathology, and treatment of deformities in the human body," *Lancet*, 1846, no. 1, 122–25, 323–26; Todhunter, *A History of the Theory of Elasticity*, Vol. 1, p. 712.

41. See Todhunter, *A History of the Theory of Elasticity*, Vol. 2, Part I, p. 577.

42. Michel Foucault, *The Birth of the Clinic*, trans. A. M. Sheridan Smith (New York: Vintage Books, 1975).

43. For a discussion of readiness to perceive, see Ludwig Fleck, *The Genesis and Development of a Scientific Fact* (Chicago: University of Chicago Press, 1979). I thank Jean Robert for teaching me about Fleck and his significance for a history of the body. See also William James, *Principles of Psychology*, Vol. 1 (1890; reprint, New York: Dover, 1950), p. 439, for the similar concept of "preperception."

44. Peterson, *The Medical Profession*, p. 173.

45. "The lectures of Professor Matteucci," *Lancet*, 1847, no. 1, 624. This dispute over the appropriateness of lectures on mechanics in a medical journal raises an interesting point in this history of the engineering mentality and its spread. Jean Robert has indicated to me that in order to understand the construction of modern certainties, we must look not only to scientific popularizers, such as Helmholtz and Huxley, but also to the active reception of the nonscientific "public." The *Lancet* in this instance is a good place to look, since although it was a medical journal, medicine in Britain had not yet insulated itself from the popular mind with scientific explications. George Beard described how the *Lancet* was on sale at newsstands next to more popular magazines. The *Times* in the Skey controversy provides an even more direct example of the constitution of the engineering mentality "from below" as it were. Robert writes: "(a) the 'science of the new age' (die Wiessenschaft der Neuzeit: a very common expression around 1860 . . .) casts a new kind of shadow; (b) the ground that receives that shadow is itself active in a very peculiar fashion" (personal communication, 1990). I think that the loss of the familiar, loss of custom, loss of connections with the knowledge that comes from tact and taste, loss of belief in orally transmitted knowledge, created a mental void and an anxious hunger for guidance

by the new experts. That this hunger existed I infer; that it exists now is evident, especially in matters concerning birth, sexuality, illness, death, learning, etc.

46. Erwin Ackerknecht, *A Short History of Medicine*, rev. ed. (Baltimore: Johns Hopkins University Press, 1982), p. 170.

47. T. Clifford Allbutt, "Over-stress of the heart," in T. C. Allbutt and H. D. Rolleston, eds., *A System of Medicine*, 2nd ed., Vol. 6: *Diseases of the Heart and Blood-Vessels* (London: Macmillan, 1909), p. 212.

48. C. Lawrence, "Moderns and ancients: The 'new cardiology' in Britain 1880–1930," in Bynum et al., eds., *The Emergence of Modern Cardiology*, p. 4.

49. Anson Rabinbach, "The european science of work: The economy of the body at the end of the nineteenth century," in S. L. Kaplan and C. J. Koepp, eds., *Work in France: Representations, Meaning, Organization, and Practice*, (Ithaca, NY: Cornell University Press, 1986), p. 479. See also Rabinbach, *The Human Motor: Energy, Fatigue, and the Origins of Modernity* (New York: Basic Books, 1990).

50. Greg Myers, "Nineteenth century popularization of thermodynamics and the rhetoric of social prophecy," *Victorian Studies* 29, no. 1 (1985), 35–66.

51. William Dampier, *A History of Science* (Cambridge: Cambridge University Press, 1971), p. 262.

52. T. Clifford Allbutt, "On the hypodermic use of morphia in diseases of the heart and great vessels," excerpted in *Retrospect of Practical Medicine and Surgery* 61 (July 1870), 61.

53. Samuel Haughton, "The relation of food to work done by the body, and its bearing upon medical practice," *Lancet*, 1868, no. 2, 641–51.

54. Samuel Haughton, "On the mechanical work done by the heart," *Dublin Quarterly Journal of Medical Science* 49, (1870), 74–85. (see reply by Andrew Buchanan, "On the force of the human heart," *Lancet*, 1870, no. 2, 665–66); and "On the action of the human heart," *Retrospect of Practical Medicine and Surgery* 64 (January 1872), 66–70.

55. Haughton, "On the action of the human heart," p. 70.

56. Haughton, "The relation of food to work," 647. See also W. R. Lee, "Occupational medicine," in *Medicine and Science in the 1860s* (London: Wellcome Institute of the History of Medicine, 1968), pp. 151–81.

57. Haughton, "The relation of food to work," p. 645.

58. J. Forbes, *Laennec's Diseases of the Chest* (1834). See also, for example, "Aetiology of diseases of the heart," *Lancet*, 1845, no. 2, 596. In the United States, Bowditch described a case of "hypertrophy of the heart, with aortic valvular disease" in 1859. He urged "physicians to caution youths not to overexert themselves in boat-racing, to which the present tendency of fashion seems to lead. Dr. Bowditch believed that in these cases, owing to the inordinate action of the heart, a partial rupture of the valves takes place. This causes the immediate dyspnoea and palpitation, and gradual hypertrophy." H. I. Bowditch, "Diseases of the heart in consequence of violent exertion in running," *Boston Medical and Surgical Journal* 59 (1858–59), 456.

59. George B. Wood, *A Treatise on the Practice of Medicine*, 3rd. ed. (Philadelphia: Lippincott, Grambo & Co., 1852), Vol. 2, p. 157.

60. Joel D. Howell, " 'Soldier's heart': The redefinition of heart disease and specialty formation in early twentieth-century Great Britain," in *The Emergence of Modern Cardiology*, p. 35.

61. Edward H. Clarke, "Practical medicine," in E. H. Clarke, H. J. Bigelow, S. D.

Gross, et al., eds., *A Century of American Medicine*, (1876; reprint, New York: Burt Franklin, 1971), p. 34.

62. Jacob M. DaCosta, "On irritable heart: A clinical study of a form of functional cardiac disorder and its consequences," *American Journal of the Medical Sciences* (1871), 19.

63. Jacob M. DaCosta, *On Strain and Overaction of the Heart* (Washington, DC: Smithsonian Institution, 1874), p. 2.

64. J. B. Treadwell, "Observations upon overwork and strain of the heart," *Boston Medical and Surgical Journal* 10 (1873), 157–60; 179–84.

65. Douglas Guthrie, *A History of Medicine* (Philadelphia: Lippincott, 1946), p. 366. See also Humphrey Davy Rolleston, *The Right Honorable Sir Thomas Clifford Allbutt: A Memoir* (London: Macmillan, 1929).

66. T. Clifford Allbutt, "The effect of overwork and strain on the heart and great blood-vessels," *St. George's Hospital Reports* 5 (1870), 23–53, excerpted in *Retrospect of Practical Medicine and Surgery* 64 (January 1872), 73.

67. Ibid., pp. 72–78.

68. Ibid., p. 75.

69. Ibid., p. 78.

70. In Haughton quotation above, p. 121, and in the letter of "Broad Blue" to the *Times*, quoted above, p. 112.

71. Allbutt, "The effect of overwork," p. 76.

72. For example, Haughton, "On action of the human heart," Allbutt, "The effect of overwork"; DaCosta, "On irritable heart," and Treadwell, "Observations upon overwork."

73. J. Milner Fothergill, "Strain in its relation to the circulatory organs," *British Medical Journal*, 1873, no. i, 182.

74. "Overstrain of the heart and aorta," *British Medical Journal*, 1873, no. i, 299–301.

75. "Heart disease from over-exertion," *Medical News* 31 (1873), 98–99.

76. "Overstrain of the heart and aorta," p. 299.

77. Ibid., p. 300.

78. Ibid.

79. Ibid.

80. The *Medical News* ("Heart disease from over-exertion,"), reporting Allbutt's 1873 lecture, urged American physicians to consider the topic, because athletics were causing injuries. Treadwell and DaCosta wrote on heart-strain, the former deriving evidence from research done while a member of the Boston Board of Pension Surgeons, and the latter from his wartime experience.

81. DaCosta, "Observations upon overwork," pp. 2–3.

82. George William Balfour, *Clinical Lectures on Diseases of the Heart* (Philadelphia: Lindsay & Blakiston, 1876), p. 72.

83. C. S. Roy and J. G. Adami, "Remarks on failure of the heart from overstrain," *British Medical Journal* 1888, no. ii, 1324.

84. Benjamin Ward Richardson, "On physical disease from mental strain," *Journal of Mental Science* 15 (October 1869), 351.

85. Ibid., p. 362.

86. Herbert Spencer, *An Autobiography* (New York: D. Appleton, 1904), Vol. II, pp. 492–93.

87. T. Clifford Allbutt, "On brain forcing," *Brain* 1, no. 1 (1878), 67.

88. Silas Weir Mitchell, *Blood and Fat, and How to Make Them* (Philadelphia: J. B. Lippincott, 1877), and *Wear and Tear, or Hints for the Overworked* (Philadelphia: J. B. Lippincott, 1887).

89. Spencer, Vol. I, p. 554.

90. Ibid., Vol. II, p. 499.

91. Anson Rabinbach, "The body without fatigue: A nineteenth-century utopia," in *Political Symbolism in Modern Europe: Essays in Honor of George L. Mosse*, eds. S. Drescher, D. Sabean, and A. Sharlin (New Brunswick, NJ: Rutgers University Press, 1982), p. 44.

92. Ibid., p. 57.

93. Spencer, *An Autobiography*, Vol. I, pp. 543–44.

94. William Rathbone Greg, "England as it is," in *Essays on Political and Social Science* (London: Longman, Brown, Green, and Longmans, 1853), Vol. I, pp. 324–25.

95. Wilks, "On overwork," *Lancet*, 1875, no. 1, 886.

96. Robson Roose, "The wear and tear of London life," *Fortnightly Review* 39 (Jan.–June 1886), 200–201.

97. George Drinka, *The Birth of Neurosis: Myth, Malady, and the Victorians* (New York: Simon & Schuster, 1984).

98. T. Clifford Allbutt, "On neurasthenia," in *System of Medicine*, 2nd ed., eds. Clifford Allbutt and Humphry Davy Rolleston, Vol. 8: *Diseases of the Brain and Mental Disease* (London: Macmillan, 1910), pp. 727–791.

99. Allbutt, "Nervous diseases and modern life," *Contemporary Review* 67 (Jan.–June 1895), 224–25.

100. Michael LaValle, *Facing the Mirror: Narcissism and the Psychological Discovery of Faith*, Ph.D. dissertation (Irving: University of Dallas, 1986). As LaValle points out, fatherless society does not produce self-governance but rather a "culture of narcissism," to use Lasch's phrase: "No internalized voice gives permission to focus one's energies on a concentrated task" (p. 217).

101. Hugh Miller, *The Old Red Sandstone* (1857; reprint, New York: Arno, 1978), p. 1.

102. John Charles Bucknill and Daniel Tuke, *Manual of Psychological Medicine* (Philadelphia: Blanchard & Lea, 1858), p. 49. Emphasis added.

103. William Osler, "On angina pectoris," *Lancet*, 1910, no. 1, 843, 697, and 839.

6

Before Engineered Grief

Engineered grief did not exist prior to the nineteenth century. We find none of the conditions for its appearance, which depended upon the confluence of several factors: industrial development, with its social displacements and transformations of the lifeworld; the engineering mentality; the anatomical gaze, making the body's interiority visible and identical to nonliving matter; the harnessing of the will for work, progress, success; the lively awareness of living in a time of transition, during which the external supports of authority and tradition were in decline. The common denominator in all of those factors is grief over unresolved losses.

Signaling the great rupture which rendered experienceable such grief was the beginning of what Foucault calls biopower. Biopower is the entrance into the political arena of those areas of human nature which had hitherto been beyond the scope of political power. The entry of "life" into political discourse coincided with a definition of life as "the sum of the forces that resist death" (to cite Bichat's famous formula). In the nineteenth century, the new science of biology conceived life as a dynamic power, as essentially a phenomenon of development and force. The history of engineered grief that we have surveyed suggests that the ground of the notions of strain and stress is life as a force, and further, the ground is a life-force understood as a manifestation of the will.[1] As is abundantly evident from the previous chapters, stress and strain are phenomena of force, the absence of which is death. What began in the nineteenth century as strain resulting from life at high pressure has become, in our own day, the stress of trying to be pure energy. The generator of this power is the grief of adapting without mourning

to the accelerating series of losses of the familiar that is the distinctive feature
of modernity. The beginnings of stress, then, coincide with the beginnings
of speculation and research into life as a force against death, which came into
being around 1800. Let us say that stress is a far-flung child of the French
Revolution.

We cannot simply say that the successive discourses on strain, anxiety, and
stress displaced an earlier moral discourse, although to a degree that is ac-
curate. But because the older moral discourse (of the will) did not belong
to a world of transition from the medieval to the modern—from a body of
the flesh to that of energy—the newer formulations of the meaning of suffering of loss did not play the same role the older discourse had. The world
of high pressure, of hurry and change, could not sustain the older discourse
and its conceptual foundations; it had no place for them. That language made
less and less sense as the modern age built up a head of steam. But if a series
of discourses of force superceded a medical-moral discourse, what was that
older discourse? Can we, following the path we have traced, find any family
resemblance between nineteenth-century strain and whatever preceded it as
a source of anxiety about civilized life? We will need to prepare the ground
for that sketch.

This chapter first gives an overview of the incipient changes in the science
of strength of material. The purpose of this overview is to determine when
modern building materials and methods were introduced. This determination
will give us the earliest possible date at which an engineering mentality can
be said to have been forming, for the extension of engineering considerations
and the use of metaphors from engineering were impossible without engineered things and practices already in existence. Second, we examine the
eighteenth century's developing conceptions of the body and of matter, in
order to see how the flesh was being imagined anew. This part of the discussion will reveal how images of the body, which are taken for granted
today and through which we perceive ourselves as under stress, were appearing for the first time in Western thought. We shall find that these images
are tied to specific practices, especially those that promote our willing sub-
jection to technological medicine. Third, we consider the transformations of
the sense of time and luxury that presaged the hurry of the coming age. With
that, we will have beheld the advent of the age of strain and stress. But it is
not my sole intention to show that the eighteenth century prepared the soil
for the seeds of stress. More important, we can view clearly the essentially
foreign concerns of this age before stress, how its complaints and worries,
how its heart and will could find expression, and people reckon with their
lives, without either stress or coping.

STRENGTH OF MATERIALS

Before it could appear in medicine, the engineering mentality had to come
into being. Its beginnings as a science date from Galileo's studies published

in 1638. Galileo laid the mathematical foundation for the science of the strength of materials with investigations into cantilever beams and related problems of weight-bearing loads. Among his observations were those dealing with size and weight. Timoshenko summarizes the thesis on the limits of size: "beams become weaker with increase in dimensions and finally, when they are large, they may fail under the action of their weight alone."[2]

Galileo concluded:

You can plainly see the impossibility of increasing the size of structures to vast dimensions either in art or in nature; likewise the impossibility of building ships, palaces, or temples of enormous size in such a way that their oars, yards, beams, iron-bolts, and, in short, all their other parts would hold together.[3]

In a related conclusion, Galileo

discusses the strength of hollow beams and states that such beams 'are employed in art—and still more often in nature—in a thousand operations for the purpose of greatly increasing strength without adding to weight....' Comparing a hollow cylinder with a solid one of the same cross-sectional area, Galileo observes that their absolute strengths are the same.[4]

These—shall we call them asides?—while they did not make an immediate difference to engineering or architecture, suggest that at its very beginning, the engineering mentality had the intuition that materiality in the sense of weight and heft is not directly related to strength. It seems that the engineering mentality, along with the mathematical theory (that only much later was applied by engineers) inspired the production of "matterless matter"[5] and the gravity-defying designs of our age. In the origins of the engineering mentality, questions about force, the limits of strength, and the possibility of increasing strength were all raised.

While theoretical advances relating to strength of material and elasticity were made in the seventeenth century, notably by Robert Hooke (1620–1684), only in the eighteenth century did the scientific method take root in engineering. France led the way with the establishment of technical training schools, especially the Ecole des Ponts et Chaussees (1747) and the Ecole Polytechnique (1795). In the latter, the apprentice system was discarded for a formal education system beginning with two years instruction in the basic sciences, followed by applied courses. The invention of devices to test the strength of materials also appeared in the mid-eighteenth century: Lodoli and Poleni tested building materials with instruments that measured the breaking point; Musschenbroeck experimented with such machines; and in 1770 the engineer Gauthey utilized a stress-testing machine for the selection of materials for the reconstruction of Sainte-Geneviève (later the Pantheon) in Paris. Soufflet, the architect who consulted Gauthey (who taught at the

Ecole des Ponts et Chaussees), broke with the traditional way of supporting a dome, abandoning "massive abutment-towers or bastions within the body of the church at the four corners of the crossing."[6] Soufflet decided to "support the great arches beneath the dome on four clusters of columns sufficient to take the vertical load. . . . In channels within the joints of the masonry he proposed, where necessary, to bury cages of wrought iron bars, linked together to form virtually a system for open-framed girders." Gauthey's use of a testing machine "was the first time that a testing machine . . . provide[d] information required in the design and erection of an actual building." Tradition-minded architects were scandalized by the design, which "had been checked only by Gauthey's arguments backed by the results of the tests."[7] Cracks did appear, and Jean Rondelet, the architect who completed the building after Soufflet's death, had to thicken the piers. But the testing machine was copied and improved upon, making the reconstruction of Sainte Geneviève an important moment in the appearance of the engineering mentality.[8]

Soufflet's use of wrought iron came from a late-eighteenth-century Parisian innovation. Wrought iron, cast iron, and later cement and steel were materials that came to embody the new engineering mentality. While there are no simple linear relations among theory, practice, and available materials, between 1750 and 1850 all three assumed their modern forms. For instance, iron and steel production expanded:

The period from 1750 to 1850 was marked by fundamental changes in the iron industry. Coke and coal were substituted for charcoal as fuel. Water was replaced by steam as a motive-power. Cast iron, which hitherto had constituted less than 5 percent of furnace-production, was produced in increasing quantities for machinery and constructional purposes. Production of wrought iron or bar iron also increased considerably after Henry Cort's invention of puddling. . . . A more homogeneous steel was produced by the crucible process invented by Benjamin Huntsman.[9]

Wrought iron, increasingly in demand, was the most widely used construction metal for most of the nineteenth century, used notably for the Crystal Palace (1851) and the Eiffel Tower (1889). A new process for making steel—and for making it cheaply—was developed in the 1850s by William Kelly and Henry Bessemer. The steel industry then grew rapidly, and "the world's annual output of steel increased from a little more than half a million tons in 1870 to almost 28 million tons in 1900."[10] The first patent for concrete was taken out by Joseph Aspdin in 1824, although only after 1850 did it come into wide use. By 1900 reinforced concrete was well established in engineering practice.

The appearance of new material had an impact on construction. By 1800, iron was being used in bridge and building construction in a structural way. With Elisha Graves Otis's invention of the elevator, the way was cleared for tall buildings (those more than five stories). Hamilton explains the problem with such buildings and the solution found in the 1880s:

> To support the weight of a lofty building on walls of brickwork they would have to be immensely thick in the lower stories and thus occupy a large amount of space. Even with the weight of the interior carried by cast iron columns, a thick, very lofty, external wall capable of carrying its own weight could spare only a limited area for window-openings. When, therefore, William Le Baron Jenny (1832–1907) was commissioned in 1883 by the Home Insurance Company to build for them at Chicago a 10-story block of offices . . . he used in the external walls cast iron columns encased in brickwork. The six lower floors were carried by wrought iron beams, but for the work above that level he used beams of Bessemer steel. This was possibly the first use of that material in quantity in an important building.[11]

When steel replaced iron in construction, walls were freed from load-bearing duties, enabling the erection of skyscrapers, so commonplace as the site of psychological and social stress.

The theory of strength of materials developed alongside the changes in material and building design. Only in the late nineteenth century did the three come together, when engineering became a profession. By that time there existed a mathematics of strength of materials; devices and techniques to test them; new materials whose application to bridges, railroads, machinery, and buildings required more precise knowledge of elastic limits; technical training for engineers; and employment for engineers by industry and government. Thus, the fundamental question of how much load can the material carry had a complex network within which to flourish. This review of the history of the topic indicates that the engineering mentality began in the area of building construction some 50–75 years before its application in medicine. It is interesting to discover that first matter became subjected to this mentality, then the human body and mind. It is not surprising, however, because we discover who we are through the things that we use. Self-discovery is an act mediated by the world in which we live; it is not an act, in the first instance, of turning away from the world into a pure interiority, a la Descartes. "I am myself and my circumstances," as Ortega y Gasset wrote, and I come to know myself via my circumstances first.[12]

THE ATOMIZATION OF MATTER

At the same time that engineering testing machines and modern building materials began to be used, matter was subjected to another type of scrutiny that greatly affected subsequent medical perception of the body. The science of chemistry began, examining matter in such a way as to break it down into atoms. Ackerknecht summarizes the results:

> In 1757 carbon dioxide was rediscovered by Joseph Black of Glasgow. In 1766 Cavendish discovered hydrogen, and six years later Rutherford discovered nitrogen.

Oxygen was discovered by Schule in 1772 and by Priestley in 1774, although its true nature was realized only by Lavoisier in 1775.... In 1780, together with the astronomer Laplace, [Lavoisier] showed that in respiration the same amount of oxygen is used, and the same amount of heat is produced, as in the burning of coal.... In 1789 he worked with Seguin to measure the changing oxygen intake during work, eating, and rest.[13]

I invoke a question that J. H. van den Berg asks in his historical study of our "divided existence": What is happening to matter at this time?[14] Both engineers and chemists gaze at it with their new techniques and ways of perceiving and discover that matter breaks apart. Does it not seem evident that in a deep sense matter was being challenged to show both its breaking points and its structure when broken into atoms? Speaking of Lavoisier, van den Berg writes that he discovered "the matter of his time," the time of the breakup of the *ancien regime*, the time of emergence of atomistic (possessive) individuality.[15] The materiality of existence lost its former coherence, as the existential ground no longer sustained the types of social relationships that existed in the pre-modern world. The questions put to matter—"How much can it take before breaking?" and "What are its essential components when broken up?"—thus reflected, sparked, and responded to changes occurring in the human order. The coherence of human atoms, the bonds between them, the elasticity of human "stuff" in the face of deforming forces, all became necessary questions of the age. Thus do we discover the existential origins of the engineering mentality. The valence of the mentality was, as today, bipolar. On the one hand, it made breakdown, dissolution, and atomization real and imaginable; on the other hand, it expressed a will to build dwelling places with this new matter, as a sign of hope in the face of the crumbling of the old regime. The Crystal Palace, the Eiffel Tower, and above all the skyscraper embody this will to endure in the a face of the breakdown of the familiar and of all that once mattered.

As with the testing of breaking points, the development of chemistry signals the late eighteenth century as the crucial point when "things fall apart." Before that time, the breakdown was not yet; after it, especially in the Victorian period, it became visible in the medical and social spheres of life, as we have seen with the astute observations of Allbutt, who recognized overstrain of the heart and the death of external authority. The terminus a quo of the mentality that generated stress belongs to the period 1750–1800.[16]

THE MEDICAL GAZE AND THE MATERIAL OF THE BODY

In order to ask engineering questions of the body, physicians had to be able to see the body as similar to testable building material. In the nineteenth century, as we saw, bodily tissue was first subjected to stress testing and later, strength of material concerns were asked about various organs and organ systems. In the eighteenth century we find the background that made such testing possible. The major development was the science of pathological anatomy. The modern study of anatomy dates from the fourteenth century, and came into its own with Vesalius's 1543 *De humani corporis fabrica*. However, as late as 1800 medical appreciation of anatomy was not universal. Anatomy requires a perceptual style that equates what exists and happens inside a person with what exists and happens outside. The manner of "what exists" has a strict specification: What exists is understood in terms of the natural sciences of matter. That this perceptual style is an elaborate construct possible only in the modern world is the conclusion of seminal studies of the past 50 years, dating from the phenomenological investigations of Jean-Paul Sartre, Maurice Merleau-Ponty, Erwin Straus, and others. Fundamental to my analysis is what I take to be a central conclusion of those studies: The objectified (anatomized) body is a way of perceiving the body; it is a metaphor for the flesh that occludes perception of the person of the body. It enables perception of only the corpse, abstracted from the "thou" of the person whom I face. This limitation of the anatomical perceptual style is also the source of its power. It made possible among other things the application of engineering considerations of the body and led ultimately to the construct of stress.

Let us now peer back just far enough in time to view the emergence of engineering as a mode of perceiving the body. The time is 1800. Laennec's stethoscope played a critical role in the construction of overstrain of the heart, as we have seen. His teacher, Jean-Nicolas Corvisart (1755–1821), stands just on the other side of the engineering mentality. Corvisart's text, *An Essay on the Organic Diseases and Lesions of the Heart and Great Vessels*, appeared in 1806, and in English translation in 1812. His approach fully incorporated pathological anatomy, pioneered earlier in the eighteenth century by Morgagni (1688–1771). Morgagni had sought to correlate the signs and symptoms of disease with demonstrable organic changes visible in autopsy, and he thus created the medical gaze, which saw through the patient and his disease to the anatomical location of the disease.[17] Pathological anatomy laid the groundwork for the perceptions of Allbutt and Beard, who two generations later, saw in palpitations and fatigue the signs of overstrain of heart and nerve.

Corvisart's modernity lay not only in his use of pathological anatomy but also in his employment of Avenbrugger's method of percussion. This hands-on approach to diagnosis signaled the shift from patient narrative and physician tact as the means of medical knowledge about the patient's illness to the use of the gaze embodied in technical instruments and procedures. Percussion required both the patient's silence and the physician's examination of the anatomized body.

What is interesting in Corvisart's text was pathological anatomy without engineering questions. In their place was a host of other things, notably a medical-moral discourse on physiognomy and on the passions.

Corvisart began his discussion of the signs of heart disease with physiognomy.[18] The appearance of the patient gave a picture of the disease to the physician who had tact. Physiognomy was an art widely practiced at the time, and the tactful physician noticed not only the visual display but also olfactory and tactile manifestations as well. Moreover, physiognomic scrutiny touched upon the life context of the patient:

One of the properties on which the *tact* of the great physician is actually founded, consists chiefly in this penetration, constantly strengthened by exercise, which leads him to notice in a patient, the scene of moral affections, as he observes all the physical phenomena which either develop, produce, or follow them.[19]

Diagnosis, then, was one part tact. Corvisart's English translator added a quotation from Joseph Andre Roubard as a footnote to this passage:

the word *tact* is now, in general employed to express a decision of the mind, prompt, subtle, and just; a decision which seems to anticipate the slow process of reflection and reasoning, and to proceed from a sort of instinctive suggestion, conducting us instantaneously and unerringly to the truth.[20]

The note differentiated taste (deemed basically innate) and tact ("appropriate to things in which the power of judging is wholly acquired"). Tact like taste deals with perceptions of beauty, and the tactful person, a connoisseur, can, for example, distinguish the paintings of different masters. "It is applied also to a quick perception of those delicate shades of character and manners, which are objects of study to the man of the world." These passages are important because they indicate a way of being a physician greatly attenuated in today's technologically dominated world.

But not only physicians differ from their forebears in this regard. Hans-Georg Gadamer has provided a seminal account of the shift in the human sciences around Corvisart's time. In the eighteenth century, the Humanist tradition provided a foundation for knowledge of human things not in a scientific method, but in character formation expressed in the concept of taste. Taste was a means of knowing distinct from pure reason and instinct. Taste (and tact) gave understanding of the good, the true, and the fair in human behavior and artifacts. On its own ground it was indubitable. In the nineteenth century, that traditional ground of knowledge seemed increasingly less secure and certain, and there developed, notably in the work of John Stuart Mill and Hermann von Helmholtz, human sciences modeled after the physical sciences. Thus, modern psychology and sociology appeared on the corpse of taste and tact. I would append to Gadamer that modern medicine did also so appear (Mill being no stranger to the readers of the *Lancet* and the *British Medical Journal*). Taste and tact declined with the rise of instruments and scientific methods, the stethoscope symbolizing the shift from tact to method. But the aside—as it were—of Corvisart and its notice by the translator provided a window into a medical world prior to that which cultivated engineered grief. Physiognomy enabled the tactful physician to behold in the flesh what was good, fair, and true in the patient. So the medical-moral discourse that existed in the eighteenth century verbalized not only a material existence radically different from that of a century later, it also had its dwelling in a network of social relationships (especially between physician and patient) that relied on face-to-face encounters, stories of illnesses, and perceptions of character.[21]

Corvisart's text displays the pre-engineering discourse that atrophied in the nineteenth century. Given the necessity of tact (and in England the classical education that arguably trained elite physicians to possess it), the medical-moral discourse that Corvisart employed occurred where later we would expect to find discussion of strength of materials and thermodynamics. Corvisart, like any good eighteenth-century physician, was aware of the social causes of illness. In the wake of 1789 he wrote:

The bloody scenes of the revolution, ruin of fortune, emotions, and chagrin which followed, do, at this period, furnish numerous proofs of the influence of the moral affections concerning the evolution of the organic diseases in general, and of those of the heart in particular. How many persons previously opulent, have we not seen, in the hospitals, reduced to beggary, desire, as a termination of their afflictions, a sudden death which the organic lesions of the heart brought too slowly for their gratification.[22]

Moreover, for Corvisart, there was a direct relation between the passions and the heart: "This organ is the point in which the effects of all the moral affections, gay or melancholy, seem to be concentrated. No moral affection can be experienced, without the acceleration, diminution, or derangement of the motion of the heart."[23]

What is striking is the ease with which he discusses the passions in relation to heart disease. Even more striking is a description of the heart's motions themselves in terms of the passions. Allan Burns's *Observations on Some of the Most Frequent and Important Diseases of the Heart* (1809), a text like Corvisart's grounded in pathological anatomy, contains the following (from a review):

Where the heart is enlarged by an addition of solid muscular substance, the balance between this organ and the arteries is destroyed. "There is a confusion and a struggling in the chest; there is also an inexpressible anxiety and inquietude about the heart; and, as one would expect, there is a weak, irregular, intermitting, fluttering pulse."[24]

This passage—and ones like it in Corvisart—were transitional to an engineering perspective. On the one hand, there was the perception of the heart as a sense organ, as the center of expression of the passions. On the other hand, thanks to pathological anatomy, there was estimation of the relative strength of the heart and arteries, or heart and other organs, a strength which was critical for health—and health was conceived (by Corvisart) as equilibrium.

But when Corvisart wrote of equilibrium, he referred to temperament as much as to relative strength of the organs. The concept of temperamental equilibrium, a perennial notion of pre-modern medicine dating back to Galen, was in the process of eclipse, with an engineering conception of equilibrium on the ascendant. Equilibrium appears to have played a Janus-like role in texts such as Corvisart's, helping to obscure the transition from balance understood in a moral sense to that among physical forces.[25]

The medical-moral discourse of the late eighteenth century dwelt upon balance, a perennial topic in such discussions that extended back to the Greek notion of moderation. Two observations from Francis Hutcheson (1694–1764), a prominent British moral philosopher, indicate the purview of the discourse. First, he defined passion: "When more violent *confused Sensations* arise with the *Affections*, and are attended with, or prolonged by bodily Motions, we call the whole by the Name of *Passion*, especially when accompanied with some *natural Propensities*."[26] Passion is at once moral and physical. While Hutcheson concentrated on the moral aspects, he did not ignore the physical entirely, pointing out "that probably certain *Motions* in the Body accompany every Passion by a fixed Law of Nature."[27] This secondary consideration in ethics became primary in medicine, while the moral aspects took up a secondary though still present place. Moral and physical matters clung together, even if neither physicians nor philosophers of the time presumed to account for how the immaterial and material parts of human nature did indeed cleave to each other. The issue from the side of medicine is complicated by the eighteenth-century debate between mechanists and vitalists, the latter dominating toward the end of the century.[28] For present purposes, however, that debate is secondary, as both positions used the same anatomically informed discourse to depict bodily motions. Second, Hutcheson addressed balance in the moral sphere in terms of his (controversial) position that we have both selfish and altruistic (public) passions by nature. The two are ideally in balance, but he considered an "adjust balance very rare."[29] Hutcheson gave voice to moral considerations common to the time, and in such a fashion as to make medical discourse congruent with them. Thus, when Corvisart and other physicians spoke of balance or equilibrium, those concepts belonged to a discourse natural to the age.

Hutcheson's *Essay* was one of the last of its type. By the end of the eighteenth century ethical discourse had begun to contain the utilitarian perspective of Bentham. "The long reign of the usefulness of the concept of 'passion' was . . . nearing its end."[30] That new discourse of Bentham, Mill, and Alexander Bain would itself be supplemented (without loss of the perspective) in the second half of the nineteenth century with metaphors from thermodynamics, yielding the commonplace (today, for example, in Piaget) that emotions are motivators, supplying the energy for cognitive structures. Coupled with the loss of "passion," following Gadamer's analysis, was the separation of aesthetics from cognition. The entire framework of the medical-moral discourse crumbled in the early nineteenth century.

The upshot was that just as the engineering mentality and discourse was forming, the medical-moral discourse that once informed medical perception was breaking apart. Given the methods pioneered by Corvisart and his pupil Laennec, and the way they revealed the body, the development of engineering discourse in medicine seems in retrospect at least as natural as the development of anatomy.

MEDICAL-MORAL DISCOURSE OF THE EIGHTEENTH CENTURY

The eighteenth century saw many attempts at a mechanical model of mental phenomena. This trend joined with ideas sparked by the Enlightenment after 1750, and produced further seeds of stress. I focus on some work of Benjamin Rush (1745–1813), a Philadelphia physician and signer of the Declaration of Independence. Rush has been singled out by historian George Rosen as one who addressed "social stress and mental disease." Given the renown Rush had in his day, both in the fledgling United States and in Great Britain, his work provides a window into another aspect of existence prior to engineered grief.

Rush understood the mind to have its ground if not its being in the brain. No reductionist, he argued in a public lecture that "the immortality of the soul depends upon the *will* of the Deity, and not upon the supposed properties of spirit."[31] Rush addressed the physical conditions which operated upon the moral and intellectual faculties as a physician and a Christian. As Rosen remarks vis-a-vis Thomas Jefferson, for Rush too "the biological, social, psychological, and moral relations of man to his environment were so interlocked that they were all one."[32] Rush developed a theory of disease different from that of William Cullen (1710–1790), his teacher at Edinburgh. Cullen had developed a complex system of disease classification; Rush held that all disease is fever resulting from disordered action of the circulatory system:

[Rush] thought in terms of a state of "general debility" that resulted from the reduction to pathological levels of "the excitement of the system." ... With the system so predisposed, the continued action of stimuli led to "reaction" that was the disease or fever. This "reaction" occurred "primarily in the blood vessels, and particularly in the arteries," and consisted of "irregular" or "convulsive" motions, also termed "morbid excitement." This activity was "mechanical" in nature and was a result of the "elastic and muscular texture" of the blood vessels.[33]

This theory focused on the tension of the circulatory system, and it prefigured nineteenth-century concerns about strain. That tension could help explain disease was integral to the theory of physicians of the Scottish school, notably Cullen and John Brown.[34] Cullen held that the tension of the circulatory system kept the supply of nourishment flowing and stimulated excretion. Moreover, the nervous system, for Cullen the source of the generation of life, had two mechanical properties, "sensibility" and "irritability," whose excesses or deficiencies produced disease. Cullen "conceived of the normal and abnormal instances of excitement and collapse as being due to variations in the 'mobility and force' of the nervous power."[35] Brown held that disease was either "*sthenia*, a result of overstimulation, or *asthenia*, inability to respond to stimulation."[36] Cullen's and Brown's theories show that mechanistic principles, which considered strength of material, were circulating in the late eighteenth century, although they were not yet engineering notions. Rather, as eighteenth-century notions of strength and weakness, they were issues of balance. To illustrate the difference, consider this: Beard popularized neurasthenia a century after Brown and Cullen; there was no corresponding pathology of neur-sthenia.

Rush coupled his theory of disease etiology with moral philosophy largely derived from the thought of the Scottish Enlightenment. Hence, it was a "faculty psychology" that was grounded in the mechanics of the body. In addressing "The Influence of Physical Causes upon the Moral Faculty" (1786) and "The Influence of Physical Causes in Promoting an Increase in the Strength and Activity of the Intellectual Faculties of Man" (1799), Rush provided a theological ground for the medical-moral discourse. To late-twentieth-century eyes, Rush may seem to prefigure systems thinking in speaking of such influences, but actually Rush embraced religious thought as his central inspiration:

Nor let it be supposed . . . that I entertain an idea of the *necessary* influence of physical causes upon the freedom of the will. I believe in the prescience of the Deity, because I conceive this attribute to be inseparable from his perfections; and I believe in the freedom of the moral agency in man, because I conceive it to be essential to his nature as a responsible being.[37]

It was thus a "natural" transition from speculations about physiological mechanisms to those about moral and mental acts. The two "levels" were neither confused nor reduced one to the other, nor did the same terminology apply to both (all of which are true in systems thinking). Nevertheless, their relations, whose "naturalness" withers upon close scrutiny with twentieth-century eyes, sustained perceptions in that epoch.

Foucault has called attention to the beginnings of biopower in the Enlightenment, and along this line Rush stands as a founding father. Rosen shows how Rush and his peer Thomas Jefferson held similar views on the relationships between individual health and the well-being of the political order. The Enlightenment, as Ackerknecht writes, "stimulated that field of medicine now called public health."[38] For Rush as for Jefferson, "human health was fostered by good social institutions."[39] For both, republican institutions and an agrarian society were the guarantors of health. Rush wrote:

There is an indissoluble union between moral, political and physical happiness; and if it be true, that elective and representative governments are the most favorable to an individual as to national prosperity, it follows of course, that they are most favorable to animal life.[40]

Rush belongs to a long line of Enlightenment physicians who campaigned against social evils in the name of health. Rush espoused "the emancipation of slaves, antialcoholism, the abolition of the death penalty, and money reform."[41] This medical humanitarianism and its mandate to intervene in the politic of society is implicit in the discourse on stress, with its implicit equation of personal and corporate stresses.

THE APPEARANCE OF CLOCK TIME

In Rush, Cullen, and their medical contemporaries we find scattered seeds of theory and thought that sprouted into the constructs of strain, anxiety, and stress. The ground in which these seeds were embedded held them not as separate elements but as part of a form of living that could not sustain engineered grief. There was neither the occasion for such grief nor the ability to mold loss into anything like stress. Nevertheless, the ground was shifting; things were germinating. Thus far in this chapter, we have considered the conditions for engineered grief in the material and medical domains. Now we turn to the most fundamental changes that were beginning to occur, that made possible the harnessing of the will to adapt: the changing existence of time and work.

The pressures of time underlie the stressful world, especially insofar as the demand to adapt has roots in a twofold organization of time: (1) clock-time, with its disciplining effect on behavior, and (2) the notion of historical progress, the sense that the present age is superior and more civilized than the past. We will address both structures of temporality.

E. P. Thompson describes the proliferation of clocks and watches through the seventeenth and eighteenth centuries. They had become fairly abundant in England by 1800: "a general diffusion of clocks and watches is occurring (as one would expect) at the exact moment when the industrial revolution demanded a greater synchronization of labor."[42] What machinery's efficient operation necessitated and clocks made possible was continuous work, which in turn demanded punctuality and regularity on the part of labor and management. A vast orchestration of society, with the clock as metronome and conductor, took form over the course of industrial expansion. Time "management" emerged, replacing an older and probably ancient form of work

characterized by "alternate bouts of intense labor and of idleness."[43] In contrast to clock-time discipline, the older form of work is irregular, but underlying it was a sense of time as suitable for the occasion, with qualitatively
different tempos and rhythms: *kairos* (the occasion for an activity, such as
fall being the occasion for harvesting, or death being the occasion for mourning) as well as *chronos* (chronological time, irreversible, linear, ever-flowing
time) played a role in it. This older temporality, Thompson implies, retreated
into the home during the Industrial Age. And the home as haven, especially
since the advent of radio and television, seems less secure these days. The
older sense of time survives in everyday experience, as phenomenological
studies of lived time show.[44] Its survival is not in question, rather its social
worth: It has been relegated socially to the domain of the "subjective" wher-
ever time is money. Where time is not dominated by the clock and budget,
then *kairos* survives.

And not only *kairos* exists in the context of undominated time; idleness
exists too. The economist Staffan Linder argues that as work time has become
increasingly productive in industry, there are numerous incentives to increase
the productivity of other time uses (which he divides into personal and
consumption times). Only among the very poor and in nonindustrial societies
does real free time exist: "It is conceivable that people in poor countries are
subjected to free time in the strict sense of the word, i.e., time that is not
utilized. . . . We will call this . . . category of time idleness."[45] Thus, before
clocks became so important to the organization of living, idleness was abundant, time was plentiful. In the pre-stress world, despite its hardships, time
was not scarce, which scarcity is a necessary condition for the existence of
engineered grief.

As Thompson notes, external demands for punctuality are one thing, inner
discipline another. He turns to Weber's *The Protestant Ethic and the Spirit of
Capitalism* to suggest that from the seventeenth to the nineteenth centuries,
people in industrial societies were internalizing the new time sense, epitomized by Benjamin Franklin's maxim "time is money." The historical record
is hard to read, but it is true today that under stress we are encouraged to
discipline ever more domains of life to the clock. It is sufficient for the limited
task of this chapter to observe that the three conditions for such discipline
came together in a gathering storm in Britain and later in the United States
toward the end of the eighteenth century. The three conditions were readily
available clocks and watches, labor demanding clock-time punctuality, and
moral exhortations to be frugal and industrious. All three did exist; in fact,
the moral condition actually preceded the first two, as Thompson's study
reveals.[46]

Anson Rabinbach shows that during the nineteenth century fatigue ceased
to be perceived as a natural limit and came to be seen as a disease. The
harnessing of human labor by both clock and industrial organization made
this shift possible. Then and only then could fatigue or "overwork" become

a disease, and overstrain a medical concern. The disease of overwork in particular was a sign of internalized time discipline, a disease of the emerging "time famine" society, to use Linder's phrase.

THE CHANGING NATURE OF LUXURY

The discourses on strain, anxiety, and stress contain complaints that civilization causes disease and distress. These refrains, such as the contemporary commonplaces of the archaic body and the exile, address the discipline imposed by the modern organization of work in terms of time and competition. Prior to these complaints, medical men observed very different consequences of civilized life. In the eighteenth century, in a tradition extending from antiquity until 1750 (and beyond), luxury was considered a source of illness. The critique of luxury has both Judeo-Christian and classical Greek origins and was a staple of social and moral analysis in Western thought. The meaning of luxury was rather diverse, but in essence it signified desires beyond one's needs or position. Thus, it could mean licentiousness or, as it occasionally did in eighteenth-century Britain, rebelliousness among peasants who rioted over increases in food prices.[47] In this long tradition, cities were said to provide men with luxuries and thus ruin their health and morals. Eighteenth-century physicians inveighed against luxurious habits, although not always for the same reasons. Their explanatory models varied but in essence said that luxury produces weakness and effeminacy, making the body too delicate and sensitive to stimuli. This sensitivity made for increased susceptibility to nervous diseases. Luxury belonged to a medical-moral discourse.

The moral tone is evident, for example in George Cheyne's famous book, *The English Malady* (1733). Reflecting on the fall of Rome, he gives a standard account of the ill-effects of luxury:

But afterwards, in Proportion as they advanced in Learning, and the Knowledge of the Sciences, and distinguished themselves from other Nations by their Politeness and Refinements, they sunk into *Effeminacy, Luxury*, and *Diseases*, and began to study *Physick*, to remedy those Evils which their Luxury and Laziness had brought upon them. ... As *Celsus* observes, where he is giving some Account of the Rise and Improvement of Physick, according to the Prevalency of these two general causes of Disease, *Idleness* and Intemperance; *that these two had ... spoil'd the Constitutions.*[48]

So in the eighteenth century, Cheyne contended, luxury was causing an increase of disease, which was so peculiar to the new wealth of England that he called it the English malady.

Cheyne's work was groundbreaking. Only beginning in the eighteenth century could one suffer from "nerves," and Cheyne's work was important in establishing nervousness as a category of illness.[49] That luxury caused nervousness became a staple of medical speculation in the eighteenth century.

In 1807, the naval surgeon Thomas Trotter wrote *A View of the Nervous Temperament*. He stated that nervous diseases had increased dramatically during the eighteenth century: Sydenham in 1700 found two-thirds of all illness were fevers, nervous diseases being rare; Cheyne in 1733 found one-third of all illness were nervous; Trotter said he himself found two-thirds of all illness had a nervous origin. Why, he asks, have nervous diseases increased so dramatically? These diseases "are the progeny of wealth, luxury, indolence, and intemperance."[50] Luxury weakens both morals and the body, making its victims susceptible to illness.

The decline of the traditional critique of luxury in the late eighteenth century had numerous sources, but chief among them was a defense of luxury by thinkers such as David Hume who were defending political freedom and the development of a market economy. Sekora notes that the defenders of luxury tended to recast the arguments from morals to economics. He summarizes Hume's defense in these terms:

Hume's study of English and European history yielded his fundamental premise: the rise of materialism, individualism and economic power outside the court had stimulated political freedom and parliamentary government. Indeed the increase of European power and grandeur during the previous two hundred years was directly attributable to the fruits of luxury. In contemporary England, the interests of the class of tradesmen and merchants, "the middling ranks of men," had a liberating influence upon the policies of the House of Commons.[51]

Luxury had been perceived as the vice of not knowing one's limits, materially or socially. The defense of luxury in part supported the rising commercial class against the landed aristocracy.

When luxury became a good, desire was stimulated without bounds, and this enticement was considered beneficial. In *Fable of the Bees* (1721), an early defense of luxury, Bernard de Mandeville observed "if once we depart from calling everything Luxury that is not absolutely necessary to keep a Man alive . . . then there is no Luxury at all; for if the wants of Man are innumerable, then what ought to supply them has no bounds."[52] Where once moralists inveighed against luxury, in our own day politicians praise growth, a creative renaming of the old term.

The new assessment of luxury affected medical thinkers. Whereas in the eighteenth century, illness was an effect of luxury, in the nineteenth century illness resulted from the pursuit of luxury. William Rathbone Greg stated the new view with passion:

If we could all be suddenly endowed with wisdom to perceive how few of the worthier objects of earthly existence require wealth for their attainment . . . we should discover that the excessive toil and the severe struggle of life which we all unite to deprecate and deplore is, in truth, a self-imposed necessity.[53]

In his later and influential address, "Life at High Pressure," Greg repeated the charge, claiming that the hurry of the new age produces nervous diseases and "an accelerated action of the heart, of which, in a few months or years, most of us become unpleasantly conscious."[54] High-pressure life, the pursuit of luxury, thus produces the two major diseases of overstrain, those of the heart and nerves. Greg captured the new nonmoral basis for the warnings against high-pressure living when, in urging simplicity as the remedy for strain, he made it clear that "we are dealing with what is rational, not with what is right—not with what duty would ordain, but with what sagacity and enlightened selfishness suggest."[55] Physicians contemporary with Greg—including William Ward Richardson, Robson Roose, George Beard, Robert Farquharson—all warned against overstrain in terms similar to Greg, as we have seen. What is noteworthy is that strain replaced luxury in the shift from a medical-moral discourse to a discourse of strain within an engineering mentality. In this sense, luxury held, in the eighteenth century, the place of strain and stress in the eighteenth century. Luxury is, in this sense, an ancestor of stress. But the differences between them far outweigh their commonalities. Whereas luxury was foreign to the good life in the traditional view, stress is necessary for it in the present day.[56]

CONCLUSION

In the second half of the eighteenth century, the ground was being prepared for the rise of engineered grief. Various aspects of that future began to appear: engineering, pathological anatomy, biopower, time and work discipline, the reassessment of luxury. To that extent, the period between 1750 and 1800 has a family resemblance to our own. But in other respects, how foreign a place it was. Modern materials did not yet exist; buildings were not planned in engineering terms; a medical-moral discourse reigned, and physicians learned of their patients' diseases primarily via narrative; overwork and strain did not exist as a medical matter, luxury did, a vice of a period before hurry and clock time dominated our time consciousness. Eighteenth-century physicians could not have and did not concern themselves with anything like strain or stress. How could they have?

NOTES

1. See Leo Strauss, "The three waves of modernity," in Hilail Gildin, ed., *Political Philosophy: Six Essays by Leo Strauss* (Indianapolis: Pegasus, 1975), pp. 81–98.

2. Stephan Timoshenko, *History of Strength of Materials* (New York: McGraw-Hill, 1953), p. 13.

3. Galileo, quoted in ibid., p. 13.

4. Timoshenko, *History of Strength of Materials*, pp. 14–15.

5. See J. H. van den Berg, *Complex Society and Dividend Existence* (Pittsburgh: Duquesne University Press, 1974).

6. S. B. Hamilton, "Building and civil engineering construction," in Charles Singer, E. J. Holymard, A. R. Hall, and Trevor I. Williams, eds., *A History of Technology*, Vol. IV: *The Industrial Revolution, c 1750 to c 1850* (Oxford: Clarendon Press, 1958), p. 480.

7. Hamilton, "Building and Civil Engineering," p. 481, (for all three quotations).

8. Jean Robert, in response to this paragraph, writes: "The architects arguments against Gauthey . . . are prefigurations of the arguments of M.D.s against diagnosis in the lab, outside of the doctor-patient clinical relationship" (personal correspondence, 1990).

9. H. R. Schubert, "Extraction and Production of Metals: Iron and Steel," in Singer et al., eds., *A History of Technology*, Vol. IV, p. 99.

10. H. R. Schubert, "The Steel Industry," in Singer et al., eds., *A History of Technology*, Vol. V: *The Late Nineteenth Century c 1850 to c 1900* (New York: Oxford University Press, 1958), p. 61.

11. S. B. Hamilton, "Building Materials and Techniques," in Singer et al., eds., *A History of Technology*, Vol. V, pp. 478–79.

12. I am simply restating here the understanding of the act of self-knowledge as presented in the works of hermeneutical phenomenology. See especially Hans-Georg Gadamer, *Truth and Method* (New York: Seabury, 1975) and Paul Ricoeur. For psychological presentations of this theme, see J. H. van den Berg, *Complex Society and Divided Existence*, p. 169; and Robert Romanyshyn, *Psychological Life: From Science to Metaphor* (Austin: University of Texas Press, 1982), pp. 38–53.

13. Erwin Ackerknecht, *A Short History of Medicine*, rev. ed. (Baltimore: Johns Hopkins University Press, 1982), pp. 138–39.

14. J. H. van den Berg, *Complex Society and Divided Existence*, pp. 131–32: "But what then would have happened if the desire to divide had not made its appearance? Lavoisier would never have discovered that water (air, earth, etc.) is divisable. We would have had entirely different ideas about matter without being aware that we missed something."

15. Ibid., p. 128. For atomistic individuality, see C. B. MacPherson, *The Political Theory of Possessive Individualism* (London: Oxford University Press, 1962), Louis Dumont, *From Mandeville to Marx: The Genesis and Triumph of Economic Ideology* (Chicago: University of Chicago Press, 1977), and Ivan Illich, *Gender* (New York: Pantheon, 1982).

16. Van den Berg, *Complex Society and Divided Existence*, dates the beginning of "divided existence," his term for the existential condition of possibility for stress, from 1733, when the Baroque period ended and Cheyne's *English Malady* appeared. See J. H. van den Berg, *Things* (Pittsburgh: Duquesne University Press, 1970).

17. See Michel Foucault, *The Birth of the Clinic* (New York: Vintage Books, 1973), for the origins of the medical gaze.

18. The study of physiognomy was prominent in the eighteenth century, notably with the work of Lavater.

19. Pierre Joseph André Roubard, quoted in Jean-Nicolas Corvisart, *An Essay on the Organic Diseases and Lesions of the Heart and Great Vessels*, trans. J. Gater (1812; reprint, New York: Hafner, 1962), pp. 19–20.

20. Corvisart, *An Essay on the Organic Diseases*, pp. 19–20.

21. See Stanley Joel Reiser, *Medicine and the Reign of Technology* (Cambridge: Cambridge University Press, 1978) for discussion of narrative as the basis of the

physician's knowledge of disease in the eighteenth century. See also Barbara Duden, *The Woman Under the Skin* (Cambridge: Harvard University Press, 1991) for the kind of knowledge that narrative revealed in essentially premodern German villages.

22. Corvisart, *An Essay on the Organic Diseases*, p. 276.

23. Ibid., p. 275.

24. Allan Burns, *Observations on Some of the Most Frequent and Important Diseases of the Heart* (reviewed) *Edinburgh Medical and Surgical Journal* 5 (1809), 345.

25. On equilibrium, see George Rosen, "Political order and human health in Jeffersonian thought," *Bulletin of the History of Medicine* 26 (1952), 32–44; R. Rosalie Stott, "Health or virtue: Or, how to keep out of harm's way. Lectures on pathology and therapeutics by William Cullen c. 1770," *Medical History* 31 (1987), 123–142; and Edward H. Kass, Review of Russell C. Maulitz, *Morbid Appearances: The Anatomy of Pathology in the Early Nineteenth Century, Journal of Interdisciplinary History* 20, no. 1 (1989), 138.

26. Francis Hutcheson, *An Essay on the Nature and Conduct of the Passions and Affections; with Illustrations on the Moral Sense* (Gainesville, FL: Scholars' Facsimiles and Reprints, 1969), p. 61.

27. Ibid., p. 57.

28. Elizabeth Haigh, *Xavier Bichat and the Medical Theory of the Eighteenth Century, Medical History*, Supplement No. 4 (London: Wellcome Institute for the History of Medicine, 1984).

29. Hutcheson, *An Essay on the Nature*, p. 56.

30. McReynolds, introduction to ibid., p. ix.

31. Benjamin Rush, *Two Essays on the Mind: An Enquiry into the Influence of Physical Causes upon the Moral Faculty, and On the Influence of Physical Causes in Promoting an Increase of the Strength and Activity of the Intellectual Faculties of Man* (1786; reprint, New York: Bruner/Mazel, 1972), p. 14.

32. Rosen, "Political Order," p. 33.

33. Stanley Jackson, *Melancholia and Depression from Hippocratic Times to Modern Times* (New Haven: Yale University Press, 1986), pp. 150–51.

34. For Rush's indebtedness to Brown, see the review of Rush's "Three lectures upon animal life," in *Medical Repository*, 1800, 190.

35. Jackson, *Melancholia and Depression*, p. 125.

36. Ackerknecht, p. 131.

37. Rush, *Two Essays,* p. 15.

38. Ackerknecht, *A Short History of Medicine*, p. 141.

39. Rosen, "Political Order," p. 33.

40. Benjamin Rush, *Selected Writings*, in Rosen, 34–35.

41. Ackerknecht, *A Short History of Medicine*, p. 222.

42. E. P. Thompson, "Time, Work-discipline, and Industrial Capitalism," *Past and Present* 38 (1967), 69. For critiques, see Richard Whipp, " 'A time to every purpose': An essay on time and work," in P. Joyce, ed., *The Historical Meanings of Work*, (Cambridge: Cambridge University Press, 1987), pp. 210–223.

43. Thompson, "Time, Work-discipline," p. 73.

44. See for example, Eugene Minkowski, *Lived Time* (Evanston: Northwestern University Press, 1970).

45. Staffan Linder, *The Harried Leisure Class* (New York: Columbia University Press, 1970), pp. 14–15.

46. Thompson, "Time, Work-discipline," p. 73.

47. For an overview of the concept of luxury and a sound intellectual history, see John Sekora, *Luxury: The Concept in Western Thought, Eden to Smollett* (Baltimore: Johns Hopkins University Press, 1977). See also Anson Rabinbach, *The Human Motor* (New York: Basic Books, 1990), pp. 19–38.

48. George Cheyne, *The English Malady* (1733; reprint, New York: Scholars Facsimiles & Reprints, 1976), p. 39.

49. See W. F. Bynum, "The nervous patient in eighteenth and nineteenth century Britain: The psychiatric origins of British neurology," in W. F. Bynum, Roy Porter, and Michael Shepherd, eds., *The Anatomy of Madness: Essays in the History of Psychiatry*, (London: Tavistock, 1985), Vol. I, pp. 89–102; George Drinka, *The Birth of Neurosis: Myth, Malady, and the Victorians* (New York: Simon & Schuster, 1984).

50. Thomas Trotter, *A View of the Nervous Temperament* (London: Longman, Hurst, Rees & Orme, 1807), p. 23.

51. Sekora, *Luxury*, pp. 119–120.

52. Mandeville, *Fable of the Bees*, Vol. 1, 107–8, quoted in ibid., p. 115.

53. William Rathbone Greg, "England as it is," in *Essays on Political and Social Science* (London: Longman, Brown, Green & Longmans, 1853), Vol. I, pp. 326–27.

54. William Rathbone Greg, "Life at high pressure," in *Literary and Social Judgments* (London: Trubner & Co., 1877), Vol. II, p. 268.

55. Ibid., pp. 281–82.

56. Anson Rabinbach provides a related analysis of idleness in *The Human Motor*: "fatigue, not idleness, was the primary discontent of industrial labor. By the 1860s and 1870s a new literature stressing the hygienic aspects of work began to appear. . . . A careful examination of these texts reveals, however, that a more scientific evaluation of work, often materialist in emphasis, gradually replaced the old moral discourse. More important, these texts placed the working body at the center of attention and treated the labor of the body as a physiological process abstracted from the conditions of work or political economy and from the specific qualities of a trade or occupation" (p. 36).

7

The Two Ends of Engineered Grief

Technology will not be overcome by men. On the contrary, the coming
to presence of technology will be surmounted in a way that restores it
into its yet concealed truth. This restoring surmounting is similar to what
happens when, in the human realm, one gets over grief or pain.
—Martin Heidegger[1]

Stress not only has a history, not only orders perceptions in the present, it
also casts its shadow on the future. In this final chapter, I will address the
two ends toward which stress leads us. The first, a continuation and elaboration of the metaphor of stress for our grief, will make us monsters that
cope. The second, which we arrive at by working through the grief rather
than exploiting its "energy," enables us to mourn.

Stress is a reality in the contemporary life world, and we have come to
understand it as a metaphor, derived from engineering, for a kind of grief
unique to the modern age. The metaphor of stress names an existential
condition characteristic of a world that is constantly changing, chiefly from
the pressures of technological change and the social dislocations that accompany it. Stress happens in a world that is without form or proportion, a time-
space of "white noise," in which temporal and spatial boundaries collapse.
Because time is scarce, and because there is always work to do, temporal
boundaries fail. The future especially floods the present as "things to do"
crowd in, eliminating the present as a time to be. Spatial limits disappear
because people perpetually find themselves on the go, never dwelling. Speed

provides the means to occupy the stressful world. Its occupants experience themselves less as flesh-and-blood creatures than as sources of energy; they consume time, money, and calories, and swim in a flood of information. They find that they desire stress; in controlled amounts it makes them feel alive, productive, important. It promises to transform them into quasi-immortal beings who cope and prosper, but at a price: they must generate increasing amounts of energy and take in increasing amounts of information to make it through the week. At some point, some find that they cannot take it anymore. They make lists. They develop symptoms. Stress is costly, since despite their best efforts, their hardiness, their buffers, and their supports, human beings are not pure energy. They in turn become threatened with a realization that the world to which they have adapted does not nurture or sustain their lives without extraordinary effort and resources on their part. The world is alien and hostile, bombarding them with stimuli, demands, and data as if they were astronauts flung adrift in the reaches of outer space.

Stress is also a style of discourse, a way of narrating the meaning of life and directing it in certain channels. As a discourse, stress resembles a chain of associations, such as those the old empiricists analyzed, such that when one term in the chain appears, certain others follow it habitually. Stress is, we can say, a bad habit we have developed for making sense of our time-scarce, energy-hungry life style. The associative chain contains key rhetorical terms which carry persuasive power, given the backdrop of accelerating change in our lives. The terms *energy* and *boundaries* it makes possible serve as lighthouses in the rough and foggy waters of daily life. These two terms inform us that our precious individuality is maintained at the cost of consumption, and that the protection of boundaries promises health and hints at immortality. *Control*, the next term in the chain, guides us in how to preserve our boundaries and gain access to the energy and information we desire. The rhetoric of control is bound in a net of engineering, military, and administrative metaphors which, because they seem so natural, entice us to take up an attitude of instrumental rationality in all our dealings. The individual becomes a modern microcosm, a copy of a corporate office or governmental agency, doing cost-benefit analyses of time allocation and energy production. Control may be illusory, but that does not matter. So long as we feel in control, all the benefits of sound management appear ours for the taking.

But control is necessary because the world subjects us to random terror. The stressful world is traumatic, which in the discourse means that we are overloaded beyond the limits of our defenses. This message of overload, however, is not the complete story, and a deeper look reveals that we suffer painful events as traumas because the world is meaningless, because we have no context in which to place them. We are exposed as victims to the extent that we deem control and energy so vital to well-being.

At the origin of the chain, we find the topic of loss. Stress names in a capsule the meaning of losses that modernity forces upon us. This is the narrative at the heart of the discourse. Two variants of the narrative on loss exist: the archaic body and the exile. In the first version, we have lost nature, rendering our bodies outmoded. In the second, we have lost tradition, leaving us exposed without a sacred canopy over our heads or the past beneath our feet. Generalizing, we can say that the narratives announce that we have lost the familiar, with all the resonances of that term. Probing the heart of stress, then, we discover that the discourse points in a distorted way to a grief endemic in the contemporary world. Its rhetoric entices us not to resolve the grief, but to adapt even further. Freeing ourselves from the discourse may open up other possibilities.

Whence this discourse, this distorting metaphor? It was a child of World War II, an experience of being ungrounded, of being an airman subjected to emergencies without the old familiar ground beneath the feet. It was an expression of being supported not by the earth but by systems, mechanical and bureaucratic, upon which the airman depended for survival. It named a response to attack, in which one must adapt or die. It named, finally, a belief in the infinite adaptability of human material, such that with training and morale-boosting, people could learn to live in any kind of nonterrestrial environment.

The immediately preceding period prepared the way for the appearance of stress, whose precursor came into being in no-man's land, in a felt fatigue and shock. In the early twentieth century, the realization of being cut off from the past already existed, as did the engineering discourse that articulated a response to groundlessness. The way was prepared for stress, moreover, in the optimistic assessment of human potential, especially potential energy, that this age of anxiety made. Finally, the explicit rejection of Victorian conceptions of the body split the flesh into mechanical body and energetic psyche, a division that the age sought to heal but ultimately did not. Only with systems thinking in the post–1945 period did this split seem to heal.

Professional groups sustained the perceptions of both periods. In the wake of World War I, psychiatry and the fledgling psychology provided institutional backing and education for the split-flesh, energy-rich person who sustained the shocks and weariness of the age. Following World War II, clinical psychology, psychiatry, and a host of fellow professions provided the wherewithal to sustain the stress field.

In the nineteenth century we discovered the roots of the discourse and experience of stress. Then, it was an age of strain, of overwork, as the West underwent the transition from medieval to modern. The ultimate roots of stress extend back to the period around 1750, when engineering, pathological anatomy, industrial development, and the defense of luxury began. The roots have proven diverse, and to discover them, we have had to consider not only medical thinking but also thinking about building material, since the world of stress is as much a material world as it is a medical one. Modern "stuff"

began to appear in the eighteenth century, as did distinctively modern institutions and techniques. In terms of discourse, the shift from a medical-
moral to an engineering discourse proved decisive for the emergence of strain
and stress as existential categories.

The lessons of this history are numerous. I suspect that many of our
ancestors would listen to our complaints about stress and tell us that we are
suffering from the effects of luxurious living. It is not stress, whatever that
word means, they would say; you are suffering from sin. Luxury breeds all
these woes. Repent and reform. Fine for you, we would reply. You did not
have to drive on the freeway to work and deal with drugs in the schools and
the air conditioning not working and the divorce rate soaring. Do not speak
of sin until you drive a mile in our cars, we might reply. It is just as well
that the conversation is impossible, but the historical analysis does show the
extent to which our material life, our social institutions, especially the clock,
mechanized transportation, and the necessity to strive for a living and for
social place, sustain our being under stress. Stress is indeed a metaphor for
unresolved grief, but a metaphor that has the force of the design of the
contemporary world behind it. There is no easy way around it, neither con-
ceptually nor materially. So what do people today do?

MANAGING STRESS AND ITS DISCONTENTS

They do two things. First, they die of stress. Stress is a modern demon
taking its toll on the freeway of life. It has achieved legal status by becoming
the basis for workers' compensation claims. In this way and others stress
proves costly to the American economy. The second thing people are doing
about stress these days is the management of stress, which has become a
profitable enterprise: stress reduction is good for corporate health. Happy,
healthy employees produce better and more efficiently than do stressed-out
ones. The message has penetrated deep into consciousness as people (primarily managers) take up stress management as a form of self-discipline, as
the spiritual exercise of the day. Stress management is a martial art, protecting
people from the ravages of white noise.

Terry Monroe, the president of a stress management firm, states that "the
single most important cause of stress stems from our absolute depressed
feelings about our inability to change—a sense of lack of control over our
lives."[2] His comment is profound in that it points up the dilemma of stress.
On the surface, it might appear that what he says is false: All we do is change,
insofar as we constantly and often eagerly adapt to the new. Even those
among us who do not idolize progress seek information to help us cope. But
all this adaptation is not the kind of change needed to slip from the yoke of
stress. At the heart of stress lies a helplessness, a kind of despair over the
incessant series of losses whose rapid succession does not leave room for
mourning. Despite the energizing effect of going with the changes and the

comforts they offer, under stress people do feel helpless, since they must be hooked into systems beyond their control or ken. As the quotation from Monroe suggests, the urge is to change ourselves in order to overcome the lack of control. That is what stress management invites: change by taking charge.

In order to evaluate stress management, we need to recall that stress is a metaphor for a specific type of grief that could not exist before the modern world of deadlines, skylines, and EEG lines. Stress names, albeit in a distorted manner, the grief of living with the constant loss of the familiar. Thus, to the extent that stress management programs do not resolve grief by making it possible for people to reformulate the meaning of their lives, the programs exacerbate the stress of living, keeping people in an endless loop of loss and adaptation. The humanistic intentions of stress management and the apparent need to help people cope with stress makes analyzing such programs necessary to the task of finding an end to stress.

THE "IDEOLOGY OF ADAPTATION"

Stress management embraces a large majority of ways of reckoning with stress. Essentially, it represents an ideology of adaptation:[3] By a series of measures, one comes to have the discipline both to accommodate to the inevitability of change, especially that bred by technological progress, and to gain mastery over the process of change. The approach is clearly holistic, ranging from diet, exercise, mental self-development, and styles of social interaction to changes in organizational systems. Stress management programs all have the common end of reducing the toxic effects of stress while maintaining enough tension in the various physiological, psychological, and social systems to provide motivation and interest.

The management of stress is a metaphor derived from business management, and it implies that stress is something to be administered. The discipline of management dates to an 1886 address, "The Engineer and an Economist," that Henry Towne delivered to the American Society of Mechanical Engineers. Towne later wrote that management's principal task is to "welcome and encourage every influence tending to increase the efficiency of our productive processes."[4] This goal remains true; indeed, the scope of management has increased, as a contemporary author underscores:

As a minimal responsibility, management must balance a multitude of individual efforts and keep peace in the corridors.... To put it in engineering parlance, a large corporation is a system in dynamic equilibrium; its parts are moving fast, and if they run in gross imbalance, centrifugal force will tear them apart.

The supervisory role is primary, then, but taken alone it is insufficient.... The manager is expected to be "creative." ... Presumably what it means ... is that management must generate energy as well as channel it.[5]

In the present, as the scope of management has expanded, the management of employee stress has become part of the mandate. Hence the manifesto-like wording of the following:

The rapidly changing nature of work presents an unprecedented challenge for today's managers to create conditions that will release the power of a work force. For too long this group has been constrained by stress associated with change, uncertainty and insecurity. To release this stress, managers must learn to free their employees from such inhibiting forces.[6]

The terms are clear: change and its anxiety generate stress which binds the power of the work force. Workers of the world, relax; you have nothing to lose but your stress.

An ideology of adaptation informs stress management, as May and Kruger admit: "As technology continues to alter and depersonalize the world, people will experience a need to interact more frequently and effectively with each other, particularly in the workplace."[7] That people must adapt to such a world is beyond question. That this world is depersonalized does not matter, since "events have no meaning in and of themselves. Meaning comes from how the event is viewed."[8] These frank admissions of the hostility and sense-lessness of the world and the need to feel comfortable within it insure that grief over the loss of the familiar and the meaningful will never be resolved, since there is always more change to come.

The scope of stress management includes virtually every aspect of living. For present purposes, I restrict the discussion to how it shapes the body and the self.

MANAGING THE BODY

In the midst of white noise, in order to function adequately and even to be happy, we need to feel calm, relaxed, composed. Like combat pilots wing-ing their way at night to bomb map coordinates, we need training and morale-boosting to accomplish our tasks, both on and off the job. For example, working parents must learn to be calm when dealing with their children after a hard day at the office; distraught parents occasionally abuse their children out of frustration or turn to drink to alleviate the anxiety. For reasons such as these, we are urged to work on our bodies to manage stress. Typically, the argument is that because of Cartesian dualism, we are out of touch with our bodies, not realizing when we are tense, anxious, out of shape. We need to get in touch with our bodies for purposes of health and happiness. Stress long endured makes us ill, but fortunately there are specific things we can do to stay (or get) healthy. The topic of the archaic body usually is invoked in the argument: The rage and the anxiety we feel arise because our bodies respond in a primitive manner to cues of danger and threat, even though there is no direct action to take in our day. The desire to beat the children or indulge in a compulsive habit are unhealthy ways to release the tension which results from our archaic bodies, and primarily life-style changes are in order. Dietary changes, exercise programs, new hobbies, and meditation are typically recommended avenues to calm the noble savage. The information about diet and exercise that moves us to do these things helps us get in touch with our bodies. The terms of this information, such as *cholesterol, immune systems, coronary arteries,* etc., have become popular terms that guide actions to manage the body.

There are more direct measures to use to get back in touch with the body— relaxation and visualization. These measures aim at cultivating a body-image for a stress-filled world. One of these techniques is "body scanning," an elaboration of progressive relaxation: "Body scanning uses your inner awareness, rather than your eyes, to examine your body. This kind of scanning involves directing your attention quickly and easily to various parts of your body."[9] The technique works insofar as it calms and centers, while at the same time it teaches its practitioners about the location of stress in their bodies. As an anxiety-reducing method, scanning and its numerous equivalents act as so many Trojan horses, for along with quietude they infiltrate into one's being an alienated image of the body:

[W]hen you scan, you will imagine various parts of your body and check to see if they are tense. Some people imagine a picture of their body, others imagine their muscles as they would be drawn in an anatomy book, and still others imagine parts of a stick figure. One individual found it easier to imagine an x-ray machine scanning his muscles.[10]

This activity of dissecting the felt body into its elements of tension and relaxation exemplifies management techniques of "getting in touch with your body."

Now if we feel better when we relax and scan, why call the technique a Trojan horse? The answer is in turn a question: What do we get in touch with? What image or set of images does stress management inculcate? I would suggest that what is inculcated is a compound image, a four-layer inscription written into the flesh. The top layer is the "information body" of systems thinking. Hence the appropriateness of the term *scan*, which has acquired the meaning of reading or analyzing patterns of lights and shadows and converting them into electrical impulses for the purpose of information processing. Now information processing is inseparably linked with control or "purposive influence toward a predetermined goal."[11] Hence what one reads or processes exerts an influence on experience and action. A basic insight of the information age is that information, tied theoretically to decision theory and to thermodynamics, is not simply "the facts," but particularly in its current usage, carries an implicit coercive force. As Barry Glassner writes of the fitness movement, so too with body-management (which subsumes fitness):

a great advantage of a fit body is that it can be entrusted to perform competently and reliably. . . . The fit body-cum-self is cognized as an information-processing-machine, a machine which can correct and guide itself by means of an internal expert system. When information from the medical and psychological sciences or from health crusaders is received via exercise and diet instructions or the media, the self-qua-information-processor is able to use that information to change its own behavior for the better.[12]

When we get in touch with the information body, we experience as self what are actually fragments of conceptual schemas. These schemas are purveyed by health experts through the media for the purpose of conforming our behavior to what these authorities have decided is "good."[13] We are told what we *need*.[14] It is illusory to believe that we can get in touch with the body without the aid of mediating images. "The soul never thinks without a mental image," Aristotle wrote.[15] The problem with the information body of stress management is the tacit coercive force of what is presented simply as data. The information shapes attitudes and behavior in the direction of personal maintenance for the purpose of fitting us into the world of white noise without detrimental impact.

The information "processed" in body-management derives from at least three scientific areas, whose history we have traced in previous chapters: thermodynamics, strength of materials, and anatomy. The sciences have contributed to the development of the discourse on stress, as we have seen. In stress management techniques, they become more fully inculcated in consciousness, and they actually comprise inscription layers 2, 3, and 4. Layer 2 exerts influence by directing consciousness to questions such as How much energy do I have? How can I get more? Since energy is the ability to do work, the questions help me shape my body to continue to perform with improved efficiency. Layer 3 exerts influence by directing attention to such questions as How much stress can I take without breaking? How can I strengthen my material? These are engineering questions. Layer 4, the bottom layer, the basic text upon which the others are inscribed, is the anatomized body. This body is, as phenomenology has taught us, an alienated body, since it is no-body, no thinking, feeling, willing body. It derives originally from the study of corpses, formerly those of criminals. (Such desecration of these bodies was a form of punishment.) Through emblems omnipresent today, courtesy of the x-ray, television, and CAT scan, we come easily to accept the corpse as the real body. Stress management is a form of training which further instills in consciousness a corpse-like body image with its successive layers of inscriptions. To what end? To the end of molding our behavior and experience; i.e., of living with loss of the familiar without getting sick or going crazy.

Nevertheless, the image of ourselves as living corpses—though we do not usually phrase it thus—calms us and reduces anxiety for several reasons. First, it fosters a sense of control. Since science reveals the inner workings of the anatomical body, to the extent that I live with such a body image, I participate in the power that knowledge brings. I take up the role of anatomist, of x-ray machine, of physician. Second, knowing my body in these terms allies me with the medical community. I become an active member of the health care team when I can describe myself in such terms. Third, the very anonymity of the image provides a measure of community. As stress isolates me in white noise, so this image of an anonymous body makes me feel that I am not alone. This image is appropriate for a stressful world, since it is not my body as lived through and familiar; it is a body I can only have, not a body I can be. But let there be no misunderstanding: such an image keeps me under stress. In no way does it negate stress; in fact, it facilitates being stressed by making the conditions which produce stress tolerable. The body is but one of the things to manage, and with this image, it becomes quite manageable. But at a price, of course: I must envision my flesh as an animated corpse. Stress management strengthens my material so that I do not break under the strain. The techniques do not throw my participation in white noise into question.

SELF-DEVELOPMENT

Management of the body implicates other aspects of personal life, which receive attention through psychological techniques of self-development. Typically these techniques promote an internal locus of control, a sense of self-mastery, effective coping skills, and other measures to offset the sense of helplessness that comes with unresolved grief. By taking up crises as challenges to master and as problems to solve, one develops into a person who can thrive in an increasingly depersonalized setting. For example, in a discussion of problem-solving therapy, we learn that an inability to solve problems causes stress. The goal of the treatment is as follows: "The client is taught how to think and behave in an autonomous, flexible, and scientific manner. Indeed, Mahoney (1974) metaphorically depicts problem-solving therapy as an educational process whereby the client learns how to function as his or her own 'personal scientist.' "[16] As with methods to manage the stressed body, psychological techniques inculcate an image: in this instance (and it is typical), it is the problem solver, the rational, autonomous, flexible analyzer of means. Specifically, this image is of a person capable of recognizing a problem, of finding alternative solutions, of evaluating means and their consequences, and finally of perceiving "cause and effect relations in interpersonal events."[17] The calculative thinking of an autonomous (independent, individualized), flexible (adaptive), scientific (detached enough to see causal networks between people) self is ideally suited to manage stress, for such a self has sufficient distance from the world not to value too highly the familiar merely because it is so.

   The image of the problem-solving self that stress management seeks to instill is deemed good partly because it represents the figures of the engineer and the choice-making exile who creates his own traditions; figures that play so important a role in the rhetoric of stress discourse. Because we have primitive bodies and because we have lost tradition, we need to be experts in problem-solving in order to navigate through the abstract space of modern life. Both the engineer and the exile choose among means. The ends that they serve are not open for discussion. Consideration of ends, meditative thinking, or contemplation makes one less adaptable. Contemplation subverts the discourse on stress.[18]

   Flexibility and detachment are two goals of stress management. Equally important is the ability to wield power. Power in two forms proves to have psychotherapeutic value. An inner locus of control—the perception that one's own actions make a difference—reduces stress. Since, in the mentality of stress, events mean nothing in themselves, an inner sense that one has power— illusory or not—goes a long way to easing the sense that events are out of control. We have seen this argument as we analyzed the rhetoric of stress and the stress discourse. In limited interpersonal spheres, my self-confidence can persuade others (and sometimes myself) that I am in control. But "out there" in the larger society, we are dealing with constant change demanded by technological developments and their social organization. There, our inner locus of control amounts to stoic acquiescence to the inevitable. Among the middle classes, who drink fully of the ideology of stress, the prison that this discourse creates has comforts beyond belief. A curious discipline of consumption of expensive goods and services conditions us to the emptiness. We jog across no-man's land in tip-top shape, health-conscious amidst devastation.

   Beyond inner locus of control, real power reduces stress. Despite the picture of the harried executive, underlings suffer more from stress than do their superiors. The Willy Lomans, not the Richard Corys, succumb to distress. As Kets de Vries discovered, a "power effect" helps to keep managers healthy: "Reduction of uncertainty, through control over information and people can be considered a countervailing force to feelings of helplessness."[19] Moreover, in a kind of voodoo operation, stress can be delegated: "Through the abuse of power, managers can induce stress in their subordinates, and for the person in charge, control over subordinates can have a stress-reducing effect. It is responsibility without control that gives rise to stress."[20] Power operates, however, within constraints, which are not only organizational. The wielders of power need also adapt to a constantly changing world. In a study of "computer anxiety among managers," for instance, two researchers investigated how managers respond to increasing expectations that they operate desktop computers. Change enters an organization, they write, "through technology, structure, or people," because an organization is a system which embraces even the top dogs. They concluded that "effective adaptation to computer technology is taking place in these companies," that managers appreciated the "increased efficiency" the computer offered, but that many complained that they had "less face-to-face contact" than previously.[21] Even powerful decisionmakers must go with the flow or face loss of position.

Instrumental thinking and attaining power are thus two important tools for managing stress. A third, which touches more intimately the human spirit, deserves attention: the management of stress through self-monitoring and meditation. "Self-observation is the first step in personal stress management," write Quick and Quick, for it helps one to learn the causes of stress in oneself.[22] Like inner locus of control, self-monitoring is another aspect of the cultivation of "innerness" typical of stress management. It has often been noted that the modern world has made people more conscious of their inner life, to the extent that the outer world has become devoid of symbol and meaning.[23] When the world cannot be altered, one can change one's self, and self-observation is a first step in that direction. Meditation proves superior to alcohol, drugs, and television for altering the self without getting sick.

Meditation in its various forms manages stress by increasing self-governance and discipline. Since outer change is inevitable, emotional calm and centeredness make these disruptions easier to take. While noting that meditation is a "contemplative state as against a calculating or analytic state of mind," Sethi reasons that meditation is also a tool to achieve relaxation and goals. Meditation frees one from stress because in realizing the illusory nature of the autonomous ego, one realizes also that the "release from stress lies through and not away from the problem—and the problem is born in, and has its sole existence, in the mind."[24] The wisdom of ages speaks in these words, yet one may wonder at the ease with which difficult disciplines such as yoga and meditation find acceptance.

Despite the personal well-being that comes from these techniques, they are means to accommodate people to live stressfully without great pain. Stress is accepted as natural. As Ellul asks: "What can limits mean when psychological devices make it possible to push back all limits?"[25] In sum, these practices of stress management have as their goal the infinite remolding of human beings to fit a world of endlessly engineered changes. Ellul captures the essence of such techniques in observing, "It makes men happy in a milieu which normally would have made them unhappy, if they had not been worked on, molded, and formed for just that milieu."[26] This intention of stress management is rarely mentioned overtly. It is characteristically disguised in an argument such as the following: "Stress is a naturally occurring experience essential to our growth, change, development and performance both at work and at home. Depending on the way in which stress is managed, it may have a detrimental effect on our well-being and health—or it may have a beneficial effect."[27] If we believe that stress is both natural and essential to growth, then of course we will cleave to it as to a lover. But the rhetoric fails when we perceive stress as a product of a blood-sucking quest for efficiency.

THE MONSTER IN THE SHADOW OF
STRESS MANAGEMENT

Stress management intends a good end—the easing of human suffering and pain, and it has not been without success. Yet trailing the good intentions, like a shadow, is a sinister presence that undoes the good and compounds the suffering by miring us deeper in stress. Stress management attempts to construct a rational, powerful, creative, calm being whose body is an animated corpse. For this being, suffering, grief, illness, and even death are not inevitable. The changes to which it adapts include medical advances that sustain its life for an increasing time and creature comforts that eliminate physical work and the discomforts of nature. The price that this being pays for these benefits, however, is enormous: a craving to become the very source of energy that preserves the formless, abstract, bodiless realm of stress. It entails, most fundamentally, not living through the work of grief, never resolving the conflict of grief, but accepting an endless series of hammer blows of loss as the condition for receiving the benefits of stress. When we adopt the metaphor of stress to describe our sufferings and to manage our lives, we become monstrous beings who feed on our own suffering and that of others.

Let us imagine the basic scene: "I" sit at home, tired and frazzled, exhausted from the pressures of the day, from fighting traffic, from stemming the flow from the checkbook, from dealing with the noise or the heat or the constant interruptions during the day, and then from trying to watch television in order to unwind. Sleep eludes "me." What "I" realize, in the typical story of salvation from stress, is that my life-style must change, not that "I" will choose to refuse to participate in the noisy world. That choice seems unimaginable. No, "I" take up stress-reducing measures and soon feel better, more relaxed, more in control.

Rather than dying to the stressful world—whatever that could mean at this juncture—"I" face it on its own terms; "I" become disciplined through management techniques to deal flexibly and calmly with the flow of change. Rather than give in, at the moment of being drained "I" bite back by becoming the center of the whirlwind, not its victim. Thereby "I" become more in harmony with stress, living on its purchasable substances: energy and information. Now stress energizes "me" rather than drains "me"; "I" do not have to die (or get sick), for "I" have transformed stress into energy.

Is it any surprise to learn that people have become addicted to lives of stress? The energizing effect of undergoing stress has the potential for compulsive activity, especially when it has power as its accompaniment. "I work best under pressure," or as Waino Suojanen, a professor of business management observes: "There is plenty of anecdotal evidence that some executives deliberately seek out the management life because they get a high out of controlling people."[28] Suojanen also asserts that some "managers become so proud of their ability to stand up under crises that they are always creating crises to stand up under, or are always starting fires in order to put them out."[29] But not only managers get addicted to stress. It is nearly universal when under stress to feed on speed, pressure, and energy. In short, to consume stress pure and simple is to be powerful, superhuman.

The phenomenon of stress addiction has arisen in recent years, in part because addiction has become a catchall term for bad habits and in part because a consumer society pushed to its limits has the addict as its ideal type. The figure of the addict so exercises the contemporary imagination that whereas in the past the addict was an other, now it appears as a figure of the self. Stress addiction, or "how to turn tension into energy," goes to the source of what addiction desires: the high, the vertical thrust that lifts us above the merely human. We stress addicts become bestial in our search for the next hit, the next sublime moment, the next crisis.

"COMPLETE FREEDOM FROM STRESS IS DEATH"

Stress management habituates us to a world of relentless change. As "I" do so, "I" lose the flesh of the familiar and feel more at home in an abstract, formless, noisy space-time. Stress thus managed promises immortality as human limits are transcended, but its truth would be the endless living of Tithonos, who in Greek myth was the human lover of Eos, the dawn. She gave Tithonos immortality but not eternal youth, and a horrid fate awaited him. Like Tithonos, we cannot actually transcend the flesh; like him we will grow decrepit, surrounded by light-bringing lovers, the life-support machines, whose allures are life extension and life enhancement. Stress management is Eos to our Tithonos. By converting the passion of grief into energy, we buy time. With our stress management programs, the profound conflict that working through grief would heal becomes harnessed instead for work.

What alternative is there? The phrase which heads this section comes from Selye,[30] although he did not mean it in quite the way I will take it. Where death has a place, stress cannot abide. So to escape from the discourse on stress and the engineering of grief, we need to give death a prominent place again. We live in a time of what Ariès calls "forbidden death,"[31] when public displays of mourning and rituals to mark solidarity with the past have been reduced to a bare minimum. We have no time for death, because time is too expensive to waste in unproductive activity. But to end the reign of engineered grief, we will need public acknowledgment of death and the waste of time required for the display of mourning. Most important, we need to de-engineer our grief, render it "unmanageable," de-develop it. Thus, we do not need more prescriptions about what to do, since escape from stress cannot be prescribed. The most that can be done in a general way is to indicate how the ground of our hearts can be prepared for grief. Three preconditions for this grief are the flesh of loss and remembering, empty time, and an empty place.

THE FLESH OF LOSS AND REMEMBERING

Then comes a sudden jab of red-hot memory.
—C. S. Lewis, *A Grief Observed*

A loss that occasions grief is a wound. This is no mere analogy, but a painful reality that the bereaved feel. Insofar as stress is unresolved grief, it is necessary to recover the felt sense of the wound of loss in order to mourn. The location of the wound varies, but typically the pain centers in the heart. With stress, however, the sense of being stricken is usually diffuse, less focused, the result of its disembodying nature. Sometimes stress bombards us from all sides; at other times, it has a peculiar precision: "employees feel like we're the anvil and everybody's beating on us with a hammer."[32] But whether the wounds come from the flak of hurry or from the hammer of criticism, the first task is to disengage these moments from the engineering mentality that asks How much can I take? Is my material adaptable enough? Can I cope? For these moments are not attacks; they are wounds in the heart. And these wounds embody the potential to bring back to reality an old idea and perception that things which matter dwell in the flesh. The work of grief that this pain facilitates can have the salutary effect of awakening us so keenly to our pain that we realize that the flesh is no animated corpse but our very selves. Loss wounds the heart (not the pump) because love and commitment dwell in the heart. When we feel the loss as loss, then we can suffer it. Taking loss to heart makes it impossible to convert the anguish of the wound into energy; it makes us "dysfunctional." Loss that is felt gives weight to the flesh: the weight of depression, sadness, anger, helplessness. These are the effects one seeks in order to escape stress. It means in the first instance that the animated corpse that stress management constructs is beginning to decay. This decaying corpse is in truth the body becoming flesh again.

The flesh is the body of the familiar. This description is true to the old echoes of "flesh" from scripture and elsewhere which bring together the self as somebody and all that belongs as part of somebody: "flesh of my flesh" (children, kin), "one flesh" (husband and wife), "the flesh is weak" (desire, passion, resistance to excesses of the spirit). Like William James's notion of the "material me," the flesh is also all that is concretely mine: clothes, dwelling, possessions, land.[33] As Merleau-Ponty writes in his philosophy of the flesh, the things of the world are enfleshed and reflect my lived body. To the extent I experience my own flesh, I can perceive the world as flesh of my flesh.[34] Under stress the flesh withers, vanishes, is transcended, so that dwelling in the flesh becomes problematic. The concept of "psychic numbing" that Robert Jay Lifton developed in his studies of Hiroshima survivors has relevance here,[35] although I do not want to conflate everyday stresses with such a disaster. But the perception of our griefs as stress numbs us to the pain that we might otherwise feel. We are numb, anesthetized by our hurrying to keep up with the changes, unable to stop and notice our own pain and that of others.

To bring the flesh back into perception, an anti-stress meditation may prove helpful. The *Secretum* of Petrarch contains a meditative exercise from a late medieval tradition. It is particularly graphic, even grotesque, flying in the face of our sanitized images of the healthy, anatomized body. It evokes the flesh in all its materiality. Petrarch provides a guide to a meditation on death that is the polar opposite of our command, "Relax!"

So here is a test which will never play you false: every time you meditate on death without the least sign of motion, know that you have meditated in vain, as about any ordinary topic. But if in the act of meditation you find yourself suddenly grow stiff, if you tremble, turn pale, and feel as if already you endured its pains . . . [and after meditating on the Four Final Things] then you may be assured you have not meditated in vain.[36]

Now to the meditation:

of all tremendous realities Death is the most tremendous. So true is this, that from ever of old its very name is terrible and dreadful to hear. Yet though so it is, it will not do that we hear that name but lightly, or allow the remembrance of it to slip quickly from our mind. No, we must take time to realize it. We must meditate with attention thereon. We must picture to ourselves the effect of death on each several part of our bodily frame, the cold extremities, the breast in the sweat of fever, the side throbbing with pain, the vital spirits running slower and slower as death draws near, the eyes sunken and weeping, every look filled with tears, the forehead pale and drawn, the cheeks hanging and hollow, the teeth staring and discolored, the nostrils shrunk and sharpened, the lips foaming, the tongue foul and motionless, the palate parched and dry, the languid head and panting breast, the hoarse murmur and sorrowful sigh, the evil smell of the whole body, the horror of seeing the face utterly unlike itself.[37]

This practice came from a mentality alien to the modern mind, although in one way at least the late medieval period resembles our own. It was a time of war and plague, when death was everpresent. In our own day, when "megadeath" has been coined in the wake of two world wars, bureaucratically organized genocides and the specter of a nuclear winter or an ecological disaster, the practice of meditating on death may not be entirely foreign to our secular mentality. And it is germane to our time for a more profound reason. Writing a generation ago, the French philosopher Gabriel Marcel discerned that the mood of our time is one of a "choking sadness."[38] Martin

Heidegger found the same mood necessary for the "turning" of technology into its truth: The restoration of technology into its truth will resemble, he wrote, "what happens when, in the human realm, one gets over grief or pain."[39] The metaphor of stress has been an impediment to the recognition of this mood.[40]

I call the meditation that comes from Petrarch an "anti-stress" exercise because it makes us neither more nor less resilient to stress. Its aim is to pierce the "I" that lives under stress and expose it to the losses that stress as a construct makes difficult to mourn. It holds up to the imagination an image of the body as bound to loss and death: not the anatomized body, fixated by embalming fluids, but the flesh with its feelings and frailties. This vision of the dying flesh, less experienceable today than in Petrarch's time, may move us from stress to a passion for living. We do not seem able to care passionately about the world or about things unless we are enfleshed, for things reflect our flesh in their own. As Ariès comments:

"We must leave behind our house, our orchards, and our gardens, dishes and vessels which the artisan engraved," wrote Ronsard, reflecting upon death. Which of us faced with death would weep over a house in Florida or a farm in Virginia? In proto-capitalist eras—in other words, in periods when the capitalist and technological mentality was being developed, the process would not be completed until the eighteenth century—man had an unreasoning, visceral love for *temporalia*, which was a blanket word including things, men, and animals.[41]

People can love things with intensity to the extent they know the impermanence of things and of themselves. Numbed, we cannot attend to the ephemeral nature of things. We need to become materialists again.[42]

Finally, all this is to say that the flesh is the archaic body, that staple of the world of stress. But it is not through reflex that the flesh fails to accommodate modern dilemmas. Its resistance constitutes a call to mourning and memory.

EMPTY TIME

To bring the flesh back into perception, we need a time for ritualized mourning. How can that be arranged in a world which leaves no time for anything, much less grieving? By a negative ritual, a content-less ritual that no one authorizes or plans, an unmanaged ritual, a ritual of empty time. In a moment of empty time, one can begin to listen to the story of one's flesh, and begin to reformulate the meaning of one's life. In the hearing of the story, past and future can begin to be reconciled. To what end? No one knows. The future, like empty time, cannot be managed. All we know for sure is that when we stop coping, we can grieve; and when we open our hearts to grief, we can love again. To the extent we stop, we step out from under stress. To stop, we must step into empty time, a ritual step for an age of technological management.

Empty time is simplified time. Critics of luxury from the eighteenth and nineteenth centuries had the right idea, at least in this sense: In order to prepare a time for mourning, we "open up" time by taking seriously again the admonitions to avoid luxury. Time is expensive and vanishes to the extent we maintain ourselves under stress. The pursuit of luxury gets us the goods but leaves us time-paupers. Whereas in the eighteenth century, luxury was said to cause disease and vice, and whereas in the nineteenth century, the excessive pursuit of luxury was declared to be contrary to enlightened self-interest, I offer neither a moral nor a rationalistic ground for the critique of luxury. The ground for our day is of necessity psychological and spiritual. We need the simple life that comes from unluxurious living in order to have the empty time for grief.

The ideal of simplicity constitutes the horizon of this meditation on engineered grief. What is simplicity? To be simple is to stay within the bounds of necessity. I do not presume to delimit what is necessary for a human life, except to say that time is necessary. We under stress are time-paupers, and simplicity gives us time.[43]

EMPTY PLACE

As empty time is necessary, so is empty place, for just as stress and its management eliminates meaningful time, so it eliminates dwelling. In a profound sense we are no place when under stress. Men under stress live in no-man's land. Whatever else *place* means, it means first and foremost where the flesh is and where human dwelling occurs.[44] In an existential sense, dwelling occurs when one is at home. Being-at-home is not only or even primarily being at ease, but it is "a radical and crucial tension that emerges . . . between openness and enclosure."[45] Being at home is thus not primarily relaxation, though that may be part of it, but it is a being bound and contained and simultaneously open to the outside, to others. Among the resonances of at-homeness that are relevant here, I want to single out being at home with oneself. Being at home in this restricted psychological sense thus refers to the act of being intimate with oneself.[46]

A place, a dwelling, an at-homeness, is necessary for the act of grieving. Because grief enables continuity between the past and the future, it needs a place to be present, to present the persistence of the past into the future. What kind of place does grief need? Not the geometric void of stress, the formless white noise where we hurry after the chimera of energy. In conjunction with the kind of time required for transforming stress into grief, the place of grief for our lost worlds will have to be by necessity a minimal place, reached by a *via negativa*. It will be an empty place. Only such a place is appropriate to a time when old cultural forms no longer nurture the soul and the spirit, when the horrors of the age render problematic appeals to old pieties, and when the cultural forms that might exist some day have not been formulated, such that for now continuity with the past is uncertain.

The ritual of establishing an empty place has this form: In the midst of the creature comforts of our age, in the midst of the infinite number of consumer goods and services, in the midst of the techniques for accommodating our anomie to the boundless stimulation of externalized desire, we must simply greet the neediness that emerges from the core of our being with a resounding "yes." We do not need to ease the pain; rather we need to acknowledge and witness it. Let us call the void that we fill with "energy" by another name—poverty. If in one respect we are like Tithonos, in another we are like Midas. All that we touch turns into energy, but nothing enriches us as creatures of flesh and bone. The "I" of stress stops when it greets with hospitality the poverty that hitherto it has called the need for energy. The hurry of stress masks this poverty, a poverty all the more profound because it exists but we do not recognize it. The alien world, the ambivalence toward loss, the accommodation to change: A stockpile of emptiness builds up, and not being recognized, not lived through in bereavement, feeds the frantic pace. Then, "wiped out," the cycle begins anew. To refuse energy in the name of poverty makes the celebration of grief possible. Mourning can thus begin and stress end when we are exhausted, stressed out, frazzled. At that moment if we embrace the ideal of simplicity we can occupy the empty place that removes us from the white noise of stress. We then greet our neediness with hospitality and not with infusions of energy. To be thus impoverished is a condition no commodity can enrich; only the gifts which come freely in celebration can answer such poverty.

What constitutes such an empty place? An image of an open grave will suffice for it: An emptiness that waits to be filled, for a human gathering to celebrate by recalling the past through story and public ceremony, by acknowledging the emptiness and sadness of the present, and by hoping for a future in which the wounds of loss will be healed, the loss comprehended by new patterns of living that incorporate the past. The flesh, the empty time, the empty place: imaged as an open grave, ready for mourners to begin.

An empty place is the location of the exile; it is that central commonplace of stress. To the extent that we acknowledge the emptiness, we are and are not exiled. We are, since the place is empty, and we cannot act heroically. We are not, in so far as it is a place, a dwelling where the past exists by being remembered in words and monuments, and where the future abides by virtue of the act of recollection that opens the door to a new day.

How to make the celebration of loss possible? How to find the empty place that will foster connection between the past, and the flesh of the past that we have already lost with our present world of white noise? The precondition for celebration is dwelling or being at home. When at home, a person can host others, and the duty of the host is to offer hospitality. The host offers guests gifts, the first of which is time. With the giving of gifts people leave the domain of scarcity, escape the grip of stress. In fact, abundance proliferates to the extent that one gives gifts. Energy is not lost, because energy cannot exist in a dwelling place, where host and guest meet. To greet the neediness with hospitality, we need to be at home to greet it.

Gifts are not scarce commodities. They are always plentiful. With arms outstretched, backs turned to the temples of scarcity, we celebrate: "A festival is essentially a phenomenon of wealth; not, to be sure, the wealth of money, but of existential richness. Absence of calculation, in fact lavishness, is one of its elements."[47] A mentality of feasting escapes the instrumental reasoning that manages stress.

Thus enfleshed and impoverished, we celebrate our losses, not nostalgic for the past, not enthralled with the brave new world. In grieving for our selves and our world, we take up a place, stepping from white noise with its swirling winds and fast lanes. Our place is filled with modern junk, surrounded by noise and speed, with fleshless, energized, calm, stress-managing people, the time-paupers, but a place nonetheless, in which to bury the dead. The absence of stress is nothing positive. It exists now as a negativity, an emptiness of time and place, in which we may be free to bid the past adieu and to hope for the future.

NOTES

1. Martin Heidegger, "The turning," in *The Question Concerning Technology and Other Essays*, trans. W. Lovitt (New York: Harper Colophon, 1977), p. 39.

2. Cited in Susan Banham, "Stress in the workplace—What can be done about it?" *Insurance Review* (May/June 1985), 12.

3. Peter Marris, "The social impact of stress," in *Mental Health and the Economy*, ed. L. A. Ferman and J. P. Gordus (Kalamazoo, MI: W. E. Upjohn Institute for Employment Research, 1979), p. 311.

4. Cited in Allen C. Bluedorn, Introduction, to "Special book review section on the classics of management," *Academy of Management Review* 11, no. 2 (April 1986), 443.

5. Carl B. Kaufman, *Man Incorporate: The Individual and His Work in an Organizational Society* (Garden City, NY: Anchor Books, 1969), p. 140.

6. Gregory D. May and Michael J. Kruger, "The Manager Within," *Personnel Journal*, February 1988, 57.

7. Ibid., p. 65.

8. Ibid., p. 57.

9. Edward Charlesworth and Ronald Nathan, *A Comprehensive Guide to Wellness* (New York: Atheneum, 1984), p. 60.

10. Ibid., pp. 62–63.

11. James Beniger, *The Control Revolution: Technological and Economic Origins of the Information Society* (Cambridge, MA: Harvard University Press, 1986), p. 7.

12. Barry Glassner, "Fitness and the postmodern self," *Journal of Health and Social Behavior* 30, no. 2 (1989), 17.

13. Irving Kenneth Zola, in "Healthism and disabling medicalization," in Illich, *Disabling Professions*, summarizes some of arguments that medicine has replaced religion as the source of authority on the good life and the inequities in this cult of healthism. "Basically my contention is that the increasing use of illness as a lever in the understanding of social problems represents no dramatic shift from a moral view to a neutral one but merely to an alternate strategy. . . . The problem being scrutinized and the person being changed is no less immoral for all the medical rhetoric. It or he is still a 'problem,' though the rhetoric may convince us that he and not the society is responsible, and he not the society should be changed" (p. 65).

14. On the creation of needs, see Ivan Illich, "Disabling professions," in *Disabling Professions* (Boston: Marion Boyars, 1977), 11–40.

15. Aristotle, *De Anima*, III, vii.

16. Donald Meichenbaum, David Henshaw and Norman Himel, "Coping with stress as a problem-solving process," in H. Krohne and L. Laux, eds., *Achievement, Stress, and Anxiety* (Washington: Hemisphere Publishing 1982), pp. 139–40.

17. Ibid., p. 138.

18. The focus on solving problems but not considering ends besides those of efficiency and power is deeply rooted in this mentality: "But in every case the rise of managerial expertise would have to be the same central theme, and such expertise, . . . has two sides to it: there is the aspiration to value neutrality and the claim to manipulative power" [Alasdair MacIntyre, *After Virtue: A Study in Moral Theory*, 2nd ed. (Notre Dame, IN: University of Notre Dame Press, 1984), p. 86].

19. M. F. R. Kets de Vries, "Organizational stress management audit," in A. S. Sethi and R. S. Schuler, eds., *Handbook of Organizational Stress Coping Strategies* (Cambridge, MA: Ballinger, 1984), p. 267.

20. Ibid., p. 269.

21. Virginia T. Geurin and Gary F. Kohut, "Dimensions of computer anxiety among managers: A field study," *Human Resource Management and Organizational Behavior Proceedings* (1987 HRMOB Annual National Conference), Vol. I, pp. 305–09.

22. James C. Quick and Jonathan D. Quick, *Organizational Stress and Preventive Management* (New York: McGraw-Hill, 1984), p. 266.

23. For a positive assessment of this development, see C. G. Jung, *Modern Man in Search of a Soul* (New York: Harcourt Brace Jovanovich, N.D.); for a critical view, see Arnold Gehlen, *Man in Age of Technology* (New York: Columbia University Press, 1980).

24. Amarjit S. Sethi, "Contemplative strategies for technostress management," in A. S. Sethi, D. H. J. Caro, R. S. Schuler, eds., *Strategic Management of Technostress in an Information Society*, (Toronto: C. J. Hogrefe, 1987), p. 297.

25. Jacques Ellul, *The Technological Society*, trans. J. Wilkinson (New York: Vintage Books, 1964), p. 324.

26. Ibid., p. 348.

27. Jonathan Quick, Rebecca Horn, James Quick, "Health consequences of stress," *Journal of Organizational Behavior Management* 8, no. 2 (1986), 19–20.

28. Quoted in Richard Lyons, "Stress addiction: 'Life in the fast lane' may have its benefits," *New York Times*, 21 July 1983, section III, p. 1:1.

29. Larry Pace and Waino Suojanen, "Addictive Type A behavior undermines employee involvement," *Personnel Journal* 67, no. 6 (June 1988), 40.

30. Hans Selye, *Stress Without Distress* (Philadelphia & New York: Lippincott, 1974), p. 32.

31. Philippe Ariès, *Western Attitudes toward Death from the Middle Ages to the Present*, trans. Patricia M. Ranum (Baltimore: Johns Hopkins University Press, 1974).

32. Curtis Austin, "DART's problems shake staff," *Dallas Times-Herald*, 2 April 1989, p. A–23.

33. William James, *The Principles of Psychology* (1890; reprint, New York: Dover Books, 1950), Vol. I, p. 292.

34. "My body is made of the same flesh as the world (it is a perceived), and moreover that this flesh of my body is shared by the world, the world *reflects* it, encroaches upon it and it encroaches upon the world . . ., they are in a relation of transgression or of overlapping" [Maurice Merleau-Ponty, *The Visible and the Invisible*, trans. Alphonso Lingis (Evanston: Northwestern University Press, 1968), p. 248].

35. Robert Jay Lifton, *Death in Life: Survivors of Hiroshima* (New York: Vintage Books, 1967). Mitchell Young and Cassandra Erickson ["Cultural impediments to recovery: PTSD in contemporary America," *Journal of Traumatic Stress* 1, no. 4 (1988), 436] write that in this time of cultural transition, "when cultural images and symbols are inadequate, individuals may become devitalized—a sense of meaning and continuity in life becomes difficult to find. Lifton . . . refers to this affective response as psychic numbing."

36. Francesco Petrarcha, *Petrarch's Secret or The Soul's Conflict with Reason*, trans. W. H. Draper (London: Chatto & Windus, 1911), pp. 34–35.

37. Ibid., pp. 32–33.

38. Gabriel Marcel, quoted in William Luijpen, *Existential Phenomenology*, rev. ed. (Pittsburgh: Duquesne University Press, 1969), p. 255.

39. Heidegger, "The turning," p. 39.

40. Scholar and psychotherapist Robert Romanyshyn, in *Technology as Symptom and Dream* (New York: Routledge & Kegan Paul, 1989), calls for an "ethic of sadness" as a way to come to terms with the depression that plagues people in a technological society.

41. Ariès, *Western Attitudes*, p. 45.

42. For the meaning of *materialist* in this sense, see Alan Watts, *Does It Matter? Essays on Man's Relation to Materiality* (New York: Vintage Books, 1970): "The commonly accepted notion that Americans are materialists is pure bunk. A materialist is one who loves material, a person devoted to the enjoyment of the physical and immediate present. By this definition, most Americans are abstractionists. They *hate* material, and convert it as swiftly as possible into mountains of junk and clouds of poisonous gas" (p. 29). Watt's book is rich with such comments, though I take issue with his depiction of the body as a swirling dance of energy.

43. In a related critique of luxury, Langdon Winner, "Techné and Politeai," in *The Whale and the Reactor: A Search for Limits in an Age of High Technology* (Chicago: University of Chicago Press, 1986), p. 57, writes: "A crucial failure in modern political thought and political practice has been an inability or unwillingness even to begin . . . the critical evaluation and control of our society's technical constitution. The silence of liberalism on this issue is matched by an equally obvious neglect in Marxist theory. Both persuasions have enthusiastically sought freedom in sheer material plenitude, welcoming whatever technological means (or monstrosities) seemed to produce abundance the fastest. It is, however, a mistake to construct one sociotechnical system

after another in the blind faith that each will turn out to be politically benign. Many crucial choices about the forms and limits of our regimes of instrumentality must be enforced at the founding, at the genesis of each new technology." Earlier in the essay, he indicates how the Founding Fathers of the United States, Jefferson in particular, warned against the heedless pursuit of luxuries as a threat to republican virtues.

44. For "place," see Edward Casey, *Remembering: A Phenomenological Study* (Bloomington: Indiana University Press, 1987).

45. Frank Buckley, "An approach to a phenomenology of at-homeness," in A. Giorgi, W. F. Fischer, and R. von Eckartsberg, eds., *Duquesne Studies in Phenomenological Psychology*, Vol. I, (Pittsburgh: Duquesne University Press, 1971), p. 207. For further reading on the phenomenology of at-homeness, see Gaston Bachelard, *The Poetics of Space*, trans. C. Gaudin (Boston: Beacon, 1969).

46. An age of stress is thus an age of depression, insofar as depression is a pathology of not being at home, of longing for a lost or even a nonexistent home. After all, under stress we are exiles. For consideration of the theme of homelessness and depression in the American psyche, see Robert Romanyshyn and Brian Whalen, "Depression and the American Search for Home," in D. M. Levin, ed., *Pathologies of the Modern Self* (New York: New York University Press, 1987), pp. 198–220.

47. Joseph Pieper, *In Tune with the World: A Theory of Festivity*, trans. R. and C. Winston (New York: Harcourt, Brace & World, 1965), p. 15.

Bibliography

Abbey, Edward, *The Brave Cowboy*. 1956. Reprint, Albuquerque: University of New Mexico Press, 1977.

Abrahams, Adolphe, " 'Soldier's heart,' " *Lancet*, 1917, no. 1, 442–445.

———, "Physiology of violent exercise in relation to the possibility of strain." *Lancet* 1 (1928), 429–35.

Achterberg, Jeanne and G. Frank Lawlis, *Bridges of the Bodymind: Behavioral Approaches to Health Care* . Champaign, IL: Institute for Personality and Ability Testing, 1980.

Ackerknecht, Erwin, *A Short History of Medicine*, rev. ed. Baltimore: Johns Hopkins University Press, 1982.

Adami, J. George, *The Principles of Pathology*. Vol. I: *General Pathology*. Philadelphia and New York: Lea & Febiger, 1908.

"Aetiology of diseases of the heart." *Lancet*, 1845, no. 2, 596.

Ahrenfeldt, Robert, *Psychiatry in the British Army in the Second World War*. New York: Columbia University Press, 1958.

Albrecht, Karl, *Stress and the Manager*. Englewood Cliffs, NJ: Prentice-Hall, 1979.

Alford, S. S., "Defective nerve-power as a primary cause of disease, with its special relation to dipsomania." *British Medical Journal*, 1881, no. i, 591–93.

Allbut, T. Clifford. "On the hypodermic use of morphia in diseases of the heart and great vessels." Excerpted in *Retrospect of Practical Medicine and Surgery* 61 (July 1870), 61–63.

———, "The progress of the art of medicine." *Lancet*, 1870, no. 2, 37–39.

———, "The effect of overwork and strain on the heart and great blood-vessels." *St. George's Hospital Reports* 5 (1870), 23–53, excerpted in *Retrospect of Practical Medicine and Surgery* 64 (January 1872), 72–78.

———, "On brain forcing." *Brain* 1, no. 1 (1878), 60–78.

———, "Nervous diseases and modern life." *Contemporary Review* 67 (Jan.–June 1895), 210–31.

———, "Over-stress of the heart." In *A System of Medicine*, 2nd ed., ed. T. Clifford Allbutt and Humphry Davy Rolleston. Vol. 6: *Diseases of the Heart and Blood-Vessels*, pp. 193–252. London: Macmillan, 1909.

———, "On neurasthenia." In *System of Medicine*, 2nd ed., ed. Clifford Allbutt and Humphry Davy Rolleston, Vol. 8: *Diseases of the Brain and Mental Disease*, pp. 727–91. London: Macmillan, 1910.

———, "The physician and the pathologist on heart failure." *British Medical Journal*, 1912, no. i, 653, 862.

———, *Diseases of the Arteries, Including Angina Pectoris*. London: Macmillan, 1915.

———, "The Lumleian Lectures and medical research: 'Innocent murmurs,' " *Lancet*, 1917, no. 2, 172–73.

———, "Medicine and the people: A review of some latter-day tracts." *British Medical Journal*, 1919, no. ii, 763.

Anderson, H. B., "Strain as a factor in cardio-aortic lesions." *British Medical Journal*, 1905, no. ii 840–45.

Andreason, N. J. C., R. Noyes, and C. E. Hartford, "Factors influencing adjustments of burn patients during hospitalization." In *Stress and Coping: An Anthology*, ed. A Monat and R. S. Lazarus. New York: Columbia University Press, 1977.

Antonovsky, Aaron, *Health, Stress and Coping*. San Francisco: Jossey-Bass, 1979.

Ariès, Philippe, *Western Attitudes Toward Death from the Middle Ages to the Present*, trans. Patricia M. Ranum. Baltimore: Johns Hopkins University Press, 1974.

Aristotle, *De Anima*.

Arney, William, *Experts in the Age of the System*. Albuquerque: University of New Mexico Press, 1991.

Arney, William, and Bernard Bergen, *Medicine and the Management of Living: Taming the Last Great Beast*. Chicago: University of Chicago Press, 1984.

Austin, Curtis, "DART's problems shake staff." *Dallas Times-Herald* (2 April 1989), p. A–23.

Bachelard, Gaston, *The Poetics of Space*, trans. C. Gaudin. Boston: Beacon, 1969.

Balfour, George William, *Clinical Lectures on Diseases of the Heart*. Philadelphia: Lindsay & Blakiston, 1876.

Banham, Susan, "Stress in the workplace—What can be done about it?" *Insurance Review* (May/June 1985).

Bartemeier, Leo H., Lawrence S. Kubie, Karl M. Menninger, et al., "Combat exhaustion." *Journal of Nervous and Mental Diseases* 104 (October and November 1946).

Baum, Andrew, Jerome Singer, and Carlene Baum, "Stress and the environment." *Journal of Social Issues* 37, no. 1 (1981).

Beck, Aaron, "Cognitive approaches to stress." In *Principles and Practices of Stress Management*, ed. Robert Woolfolk and Paul Lehrer. New York: Guilford Press, 1984.

Benison, Saul, A. Clifford Barger, Elin L. Wolfe, *Walter B. Cannon: The Life and Times of a Young Scientist*. Cambridge: Belknap Press, 1987.

Berger, Peter, Manfried Kellner, Brigit Berger, *The Homeless Mind: Modernization and Consciousness*. New York: Vintage Books, 1983.

Berman, Marshall, *All That Is Solid Melts into Air: The Experience of Modernity*. New York: Simon & Schuster, 1982.

Bertalanffy, Ludwig von, "An outline of general systems theory." *British Journal of the Philosophy of Science* 1 (1950).

Bishop, John, "On the causes, pathology, and treatment of deformities in the human body." *Lancet*, 1846, no. i, 122–25, 323–26.

Bluedorn, Allen C., "Introduction to special book review section on the classics of management." *Academy of Management Review* 11, no. 2 (April 1986).

Bogacz, Ted, "War neurosis and cultural change in England, 1914–22: The work of the War Office Committee of Enquiry into 'Shell-Shock.' " *Journal of Contemporary History* 24, no. 2 (April 1989).

Boulanger, Ghislaine, "Post-traumatic stress syndrome: An old problem with a new name." In *The Trauma of War: Stress and Recovery in Viet Nam Veterans*. Washington, DC: American Psychiatric Press, 1985.

Bowditch, H. I., "Diseases of the heart in consequence of violent exertion in running." *Boston Medical and Surgical Journal* 59 (1858–59), 456.

Bradshaw, John, *Healing the Pain That Binds You*. Deerfield, FL: Health Communications, 1988.

"Broad Blue," letter to the *London Times*, October 14, 1867, p. 10.

Brown, JoAnn, *The Semantics of Profession: Metaphor and Power in the History of Psychological Testing, 1890–1929*. Ph.D. dissertation. Madison: University of Wisconsin, 1985.

Buchanan, Andrew, "On the force of the human heart." *Lancet*, 1870, no. 2, 665–66.

Buchanan, R. A., "Gentlemen engineers: The making of a profession." *Victorian Studies* 26, no. 4 (1983).

Buckley, Frank, "An Approach to a Phenomenology of At-Homeness." In *Duquesne Studies in Phenomenological Psychology: Volume I*, eds. A. Giorgi, W. F. Fischer, and R. von Eckartsberg (Pittsburgh: Duquesne University Press, 1971).

Bucknill, John Charles and Daniel Tuke, *Manual of Psychological Medicine*. Philadelphia: Blanchard & Lea, 1858.

Burchfield, Susan, "The stress response: A new perspective," *Psychosomatic Medicine* 41, no. 8 (December 1979).

———, "Stress: An Integrative Framework." In S. Burchfield, *Stress: Psychological and Physiological Interactions*. Washington: Hemisphere Publishing, 1985.

Burnett, J., "The origins of the electrocardiograph as a clinical instrument." In *The Emergence of Modern Cardiology*, London: Wellcome Institute of the History of Medicine, ed. W. F. Bynum, C. Lawrence, and V. Nutton, Supplement No. 5. 1985. *Medical History*, pp. 53–76.

Burns, Allan, *Observations on Some of the Most Frequent and Important Diseases of the Heart* (reviewed). *Edinburgh Medical and Surgical Journal* 5 (1809).

Bynum, W. F., "The nervous patient in eighteenth and nineteenth century Britain: The psychiatric origins of British Neurology." In *The Anatomy of Madness: Essays in the History of Psychiatry*, Vol. I, ed. W. F. Bynum, Roy Porter, and Michael Shepherd, pp. 89–102. London: Tavistock, 1985.

Camfield, Thomas M., "The professionalization of American psychology." *Journal of the History of the Behavioral Sciences* 9, (1973).

Cannon, Walter B., "The stimulation of adrenal secretion by emotional excitement." *Journal of the American Medical Association* 56 (1911), 742.

———, *Bodily Changes in Pain, Hunger, Fear and Rage*. New York: Norton, 1929.

———, *The Wisdom of the Body*. New York: Norton, 1932.

———, "Biocracy: Does the human body contain the secret of economic stabilization?" *The Technology Review* 35, no. 6 (March 1933), 203–206, 227.

———, "Stresses and strains of homeostasis." *American Journal of the Medical Sciences* 189 (1935) 1–14.

Cantril, Hadley, *The Invasion from Mars: A Study in the Psychology of Panic*. 1940. Reprint, New York: Harper Torchbooks, 1966.

Casey, Edward, *Remembering: A Phenomenological Study*. Bloomington: Indiana University Press, 1987.

Caughey, J. L., "Cardiovascular neurosis—A review." *Psychosomatic Medicine* 1, no. 2 (April 1939), 311–24.

Cerullo, John, *The Secularization of the Soul: Psychical Research in Modern Britain*. Philadelphia: Institute for the Study of Human Issues, 1982.

Charlesworth, Edward and Ronald Nathan, *A Comprehensive Guide to Wellness*. New York: Atheneum, 1984.

Cheyne, George. *The English Malady*. 1733. Reprint, New York: Scholars Facsimiles & Reprints, 1976.

Clark, A., "Some observations concerning what is called neurasthenia." *Lancet*, 1886, no. 1, 1.

Clark, F., "Some remarks on nervous exhaustion and on vasomotor action." *Journal of Anatomy and Physiology* 18 (London 1883–84), 239–56.

Clarke, Edward H., "Practical medicine." In *A Century of American Medicine*, eds. E. H. Clarke, H. J. Bigelow, S. D. Gross, et al. 1876. Reprint, New York: Burt Franklin, 1971.

Cohen, S., "Aftereffects of stress on human performance and social behavior: A review of research and theory." *Psychological Bulletin* 88 (1980).

Comaroff, J., "Medicine: symbol and ideology." In *The Problem of Medical Knowledge*, eds. P. Wright and A. Treacher, pp. 49–68. Edinburgh: Edinburgh University Press, 1988.

Corvisart, Jean-Nicolas, *An Essay on the Organic Diseases and Lesions of the Heart and Great Vessels*, trans. J. Gater. 1812. Reprint, New York: Hafner, 1962.

Cousins, Norman, *Modern Man Is Dead*. New York: Random House, 1945.

Cross, Stephen, and William R. Albury, "Walter B. Cannon, L. J. Henderson, and the organic analogy." *Osiris* 3, 2nd series (1987).

Cushman, Philip, "Why the self is empty: Toward a historically situated psychology." *American Psychologist* 45 (1990), 599–611.

DaCosta, Jacob M., "On irritable heart: A clinical study of a form of functional cardiac disorder and its consequences." *American Journal of the Medical Sciences* (1871).

———, *On Strain and Overaction of the Heart*. Washington, DC: Smithsonian Institution, 1874.

Dampier, William, *A History of Science*. Cambridge: Cambridge University Press, 1971.

DeCarlo, Donald, "Stress in the workplace—An assessment of the problem." *Insurance Review* (May/June 1985), 2–7.

DeLillo, Don, *White Noise*. New York: Elizabeth Sifton Books/Viking, 1984, 1985.

Denny-Brown, D., "Shell-shock and effects and high explosives." In *Collected Lectures of the 7th Postgraduate Seminar in Neurology and Psychiatry, including a Review Course in Military Neuropsychiatry, Oct. 3, 1941–April 10, 1942*, eds. Roy D. Halloran and Paul I. Yakoley. Waltham, MA: Metropolitan State Hospital, 1942.

Diagnostic and Statistical Manual of Mental Disorders: DSM–III. Washington, DC: American Psychiatric Association, 1987.

Disraeli, Benjamin, *The Works of Benjamin Disraeli, Earl of Beaconsfield; Embracing Novels, Romances, Plays, Poems, Biography, Short Stories, and Great Speeches*, Vol. 12: *Coningsby*. London and New York: M. W. Dunne, 1904–1905.

Dowse, T. S., *On Brain and Nerve Exhaustion, "Neurasthenia"*. Rev. ed. London, Bailliere, Tindall & Cox, 1887.

Drinka, George, *The Birth of Neurosis: Myth, Malady, and the Victorians*. New York: Simon & Schuster, 1984.

Duden, Barbara, and Thomas Dunlap, *The Woman under the Skin*. Cambridge, MA: Harvard University Press, 1991.

Dumont, Louis, *From Mandeville to Marx: The Genesis and Triumph of Economic Ideology*. Chicago: University of Chicago Press, 1977.

Dunbar, Helen Flanders, *Emotions and Bodily Changes: A Survey of Literature on Psychosomatic Interrelationships 1910–1953*, 4th ed. New York: Columbia University Press, 1954.

Durkheim, Emile, *Suicide: A Study in Sociology*. New York: Free Press, 1951.

Eder, M. D., "The psycho-pathology of the war neuroses." *Lancet* 2 (1916).

"Elasticity and bearing properties of cast iron." *Lancet* 1831–32, no. 2, 187.

Ellul, Jacques, *The Technological Society*, trans. J. Wilkinson. New York: Vintage Books, 1964.

Engel, George, "Behavioral adjustment and the concept of health and disease." In *Mid-Century Psychiatry*, ed. Roy R. Grinker. Springfield, IL: Charles C. Thomas, 1953.

Eysenck, Hans, "Stress, Personality, and Smoking Behavior." In *Stress and Anxiety*, Vol. 9, eds. C. D. Spielberger, I. G. Sarason, and P. B. Defares. Washington, DC: Hemisphere Publishing, 1985.

Farquharson, Robert, "The influence of athletic sports on health." *Lancet*, 1870, no. 2, 370.

Fellman, Anita Clair, and Michael Fellman, *Making Sense of Self: Medical Advice Literature in Late Nineteenth Century America*. Philadelphia: University of Pennsylvania Press, 1981.

Figley, Charles, "Toward a Field of Traumatic Stress." *Journal of Traumatic Stress* 1, no. 1 (January 1988), 3–16.

Fleck, Ludwik, *The Genesis and Development of a Scientific Fact*. Chicago: University of Chicago Press, 1979.

Fleming, Raymond, Andrew Baum, and Jerome E. Singer, "Toward an integrative approach to the study of stress." *Journal of Personality and Social Psychology* 46, no. 4 (1984).

Fothergill, J. Milner, "Strain in its relation to the circulatory organs." *British Medical Journal*, 1873, no. i.

Foucault, Michel, *The Order of Things: An Archeology of the Human Sciences*. New York: Vintage Books, 1970.

————, *The Birth of the Clinic*, trans. A. M. Sheridan Smith. New York: Vintage Books, 1975.

————, *The History of Sexuality*, Part I: *Introduction*. New York: Pantheon, 1978.

Freud, Sigmund, *Civilization and Its Discontents*, trans. James Strachey. New York: W. W. Norton, 1961.

Friedman, B. H., *Jackson Pollock: Energy Made Visible*. New York: McGraw-Hill, 1972.

Friedman, Meyer, and Ray H. Rosenman, *Type A Behavior and Your Heart*. Greenwich, CT: Fawcett Crest, 1974.

Fromm, Erich, *To Have or To Be*. New York: Bantam Books, 1976.

Gadamer, Hans-Georg, *Truth and Method*. New York: Seabury, 1975.

Gehlen, Arnold, *Man in Age of Technology*. New York: Columbia University Press, 1980.

Gendlin, Eugene, "A philosophical critique of narcissism: The significance of the awareness movement." In *Pathologies of the Modern Self*, ed. D. M. Levin, pp. 251–304. New York: New York University Press, 1987.

Geurin, Virginia T. and Gary F. Kohut, "Dimensions of computer anxiety among managers: A field study." *HRMOB Proceedings*, Vol. I (1987 HRMOB Annual National Conference), pp. 305–309.

Gherman, E. M., *Stress and the Bottom Line: A Guide to Personal Well-Being and Corporate Health*. New York: Amacom, 1981.

Gissing, George, "Life at high pressure." In *Human Odds and Ends: Stories and Sketches*, pp. 270–76. London: Lawrence & Bullen, 1898.

Greg, William Rathbone, "England as it is." In *Essays on Political and Social Science*, Vol. I. London: Longman, Brown, Green & Longmans, 1853.

————, "Life at high pressure." In *Literary and Social Judgments* Vol. II. London: Trubner & Co., 1877.

Grinker, Roy R., *Psychosomatic Research*. New York: Norton, 1953.

Grinker, Roy R., and John Spiegel, *Men under Stress*. Philadelphia: Blakiston, 1945.

————, *War Neuroses*, rev. ed. Philadelphia: Blakiston, 1945.

Guthrie, Douglas, *A History of Medicine*. Philadelphia: Lippincott, 1946.

Haigh, Elizabeth, *Xavier Bichat and the Medical Theory of the Eighteenth Century: Medical History* Supplement No. 4. London: Wellcome Institute for the History of Medicine, 1984.

Haley, Bruce, *The Healthy Body and Victorian Culture*. Cambridge, MA: Harvard University Press, 1978.

Hamilton, S. B., "Building and civil engineering construction." In *A History of Technology*, ed. Charles Singer, E. J. Holymard, A. R. Hall and Trevor I. Williams, Vol. IV: *The Industrial Revolution, c 1750 to c 1850*. Oxford: Clarendon Press, 1958.

————, "Building materials and techniques." In *A History of Technology*, Vol. V: *The Late Nineteenth Century c 1850 to c 1900*. Oxford: Clarendon Press, 1958.

Hastings, Donald W., David G. Wright, and Bernard C. Glueck, *Psychiatric Experiences of the Eighth Air Force, First Year of Combat (July 4, 1942–July 4, 1943)*. New York: Josiah Macy, Jr., Foundation, 1944.

Haughton, Samuel, "The relation of food to work done by the body, and its bearing upon medical practice." *Lancet*, 1868, no. 2, 641–51.

————, "On the mechanical work done by the human heart." *Dublin Quarterly Journal of Medicine* 49 (1870), 74–85.

———, "On the action of the human heart," *Medical Times and Gazette* (1871), 653, also in *Retrospect of Practical Medicine and Surgery* 64 (January 1872), 66–70.

"Heart disease from over-exertion," *Medical News* 31 (1873), 98–99.

Heidegger, Martin, *The Question Concerning Technology and Other Essays*, trans. William Lovitt. New York: Harper Colophon Books, 1977.

Hilgard, Ernest, *Psychology in America: A Historical Survey*. Austin: Harcourt Brace Jovanovich, 1987.

Hillman, James, *Emotion: A Comprehensive Phenomenology of Theories and Their Meaning for Therapy*. Evanston: Northwestern University Press, 1961.

Hinkle, Lawrence, "The concept of 'stress' in the biological and social sciences." *International Journal of Psychiatry in Medicine* 5, no. 4 (1974), 335–57.

Hitt, Dick, "Making the best of traffic snarls on Dallas roads," *Dallas Times-Herald* (18 December 1988), p. B–1.

Hoagland, Hudson, "Adventures in biological engineering," *Science* (1944).

Hobfalls, Stevan E., "Conservation of resources: A new attempt at conceptualizing stress," *American Psychologist* 44, no. 3 (March 1989).

Homans, Peter, *The Ability to Mourn: Disillusionment and the Social Origins of Psychoanalysis*. Chicago: University of Chicago Press, 1989.

Houghton, Walter, *The Victorian Frame of Mind, 1830–1870*. New Haven: Yale University Press, 1957.

Hovell, D. DeB., *On Some Conditions of Neurasthenia*. London: J. & A. Churchill, 1886.

Howell, Joel, " 'Soldier's Heart': The redefinition of heart disease and specialty formation in early twentieth-century Great Britain." In *The Emergence of Modern Cardiology*, eds. W. F. Bynum, C. Lawrence, and J. Nutton, in *Medical History*, Supplement No. 5. London: Wellcome Institute of the History of Medicine, 1985.

Hutcheson, Francis, *An Essay on the Nature and Conduct of the Passions and Affections: With Illustrations on the Moral Sense*. Gainesville, FL: Scholars' Facsimiles and Reprints, 1969.

Ianni, Francis and Elizabeth Reuss-Ianni, " 'Take this job and shove it!' A comparison of organizational stress and burnout among teachers and police." In *Stress and Burnout in the Human Service Professions*, ed. Barry Farber. New York: Pergamon Press, 1983.

Illich, Ivan, "The Disabling Professions." In *The Disabling Professions*, pp. 11–40. Boston: Marion Boyars, 1978.

———, *Gender*. New York: Pantheon, 1982.

———, "Subsistence." In *The Virtues That Make Us Human: The Foundations of Medical Ethics*. Urbana and Chicago: University of Illinois Press, 1985, 45–53.

Illich, Ivan and Barry Sanders, *ABC: The Alphabetization of the Popular Mind*. Berkeley: North Point Press, 1988.

Ivancevich, John M., Michael T. Matteson, and Edward Prichards, "Who's liable for stress on the job?" *Harvard Business Review* (March–April 1985), 60–72.

Jackson, Stanley, *Melancholia and Depression from Hippocratic Times to Modern Times*. New Haven: Yale University Press, 1986.

Jager, Bernd, "Transformation of the Passions: Psychoanalytic and Phenomenological Perspectives." In *Existential-Phenomenological Perspectives in Psychology: Explor-*

ing the Breadth of Human Experience, eds. Ronald S. Valle and Steen Halling. New York: Plenum, 1989.

James, William, *The Principles of Psychology*. 1890. Reprint, New York: Dover Books, 1950.

———, "The Energies of Men." In *Essays in Faith and Morals*. New York: Longmans, Green & Co., 1943.

———, "The gospel of relaxation." In *Essays on Faith and Morals*, ed. R. B. Perry, p. 245. Cleveland: World Publishing, 1962.

Jung, C. G., *Modern Man in Search of a Soul*. New York: Harcourt Brace Jovanovich.

Kaempffert, Waldemar, "Cortisone and ACTH: An assay," *New York Times Magazine*, 16 December 1951, pp. 12, 30–31.

Kagan, Jerome, "Stress and Coping in Early Development." In *Stress, Coping, and Development in Children*, eds. Norman Garmezy and Michael Rutter. Baltimore: Johns Hopkins University Press, 1983.

Kalish, David, "Straight for the gut." *Marketing and Media Decisions* 23 (July 1988), 26.

Kass, Edward H., Review of Russell C. Maulitz, *Morbid Appearances: The Anatomy of Pathology in the Early Nineteenth Century*. *Journal of Interdisciplinary History* 20, no. 1 (1989), 138.

Kaufman, Carl B., *Man Incorporate: The Individual and His Work in an Organizational Society*. Garden City, NY: Anchor Books, 1969.

Kenner, Cornelia, Cathie E. Guzzetta, and Barbara M. Dossey, *Critical Care Nursing: Body-Mind-Spirit*, 2nd ed. Boston: Little, Brown, 1985.

Kesteven, W. H., *Work and Worry from a Medical Point of View*. London, 1884.

Kets de Vries, M. F. R., "Organizational stress management audit." In *Handbook of Organizational Stress Coping Strategies*, eds. A. S. Sethi and R. S. Schuler, p. 267. Cambridge, MA: Ballinger, 1984.

Kobasa, Suzanne C., "The hardy personality: Toward a social psychology of stress and health." In *Social Psychology of Health and Illness*, eds. G. S. Sanders and J. Sols. Hillsdale, NJ: Lawrence Erlbaum, 1982.

Koch, Howard, "The War of the Worlds." In Hadley Cantril, *The Invasion from Mars: A Study in the Psychology of Panic*. 1940. Reprint, New York: Harber Torchbooks, 1966.

Kopolow, Louis E., "Plain talk about handling stress." Rockville, MD: National Institute of Mental Health, 1983.

Korn, Errol and Karen Johnson, *Visualization: The Uses of Imagery in the Health Professions*. Homewood, IL: Dow Jones-Irwin, 1983.

Krystal, Henry, "Psychoanalytic views on human emotional damage." In *Post-Traumatic Stress Disorders: Psychological and Biological Sequelae*, ed. Bessel A. van der Kolk. Washington, DC: American Psychiatric Association, 1984.

Kugelmann, Robert, *The Windows of the Soul*. Lewisburg, PA: Bucknell University Press, 1983.

———, "The stress on 'stress' in psychology and medicine." *New Ideas in Psychology* 7, no. 1 (1989), 99–108.

Lasch, Christopher, *A Culture of Narcissism: American Life in an Age of Diminishing Expectations*. New York: W. W. Norton, 1979.

———, *The Minimal Self*. New York: W. W. Norton, 1984.

———, "Fraternalist manifesto," *Harper's Monthly* 274, no. 1643 (April 1987), 17–20.

LaValle, Michael, *Facing the Mirror: Narcissism and the Psychological Discovery of Faith.* Ph.D. dissertation. Dallas: University of Dallas, 1986.

Lawrence, C., "Moderns and ancients: The 'new cardiology' in Britain 1880–1930," in *The Emergence of Modern Cardiology*, eds. W. F. Bynum, C. Lawrence, V. Nutton, *Medical History*, Supplement No. 5 (1985).

"Lectures of Professor Matteucci, The" *Lancet* 1847, no. 1, 624.

Lee, W. R., "Occupational medicine." In *Medicine and Science in the 1860s*, pp. 151–81. London: Wellcome Institute of the History of Medicine, 1968.

Lefcourt, Herbert M., "The function of the illusions of control and freedom." *American Psychologist* 28 (1973).

———, "The locus of control as a moderator variable: Stress." In *Research with the Locus of Control Construct*, Vol. 2: *Developments and Social Problems*, ed. H. M. Lefcourt. New York: Academic Press, 1983.

Levin, David Michael (ed.), *Pathologies of the Modern Self.* New York: New York University Press, 1987.

Levine Robert, "The pace of life," *Psychology Today* 23 (October 1989), 42–46.

Lewis, Thomas, *The Soldier's Heart and the Effort Syndrome.* New York: Paul B. Hoeber, 1919.

Lewis, C. S., *A Grief Observed.* New York: Seabury Press, 1961.

Lifton, Robert Jay, *Death in Life: Survivors of Hiroshima.* New York: Vintage Books, 1967.

Linder, Staffan, *The Harried Leisure Class.* New York: 1970.

"Lord Normanby's Drainage Bill," *Lancet*, 1840–41, no. 2, 17.

Luckmann, Thomas, "On the Rationality of Institutions in Modern Life." In *Life-World and Social Realities.* London: Heinemann Educational Books, 1983.

Luijpen, William, *Existential Phenomenology*, rev. ed. Pittsburgh: Duquesne University Press, 1969.

Lynch, Kevin, *The Image of the City.* Cambridge, MA: MIT Press, 1960.

Lyons, Richard, "Stress addiction: 'Life in the fast lane' may have its benefits." *New York Times* (21 July 1983), p. III, 1: 1.

MacIntyre, Alasdair, *After Virtue: A Study in Moral Theory.* 2nd ed. Notre Dame, IN: University of Notre Dame Press, 1984.

Mackenzie, James, "The recruit's heart: A memorandum for medical examiners," *British Medical Journal*, 1915, no. ii, 563.

———, "Soldier's Heart," *British Medical Journal*, 1916, no. i.

———, *Diseases of the Heart*, 4th ed. London: Humphrey Milford, Oxford University Press, 1925.

Mackenzie, James, and James Orr, *Principles of Diagnosis and Treatment in Heart Affections*, 3rd ed. London: Oxford University Press, 1926.

MacPherson, C. B., *The Political Theory of Possessive Individualism.* London: Oxford University Press, 1962.

Mair, A., *Sir James Mackenzie M.D. 1853–1925, General Practitioner.* Edinburgh: Churchill Livingstone, 1973.

Mandler, George, "Stress and thought processes." In *Handbook of Stress: Theoretical and Clinical Aspects*, eds. Leo Goldberger and Shlomo Broznitz. New York: Free Press, 1982.

Marris, Peter, *Loss and Change*. London: Routledge & Kegan Paul, 1974.

———, "The social impact of stress." In *Mental Health and the Economy*, ed. L. A. Ferman and J. P. Gordus. Kalamazoo, MI: W. E. Upjohn Institute for Employment Research, 1979.

Mason, John, "A historical view of the stress field." *Journal of Human Stress* 1, no. 1 (March 1975), 6–12.

Matthews, Fred, "In defense of common sense: Mental hygiene as ideology and mentality in twentieth-century America," *Prospects* 4 (1979).

May, Gregory D. and Michael J. Kruger, "The manager within." *Personnel Journal* (February 1988).

Meerloo, Joost A. M., *Delusion and Mass Delusion*. New York: Nervous and Mental Disease Monographs, 1949.

Meichenbaum, Donald, David Henshaw, and Norman Himel, "Coping with stress as a problem-solving process." In *Achievement, Stress, and Anxiety*, eds. H. Krohne and L. Laux. Washington, DC: Hemisphere Publishing, 1982.

Meltzer, S. J., "Factors of Safety in the Animal Economy," *Science* 25 (January–June 1907).

Menninger, Karl, "Regulatory devices of the ego under major stress." In *A Psychiatrist's World: The Selected Papers of Karl Menninger*, ed. Bernard H. Hall. New York: Viking Press, 1959.

Menninger, William, "Modern concepts of war neuroses." *Bulletin of the Menninger Clinic* 10 (1946).

———, "Psychosomatic medicine: Somatization reactions," *Psychosomatic Medicine* 9 (1947), 92–97.

Merleau-Ponty, Maurice, *Phenomenology of Perception*, trans. Colin Smith. New York: Humanities Press, 1962.

———, *The Visible and the Invisible*, trans. Alphonso Lingis. Evanston: Northwestern University Press, 1968.

Mestrovic, Stjepan, "A Sociological Conceptualization of Trauma." *Social Science and Medicine* 21, no. 8 (1985), 835–48.

Mestrovic, Stjepan, and Barry Glassner, "A Durkheimian hypothesis on stress." *Social Science and Medicine* 17, no. 18 (1983), 1315–27.

Meyer, Donald, *The Positive Thinkers: Religion as Pop Psychology from Mary Baker Eddy to Oral Roberts*, reissue. New York: Pantheon, 1980.

Miller, Alice, *The Drama of the Gifted Child*. New York: Basic Books, 1990.

Miller, Emanuel, *The Neuroses in War*. New York: Macmillan, 1940.

Miller, Hugh, *The Old Red Sandstone*. 1857. Reprint, New York: Arno, 1978.

Minkowski, Eugene, *Lived Time*. Evanston: Northwestern University Press, 1970.

Mitchell, Silas Weir, *Blood and Fat, and How to Make Them*. Philadelphia: J. B. Lippincott, 1877.

———, *Wear and Tear, or Hints for the Overworked*. Philadelphia: J. B. Lippincott, 1887.

Monat, Alan, and Richard S. Lazarus, "Stress and Coping—Some Current Issues and Controversies." In *Stress and Coping: An Anthology*, eds. A. Monat and R. S. Lazarus. New York: Columbia University Press, 1977.

Muirhead, I. B., "Shock and the soldier." *Lancet*, 1916, no. 1, 1021.

Myers, Greg, "Nineteenth century popularization of thermodynamics and the rhetoric of social prophecy." *Victorian Studies* 29, no. 1 (1985), 35–66.

Nalbantian, Suzanne, *The Symbol of the Soul from Holderlin to Yeats*. New York: Columbia University Press, 1977.

"Nerves and Nervelessness." *Eclectic Magazine*, 69, no. 122 (February 1894), 278–81.

"Neurasthenia and Shell Shock," *Lancet*, 1916, no. 1, 627.

Niebyl, P. H., *Venesection and the Concept of the Foreign*. New Haven: Yale University Press, 1969.

O'Neill, John, *Five Bodies: The Human Shape of Modern Society* (Ithaca: Cornell University Press, 1985).

Osler, William, "Diseases of the Arteries," in *Modern Medicine, Its Theory and Practice*, ed. William Osler and Thomas McCrae, Vol. IV: *Diseases of the Circulatory System*, 2nd ed. (Philadelphia: Lea & Fabiger, 1915).

Osler, William, *The Principles and Practice of Medicine*, 4th ed. New York: D. Appleton & Co., 1901.

———, "On angina pectoris." *Lancet*, 1910, no. 1.

———, "Graduated exercise in prognosis." *Lancet*, 1918, no. 1.

———, *The Principles and Practice of Medicine*, 9th ed. New York: Appleton, 1923.

Ostberg, Olov and Carina Nilsson, "Emerging technology and stress." In *Job Stress and Blue Collar Work*, eds. C. L. Cooper and M. J. Smith. New York: Wiley, 1985, pp. 149–69.

"Overstrain of the heart and aorta," *British Medical Journal* 1873, no. i, 299–301.

Oxford English Dictionary, 2nd ed. Oxford: Clarendon Press, 1989.

Pace, Larry, and Waino Suojanen, "Addictive Type A behavior undermines employee involvement." *Personnel Journal* 67, no. 6 (June 1988).

Palmer, H. "Military psychiatric casualties: Experience with 12,000 cases." *Lancet*, 1945, no. 2, 456.

Pelletier, Kenneth, *Mind as Healer, Mind as Slayer*. New York: Dell, 1977.

Percy, Walker, *Lost in the Cosmos: The Last Self-Help Book*. New York: Farrar, Straus & Giroux, 1983.

———, *The Thanatos Syndrome*. New York: Farrar, Straus & Giroux, 1987.

Perring, R. J., "Family doctor." *Lancet*, 1949, no. 2, 1166.

Peterson, M. Jeanne, *The Medical Profession in Mid-Victorian London*. Berkeley: University of California Press, 1978.

Petrarcha, Francesco, *Petrarch's Secret or The Soul's Conflict with Reason*, trans. W. H. Draper. London: Chatto & Windus, 1911.

Pickering, George, *Creative Malady*. New York: Delta, 1974.

Pieper, Joseph, *In Tune with the World: A Theory of Festivity*, trans. R. and C. Winston. New York: Harcourt, Brace & World, 1965.

Pollock, Kristian, "On the nature of social stress: Production of a modern mythology." *Social Science and Medicine* 26, no. 3 (1988).

Porter, Dale H., and Gloria C. Clifton, "Patronage, professional values, and Victorian public works: Engineering and contracting the Thames Embankment." *Victorian Studies* 31, no. 3 (1988) 319–50.

"Provisional data from the Health Promotion and Disease Prevention Supplement to the National Health Interview Survey: United States, Jan.–March, 1985." *Advance Data* No. 113 (15 November 1985) 4146–8.114.

"Psychosomatics." *New England Journal of Medicine* 232, (1945), 19.

Quick, Jonathan, Rebecca Horn, James Quick, "Health consequences of stress." *Journal of Organizational Behavior Management* 8, no. 2 (1986) 19–36.

Quick, James C. and Jonathan D. Quick, *Organizational Strees and Preventive Management*. New York: McGraw-Hill, 1984.

Rabinbach, Anson, "The body without fatigue: A nineteenth-century utopia." In *Political Symbolism in Modern Europe: Essays in Honor of George L. Mosse*, ed. S. Drescher, D. Sabean, and A. Sharlin, pp. 42–62. New Brunswick, NJ: Rutgers University Press, 1982.

———, "The European Science of Work: The Economy of the Body at the End of the Nineteenth Century." In *Work in France: Representations, Meaning, Organization, and Practice*, eds. S. L. Kaplan and C. J. Koepp. Ithaca, NY: Cornell University Press, 1986.

———, *The Human Motor*. New York: Basic Books, 1990.

Rees, John, *The Shaping of Psychiatry by War*. New York: W. W. Norton, 1945.

Reid, David, "Participatory control and the chronic-illness adjustment process." In *Research with the Locus of Control Construct*, Vol. 3, ed. H. M. Lefcourt, pp. 361–91. New York: Academic Press, 1984.

Reinartz, Eugen, "Psychiatry in Aviation." In *Psychiatry and the War*, ed. F. J. Sladen. Springfield, IL and Baltimore: Charles C. Thomas, 1943.

Reiser, Stanley Joel, *Medicine and the Reign of Technology*. Cambridge: Cambridge University Press, 1978.

Richardson, Benjamin Ward, "On physical disease from mental strain. *Journal of Mental Science* 15 (October 1869), 351.

Rivers, W. H. R., "War neurosis and military training." *Mental Hygiene* 2, no. 4 (1918), 513–33.

Robinson, George, *Contributions to the Physiology and Pathology of the Circulation of the Blood*. London: Longman, Brown, Green, Longmans, & Roberts, 1857.

Rodgers, Daniel T., "In search of Progressivism." *Reviews in American History* 10 (December 1982).

Rolleston, Humphrey Davy, *The Right Honorable Sir Thomas Clifford Allbutt: A Memoir*. London: Macmillan, 1929.

Romanyshyn, Robert, "Psychological language and the voice of things." *Dragonflies: Studies in Imaginal Psychology* 1, no. 2 (Spring 1979), 73–79.

———, *Psychological Life: From Science to Metaphor*. Austin: University of Texas Press, 1982.

———, *Technology as Symptom and Dream*. New York: Routledge & Kegan Paul, 1989.

Romanyshyn, Robert, and Brian Whalen, "Depression and the American Search for Home." In *Pathologies of the Modern Self*, ed. D. M. Levin, pp. 198–220. New York: New York University Press, 1987.

Roose, Robson, "The wear and tear of London life." *Fortnightly Review* 39 (Jan.–June 1886).

Rosen, George, "Political order and human health in Jeffersonian thought." *Bulletin of the History of Medicine* 26 (1952), 32–44.

Roy, C. S. and J. G. Adami, "Remarks of failure of the heart from overstrain." *British Medical Journal*, 1888, no. ii.

Rubenstein, Richard, *The Cunning of History: The Holocaust and the American Future*. New York: Harper Colophon, 1975.

Rush, Benjamin, *Two Essays on the Mind: An Enquiry into the Influence of Physical Causes upon the Moral Faculty, and on the Influence of Physical Causes in Promoting an Increase of the Strength and Activity of the Intellectual Faculties of Man.* 1786; Reprint, New York: Bruner/Mazel, 1972.

Samelson, I., "World War I intelligence testing and the development of psychology." *Journal of the History of the Behavioral Sciences* 13, no. 3 (1977).

Sartre, Jean-Paul, *Being and Nothingness: An Essay on Phenomenological Ontology.* New York: Philosophical Library, 1956.

Schilder, Paul, *Medical Psychology.* New York: Wiley, 1953.

Schivelbusch, Wolfgang, *The Railway Journey: Trains and Travel in the Nineteenth Century.* Oxford: Basil Blackwell, 1979.

Schubert, H. R., "Extraction and production of metals: Iron and steel." In *A History of Technology*, Vol. IV: *The Industrial Revolution, c 1750 to c 1850.* New York and London: Oxford University Press, 1958.

———, "The steel industry," in *A History of Technology*, eds. Charles Singer, E. J. Holmyard, A. R. Hall and Trevor I. Williams, Vol. V: *The Late Nineteenth Century c 1850 to c 1900.* New York and London: Oxford University Press, 1958.

Searles, Harold, "Unconscious processes in relation to the environmental crisis." In *Countertransference and Related Subjects*, pp. 228–242. New York: International Universities Press, 1979.

Segal, Hanna, *Introduction to the Work of Melanie Klein*, 2nd ed. New York: Basic Books, 1974.

Sekora, John, *Luxury: The Concept in Western Thought, Eden to Smollett.* Baltimore: Johns Hopkins University Press, 1977.

Selye, Hans, *Stress Without Distress.* Philadelphia and New York: J. B. Lippincott, 1974.

———, *The Stress of Life.* New York: McGraw-Hill, 1975.

Sethi, Amarjit S., "Contemplative strategies for technostress management." In *Strategic Management of Technostress in an Information Society*, ed. A. S. Sethi, D. H. J. Caro, R. S. Schuler. Toronto: C. J. Hogrefe, 1987.

Shatan, C. F., "The grief of soldiers—Viet Nam combat veterans' self help movement." *American Journal of Orthopsychiatry* 43 (1973), 640–53.

Skey, F. C. Letter to the *London Times*, 10 October 1867, p. 9.

———, Letter to the *London Times*, 21 October 1867, p. 10.

Skinner, E. F., "Psychological stresses in industry." *Practitioner* 53 (1944), 37–44.

Smith, G. Eliot and T. H. Pear, *Shell Shock and Its Lessons.* (Manchester: University Press, 1917).

Sontag, Susan, *Illness as Metaphor.* New York: Vintage, 1978.

Southard, E. E., "Shell shock and after." *Boston Medical and Surgical Journal* 79, no. 3 (18 July 1918).

Spencer, Herbert, *An Autobiography.* New York: D. Appleton, 1904.

Spiegel, John, "Transactional theory and social change." In *Modern Psychiatry and Clinical Research: Essays in Honor of Roy R. Grinker*, ed. Daniel Offer and Daniel Freedman. New York: Basic Books, 1972.

Spiro, Melford, "Religious systems as culturally constituted defense mechanisms." In *Stress and Coping: An Anthology*, eds. A. Monat and R. S. Lazarus, p. 178. New York: Columbia University Press, 1977.

Starr, Paul, *The Social Transformation of American Medicine*. New York: Basic Books, 1982.

Steiner, Rudolf, *The Child's Changing Consciousness and Waldorf Education*. Hudson, NY: The Anthroposophic Press, 1988.

Stott, R. Rosalie, "Health or virtue: Or, how to keep out of harm's way. Lectures on pathology and therapeutics by William Cullen c. 1770," *Medical History* 31 (1987), 123–142.

Strahan, J., "Puzzling conditions of the heart and other organs dependent on neurasthenia," *British Medical Journal*, 1885, no. ii, 435–37.

Straus, Erwin, *The Primary World of Senses: A Vindication of Sensory Experience*. New York: Free Press, 1963.

Strauss, Leo, "The three waves of modernity," in *Political Philosophy: Six Essays by Leo Strauss*, ed. Hilail Gildin, pp. 81–98. Indianapolis: Pegasus, 1975.

Strecker, Edward, "War psychiatry and its influence upon postwar psychiatry and upon civilization." *Journal of Nervous and Mental Diseases* 101 (May 1945).

Taylor, Shelley E., "Health psychology: The science and the field." *American Psychologist* 45, no. 1 (January 1990).

Temkin, Oswei, "Metaphors of Human Biology." In *Science and Civilization*, ed. R. Stauffer, 169–96. Madison: University of Wisconsin Press, 1949.

Thom, Douglas A., "War neuroses. Experiences of 1914–1918. Lessons for the current emergency." In *Collected Lectures of the 7th Postgraduate Seminar in Neurology and Psychiatry, Including a Review Course in Military Neuropsychiatry, Oct. 3, 1941–April 10, 1942. First Seminar: Military Neuropsychiatry*, eds. Roy D. Halloran and Paul I. Yakolev. (Waltham, MA: Metropolitan State Hospital, 1942).

Thompson, E. P., "Time, work-discipline, and industrial capitalism." *Past and Present* 69.

Timoshenko, Stephen, *History of Strength of Materials*. New York: McGraw-Hill, 1953.

Todhunter, Isaac, *A History of the Theory of Elasticity and of the Strength of Materials*, ed. Karl Pearson. 1886. Reprint, New York: Dover, 1960.

Toffler, Alvin, *Future Shock*. New York: Random House, 1970.

Treadwell, J. B., "Observations upon overwork and strain of the heart." *Boston Medical and Surgical Journal* 10 (1873), 157–60, 179–84.

Trotter, Thomas, *A View of the Nervous Temperament*. London: Longman, Hurst, Rees & Orme, 1807.

Van den Berg, J. H. *The Changing Nature of Man*. New York: W. W. Norton, 1961.
———, *Things*. Pittsburgh: Duquesne University Press, 1970.
———, *Divided Existence and Complex Society*. Pittsburgh: Duquesne University Press, 1974.

Voluck, Philip R., and Herbert Abramson, "How to avoid stress-related disability claims." *Personnel Journal* (May 1987), 95–98.

Von Eckartsberg, Rolf, *Life-World Experience: Existential-Phenomenological Research Approaches in Psychology*. Washington, DC: Center for Advanced Research in Phenomenology & University Press of America, 1986.

Watts, Alan, *Does It Matter? Essays on Man's Relation to Materiality*. New York: Vintage Books, 1970.

Weeks, Jeffrey, *Sex, Politics, and Society*. New York: Longman, 1981.

Weiss, Edward, and O. Spurgeon English, *Psychosomatic Medicine*. Philadelphia: Saunders, 1952.

Whipp, Richard, " 'A time to every purpose': An essay on time and work." In *The Historical Meanings of Work*, ed. P. Joyce, pp. 210–223. Cambridge: Cambridge University Press, 1987.

White, William Alanson, *The Principles of Mental Hygiene*. New York: Macmillan, 1917.

Whitehorn, John, "Introduction and survey of the problems of stress." In *Symposium on Stress, 16–18 March 1953*. Washington, DC: Walter Reed Army Medical Center, Army Medical Service Graduate School, 1953.

———, *Psychiatric Education and Progress. The Salmon Lectures of the New York Academy of Medicine, November 30, 1955*. Springfield, IL: Charles C. Thomas, 1957.

Wiebe, Robert, *Search for Order 1877–1920*. New York: Hill & Wang, 1967.

Wilhelmsen, Frederick, and Willmoore Kendall, "Cicero and the Politics of Public Orthodoxy." *The Intercollegiate Review* 5, no. 2 (Winter 1968–69), 84–100.

Wilks, Samuel, "On overwork." *Lancet*, 1875, no. 1, 886.

Winner, Langdon, "Techné and Politeai." In *The Whale and the Reactor: A Search for Limits in an Age of High Technology*. Chicago: University of Chicago Press, 1986.

Winnicott, Donald W., "The depressive position in normal emotional development." In *Collected Papers: Through Pediatrics to Psycho-Analysis*, pp. 262–77. London: Tavistock, 1958.

Wittkower, Eric, "Historical perspective of contemporary psychosomatic medicine," *International Journal of Psychiatry in Medicine* 5, no. 4 (1974), 309–19.

Wittkower, Eric, and J. P. Spillane, "A survey of the literature of neuroses in war." In *The Neuroses in War*, ed. Emanuel Miller. New York: Macmillan, 1944.

Wolfe, Tom, *Bonfire of the Vanities*. New York: Farrar, Straus, & Giroux, 1987.

Wood, George B., *A Treatise on the Practice of Medicine*, 3rd ed., Vol. 2. Philadelphia: Lippincott, Grambo & Co., 1852.

Wood, Paul, "DaCosta's syndrome." *British Medical Journal*, 1941, no. i.

Woolfolk, Robert, and Paul Lehrer, "Clinical Applications." In *Principles and Practices of Stress Management*. New York: Guilford, 1984.

Wooton, Edwin, "Nervous exhaustion." *Knowledge* 7 (Jan.–June 1885), 435–36, 500–502, 519–20.

Young, Allan, "The discourse on stress and the reproduction of conventional knowledge." *Social Science and Medicine* 14B (1980).

Young, Mitchell, and Cassandra Erickson, "Cultural impediments to recovery: PTSD in contemporary America." *Journal of Traumatic Stress* 1, no. 4 (1988).

Zola, Irving Kenneth, "Healthism and Disabling Medicalization." In *Disabling Professions*. Boston: Marion Boyars, 1977.

Index

ABOUT THE AUTHOR

ROBERT KUGELMANN is Associate Professor of Psychology at the University of Dallas. He is the author of *The Windows of the Soul: Psychological Physiology of the Human Eye and Primary Glaucoma* (1983).